Dr. Marcia Emery's

INTUITION WORKBOOK

An Expert's Guide to Unlocking the Wisdom of Your Subconscious Mind

PRENTICE HALL
Englewood Cliffs, New Jersey 07632

Prentice-Hall International (UK) Limited, *London*
Prentice-Hall of Australia Pty. Limited, *Sydney*
Prentice-Hall Canada, Inc., *Toronto*
Prentice-Hall Hispanoamericana, S.A., *Mexico*
Prentice-Hall of India Private Limited, *New Delhi*
Prentice-Hall of Japan, Inc., *Tokyo*
Simon & Schuster Asia Pte. Ltd., *Singapore*
Editora Prentice-Hall do Brasil, Ltda., *Rio de Janeiro*

©1994 by
Marcia Emery, Ph.D.

10 9 8 7 6 5 4 3

ISBN 0-13-091688-9

PRENTICE HALL
Career and Personal Development
Englewood Cliffs, NJ 07632

Simon & Schuster, A Paramount Communications Company

Printed in the United States of America

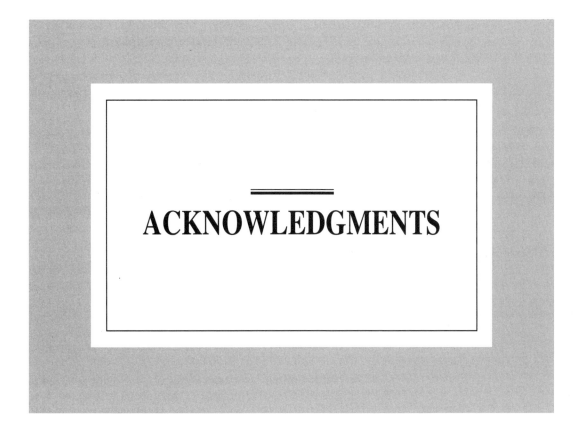

ACKNOWLEDGMENTS

When I read Einstein's quote that "Imagination is more important than knowledge," I think of how this book was created. The imagination of so many people was sparked to give it birth. Since the intuitive mind speaks in pictures, images, and symbols it becomes most challenging to retrieve appropriate words to convey the essence of intuition. That is where the imagination of many fine minds came through to help "birth" this book. My words are inadequate to express the depth of my appreciation—but if any of you can imagine my smiling face and big eyes opened in awe, you will sense the gratitude that comes right from my heart.

So many played a part in the development of this book ranging from my students over the years, to the administrators at Aquinas College in Grand Rapids, Michigan, who sanctioned both my graduate course, "Integrating Intuition and Logic For Managers," and my undergraduate course, "Intuitive Management in Decision Making." I am particularly indebted to Jack Dezek, chairman of the Masters in Management Program, for his support over the years. Bob Kunnen, former chair of the undergraduate Business Department at Aquinas, initially extended the invitation to teach an elective course in the Undergraduate Business Department and Joyce McNally, his successor, continued to support my teaching. I am grateful to all of them.

I also want to thank Drs. Weston Agor, Douglas Dean, Stanley Krippner, Lilia Logette, and Alan Vaughan. Each gave me a "professional" block on which to build the foundation for this book.

Other invaluable support and inspiration came from Kay Bazzett, Heidi DeWinter, Helen Morning Star, Kim Smith, C. Michael Smith, Jim Stark, and Joyce and Bill Townsend.

While so many played a part, I single out for recognition four stalwarts who supported my quest to articulate intuition, the silent but ever wise partner of our mind.

My editor, Ellen Schneid Coleman, intuitively knew when she first saw the manuscript that there was a diamond waiting to be polished within the pages. I feel blessed to be the recipient of her gifted editorial touch.

I will always be grateful to J. R. Jablonski. He took a chisel to my original ideas and helped me shape, mold, and incorporate those primitive views into this book.

Mary Marin, an extraordinary wordsmith, was literally the answer to a prayer, deftly applying her pen to refine the language so that the essence of intuition could be articulated.

My husband, friend, and partner, Jim Emery, was always there to light my fire when my lamp was faint. His caring, support, and assistance throughout every phase of this book was truly an act of love.

My gratitude would not be complete without acknowledging the creative or higher source, from which all my intuitive wisdom flows.

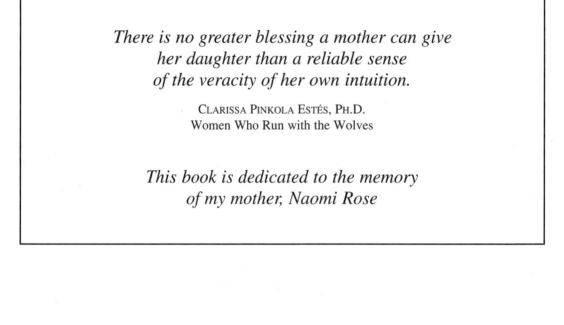

*There is no greater blessing a mother can give
her daughter than a reliable sense
of the veracity of her own intuition.*

CLARISSA PINKOLA ESTÉS, PH.D.
Women Who Run with the Wolves

*This book is dedicated to the memory
of my mother, Naomi Rose*

CONTENTS

PART ONE

UNVEILING
THE INTUITIVE MIND ◆ 1

THE FORMULA FOR SUCCESS ◆ 33

PART THREE

USING YOUR INTUITIVE TOOL BOX
FOR SUCCESS • 143

PART FIVE

ACTIVATING INTUITIVE PROBLEM-SOLVING FOR PERSONAL SUCCESS • 259

FOREWORD

Readers seeking to explore and develop their intuitive abilities will find Marcia Emery's firm but helping hand guiding them in simple and effective exercises in the *Intuition Workbook*. Even the faint of heart, those who fear they might be wrong or probably don't have such intuitive ability, will be stimulated into taking risks—following through the exercises and guided meditations to discover how deceptively simple it can be.

Emery's conceptualizations are solidly based on research findings and, more important, have a light touch that seduces the reader into making intuitive efforts. As with any other skill, intuition improves with practice. The object here is to establish a reliable track record so that intuition becomes a powerful and practical tool for decision making.

By learning to discount wishful thinking and even fearful thinking, readers can come into contact with their own higher processes of thinking that will guide them into greater harmony with the universe—with their own lives.

As Emery correctly points out, intuition is always right. If the *seemingly* intuitive answer is wrong, it means that logical thought has snuck in to masquerade as intuition. So an important focus on the book is to discover just how *real* intuition works best for the individual reader. That is something you can discover only by trying.

Dr. Emery's *Intuition Workbook* is an excellent way for beginners to put intuition on a solid footing in coping with the complexities of modern life.

ALAN VAUGHAN, PH.D.
Mind Technology Systems

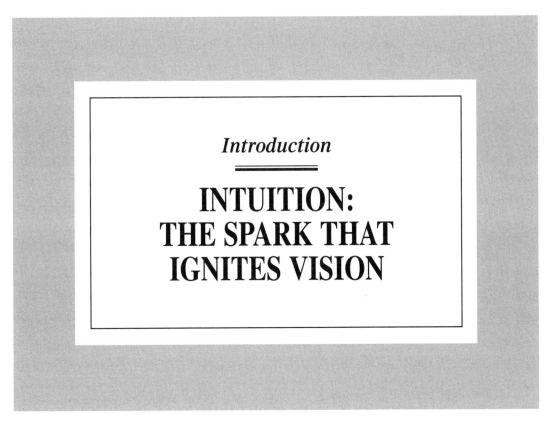

Introduction

INTUITION: THE SPARK THAT IGNITES VISION

The very essence of leadership is that you have to have a vision. You can't blow an uncertain trumpet.

FATHER THEODORE HESBURGH
Late president of Notre Dame University

LEADERS EVERYWHERE USE INTUITION—YOU CAN, TOO

Intuition is the spark that ignites vision. The hunch, gut feeling, sudden insight, or flash out of the blue are all evidence of intuition. This intuitive "Ah'ha!" impels a decision maker to take unprecedented action, go into new areas of endeavor, or retrieve innovative solutions to long-standing problems. Intuition allows for correct decisions, even before all the facts are in. In an interview,[1] Richard DeVos, the legendary cofounder of Amway Corporation, talked about his observation that total dependence on facts limits the adventurous spirit that's crucial to the process of innovation and discovery. Facts alone, he believes, often end up being nothing more than a litany of reasons for why an idea will *not* work. In essence, they often tell us to do nothing at all. DeVos joins many leaders who acknowledge that companies will advance only when intuition is integrated and used along with facts and logic in the decision-making process.

I once watched a movie about two people who met serendipitously and became close friends. One was blind; the other was deaf. Each needed help from the other, and their relationship, characterized by a healthy give and take, helped each individual work more effectively.

This analogy parallels the journey you will be taking. You have two friends "within you" that need to be reunited so you, too, can function more effectively. These friends are called "logic" and "intuition." For most people, logic is more highly developed thanks to years of practice learning how to use reasoning, verbal agility, and fact collecting as needed. Intuition, on the other hand, is usually less developed.

Each of these friends, or inner faculties, has special talents. Your logic has the wherewithal to lead you through the day, make sure you are on track, and refer you back to experience when needed. Your intuition, on the other hand, can ignite your vision to make your dreams come true.

This book honors that forgotten, newly awakened, but vital part of you—your intuition. By the time you go through all these pages and come to the end of the book, intuition and logic will be equally developed. Each will stand side by side, ever ready to lead you through the exciting and puzzling developments occurring at work and in your personal life. Remember, each is necessary to succeed in anything you do. But our focus is on strengthening the undeveloped member of this team.

We all have intuition. According to Dr. Jonas Salk, inventor of the polio vaccine, intuition is an innate quality that can be developed and cultivated.[2] When I hear students in my classes or corporate seminars deny they have this natural ability, I compare intuition to art. I remind them that everyone can draw, though some are more artistic than others. Likewise, every person has intuition, though for some, this ability is stronger than for others. Be assured that, though it may be sleeping or undeveloped, the power of intuition resides in you. Accept the challenge of arousing the sleeping giant. Strengthening your intuition will give you the power to succeed in anything you do. But always keep in mind that this developing of your intuition will be half-hearted if you don't integrate intuition with logic for more effective decision making, problem solving, strategic planning, delving into character, and generating creative solutions.

First, a word or two about intuition and how it can ignite your vision. Ken DeHaan, the dean of academic affairs at Davenport College in Michigan, says that vision takes you above and beyond today. *Having a vision is vital!* When describing ten new trends that are transforming society, John Naisbitt and Patricia Aburdene, authors of *Re-Inventing the Corporation*,[3] underscore the growing use of both intuition and vision. They point out that intuition has long been accepted in sports, but it is only now being recognized as a powerful management tool. Corporate leaders are learning to draw on their vision to guide their businesses, large and small, into the future. Acclaimed hockey star Wayne Gretsky comments on vision, saying that the best skaters don't go where the puck is but where the puck will be. It takes *vision* to identify the perfect place for action.

Isaac Newton, the brilliant scientist and inventor, wrote, "If I have seen farther than others, it is because I have stood on the shoulders of giants." These words capture the *visionary spirit* of the entrepreneur who, when viewing a barren landscape, uses *vision* to "see" the high-rise buildings and shopping and entertainment centers that will turn this bleak area into a "boom town." This is exactly what one thriving West Michigan retailer does all the time. He is known for driving to vacant spots that have been overlooked by developers and proclaiming, "This is it!" How does his vision relate to intuition? The vision emanating from his *intuitive mind* allows him to "see the right place" where another successful store in his chain will be erected.

Joel Barker, futurist and innovator of the highly successful Paradigm video series, has observed that all great leaders are not necessarily visionary, but all great leaders know visionaries. He elaborated that the difference between a visionary and a leader is that when visionaries go to the future and turn around, there is hardly anyone behind them. They are seeing the new world, and although there is not yet nearly enough data to prove it, they know they are correct. When leaders go to the future and turn around, there is a line of followers. The leaders use their intuition to judge which visionary is right.

When Dorothy Morris, C.C.E. was growing up, she had a vision of being a corporate executive or owning her own business. She knew she was up against incredible odds, but the vision of sitting in the executive chair burned bright, fueled by her intuitive mind. Now, as president and chief operating officer of the National Association of Credit Management, she has fulfilled that childhood dream.

As you work your way through this book, you will see how different individuals learned when to make a move and what direction to take by using the unbeatable combination of intuition and vision. I like the way Judeth Javorek, president of Holland Community Hospital in Holland, Michigan, metaphorically describes this teaming up of intuition and vision in the strategic planning process. She says that if you can imagine strategic planning, or vision for the future, as the boat, intuition is the rudder.

This is a unique book. As you go through these pages, you will discover how to take the necessary power steps to develop your intuition. Then you will consistently access and trust your intuition to sail through uncharted waters.

How do other people get this intuitive flash? Throughout this book you will discover how people function successfully in their daily professional, personal, and social lives by adapting and applying a vision to everything they do. It is *intuition* that kindles their *vision*. This powerful book will show you how to spark your intuition to ignite your vision.

Dan Henslee, president of Hekman Furniture in Grand Rapids, Michigan, knows firsthand how effective a hunch can be. When he came upon the latest census figures showing that the projected number of people working from their homes in the 1980s and 1990s would increase, his intuitive mind sparked a vision of an office in every home. Introducing the concept of manufacturing residential desks to his board of directors was risky for Henslee, since residential desks were not doing well at the time, but his hunch turned out to be so successful and profitable for the company that it placed an awesome burden on its manufacturing capabilities. It introduced 11 desk models and sold almost five times what its projections were.

Peter C. Cook, an internationally known and very successful regional Mazda distributor, became a successful pioneer in the import car business by relying on his interest in cars and using his intuition. He still has fond memories of his beginnings. When he was set up as a distributor by Volkswagen, Peter was told, "You will become a millionaire." Although becoming a millionaire was the furthest thing from his mind, he was given a *vision* to hold.

If Cook had adhered strictly to factual data and not kept an open mind, he probably would have missed the opportunity to introduce Volkswagen's Beetle, a small, homely, round-looking car that lacked an important styling feature characteristic of that era, namely, fins. Cook's decision to import and promote the Beetle was completely intuitive since he "clearly knew" that a little car made sense. His logical mind supported the decision by reinforcing certain facts, such as the availability of parts and service for the car and the strong desire of the Germans to enter the American market.

Cook was convinced he had a worthy product, but he experienced difficulty in establishing his organization. Finding people to become Volkswagen dealers was difficult because not everyone shared his enthusiastic vision for the Beetle. Without a proven track record or mountains of statistical data to show the benefits of the Beetle, Cook received an intuitive spark to organize his new distributorship from an unexpected source. Leon Hart, a professional football player who was then playing for the Detroit Lions, was in California for a game with the L.A. Rams. One of his friends on the Rams team took Hart and a couple of his Lions teammates to dinner in a Volkswagen. When these four big men arrived at the restaurant, they couldn't find a parking place; so they used their brawn to simply pick up the car and put it on the sidewalk next to the building. Hart couldn't get over how this little car had accommodated the four big guys. On a hunch, he soon made contact with Cook and became one of the early Volkswagen dealers in Michigan.

Peter C. Cook can certainly testify that developing a vision for tomorrow is essential. The wise ancestor who said, "The journey of a thousand miles begins with the first step" was also talking about maintaining a vision of the destination and the route to take to get there.

Actually, all of us need and rely on multiple visions to guide us through our lives. For example, we use vision

- At the start of the day to determine the steps we want to take as the day unfolds.
- To activate a strategic plan.
- To run an efficient meeting.
- To select the right partner for a project.
- To bolster a coworker's morale.
- To choose the right physical activity.
- To use spare time effectively.
- To choose the right words to motivate our children to seek their goals.

We can extend this list indefinitely as we realize the potent impact intuition can play in clarifying our visions. For example, have you ever dozed off and had a new idea for marketing a product quickly flash through your mind? Were you ever scheduled to give a talk and had a vision of who would be in the audience and how they would respond? And how often has the solution to a problem or answer to a question unexpectedly popped into your head, even when hours of intense deliberation have been fruitless?

While interviewing a group of outstanding business leaders, I discovered how valuable intuition has been in helping them create and sustain their vision. Darwin Clark, the vice president of sales, marketing, and aftersales for General Motors Europe, says vision is essential to him and his team as they develop products that won't be on the market for several years. A bad decision today could destroy the auto manufacturer's competitiveness in the market place. For Clark, intuition is a tool that provides a window to see the future and make that vision a reality.

Jim Adamson, now the CEO of Burger King, talks about his experience in the clothing business, where intuition is used to predict customer behavior in the future. "Early in my career, when I was with the GAP, I was on a buying trip in the Far East. I picked out GAP's first imported jean, and I bought far more than the numbers said. To make a long story short, when they arrived, they sold out in less than 30 days. I thought I had bought a four-month supply. I had made a good decision on style and had overbought based on my intuition. I just didn't know *how* good my intuition was."

Geoffrey Bloom, CEO of Wolverine World Wide, manufacturers of the well-known Hush Puppy shoes, underscores the importance of having vision. He points out that in the apparel business you have to sense what people want to wear, when they want to wear it, and the price they will pay for it.

Carol Valade Smith, editor of the *Grand Rapids Business Journal* and the *Grand Rapids Magazine*, uses her intuition to project what will be happening two or three months down the road that will be of interest to her readers.

Ken DeHaan, Dean of Academic Affairs Davenport College, told me that he visualizes how the various pieces of any new program will fit together. Ken gets a *gut feel* or vision of the whole picture first, and then the individual components make more sense to him.

You are the leader, the CEO, and captain of your own ship, using your intuition to guide and direct you as you execute your daily responsibilities. Here are examples of how your intuition can act as a powerful tool to help you.

- Decide who to hire, who would be "right" for the job. Marge, an office supervisor who uses intuition in hiring, says the applicants who didn't work out after she hired them were the ones she had a "gut feeling" should be interviewed further.

- Discover errors in your product that have gone undetected by others. An engineer intuitively found a problem that no one caught despite all the testing that was done. Using his intuition or inner alarm, he helped the company avoid the potential liabilities that might otherwise have occurred.

- Mend hurt feelings when you have unintentionally offended coworkers or friends.

- Use that same inner radar to help you find the best way to approach coworkers for a favor or a helping hand.

- Find the right words to motivate a child or young person to reach his or her goals.

- Lessen the risk of going into new markets by guiding you to just the right audience for your product.

- Make a good choice of partner in what many consider the greatest risk of all, marriage.

Frequently an intuitive flash will reveal a new approach or solution to a problem. Anyone with a sweet tooth will enjoy the example of Mrs. Fields Cookies. When customers failed to appear the day Debbie Fields opened her first store, a flash of intuition prompted her to grab a sheet filled with cookies, walk down the street, and offer free samples to anyone she met. Almost instantly her store was filled with patrons. Eventually, the success of that first store was multiplied as successful stores were opened across the country.

HOW THIS BOOK WILL UNLOCK
YOUR POWER OF INTUITION

There are many benefits that come from using your intuition, but two compelling reasons for learning to tap into and use intuitive input are highlighted here. First, information sent by the intuitive mind provides shortcuts that will immensely expedite your problem-solving. Many of my students and seminar participants express their amazement when, after completing the course, months of probing and prying are replaced by rapid intuitive insights. Second, you will be empowered to cope with these rapidly changing times. Anxiety and fear dissipate and are replaced with confidence and hope.

By learning to use the techniques presented in the *Intuition Workbook* you will

- Become a powerful, decisive decision maker.
- Discover tremendous new creative forces within you.
- Gain a sense of unshakable confidence.
- Become more efficient and productive in all your endeavors.
- Sharpen your strategic vision as your sense of timing becomes infallible.
- Save time, effort, and money in all your business and personal undertakings.
- Discover new perspectives on and responses to any situation.
- "Read" and clearly understand the motives and character of other people.
- Feel more confident about taking risks in crisis situations.
- Access the expansive database of your subconscious.
- Open lines of communication when an impasse is reached.
- Develop innovative ideas that put you on the "cutting edge" of your field.

By learning to use the power of your intuition, you will become more powerful and more in control for all decision-making and problem-solving activities. By using your past experience, logical analysis, and enhanced *intuitive skills*, you will move confidently into unknown areas and become more innovative.

A Treasure Chest of Discovery and Insight

This book is a treasure chest filled with nuggets of intuitive discovery. Going through each exercise will lead you on the path to developing and strengthening your intuitive ability. As you incorporate these exercises into your life, you will be able to access this source of information whenever necessary.

Your intuitive mind will become activated as you apply the *intuitive problem-solving (IPS) formula* to any issue in your life. The array of sample problems to which this IPS formula has been applied is so broad that you no doubt will be able to identify with several of the "problem" situations. As you do each exercise, you will be transported to the theater of your inner mind to tap into your intuition, which resides in your subconscious mind. Think of it as a giant data bank in which whatever solution or evaluation you need is stored. The exercises in this book are designed to give your intuitive mind a thorough workout so that eventually your intuition will work in complete harmony and unison with your logical mind.

You will learn how to

1. Identify, activate, and strengthen your intuitive skills and apply them to problems and situations that arise from your everyday work, family, and social experiences.

2. Develop your intuitive skills to assist you in coping with any change that impacts your professional affairs or personal life.

3. Differentiate real intuitive insight from subjective and emotional influences that may negatively affect the decision-making process.

4. Integrate information gathered through the intuitive process with logical analysis for effective evaluation and decision making.

5. Consistently recognize and trust your intuition.

How to Get the Most from This Book

This is your role in developing your intuition as you work through this book.

1. This is *your* book; please feel free to write in it. Complete each exercise by writing your answers in the space provided. Use blank paper if you need more space. Try not to leave any question unanswered. You can always come back and change today's "I don't know" response to a complete answer tomorrow.

2. You have to feel comfortable with what you have learned in each chapter. Therefore, proceed at your own speed. Completion of this book will undoubtedly bring you many benefits, but remember that *when* you finish is up to you. Go at your personal pace.

3. Collect "intuition-in-action" tidbits. As you work your way through this book, you will begin to remember and identify intuitive experiences of your own. Record any of these past or present experiences in this book or a separate journal to remind you that your "intuitive muscle" is working.

4. Employ the "relaxation principle" as you go through the book. Use any of the breathing and relaxation receptivity principles explained in Chapter Four to put you in the "right space" for doing your exercises.

5. Practice consistently. Let reading and/or engaging in the exercises from this book become a daily habit.

Part One

UNVEILING THE INTUITIVE MIND

Chapter One

INTUITION:
THE MASTER KEY
TO SUCCESS

A leader has to bet. And the bet is that the leader's intuition is active enough, informed enough, perceptive enough that he or she can get the company safely and successfully through the business window of the future. For every company and organization, that will be the bet of the 21st century.

JOEL BARKER
The Paradigm Pioneer

BEING OF TWO MINDS HAS ITS ADVANTAGES

I have frequently heard people talk about their frustration following a long brain-storming session because they failed to gain any significant insight into their problem. The truth is, they were sitting in that session using only half their brain. Although they applied their logical abilities to a problem or situation, they never shifted their perception so their intuition could emerge. Whole brain thinking entails integrating your intuition with logic. By the time you complete this book, you will possess that intuitive skill and the power that accompanies using both of these faculties.

You are probably familiar with the logical and rational processes. Therefore, throughout this book I will purposely focus on intuition to offset the many years your verbal and rational skills received primary attention. I want to have you validate, through the examples and exercises in this book, that intuition is separate and distinct from logic, though both are necessary ingredients in the decision-making partnership. Before going any further, let's see how these two distinct minds function.

Your *logical mind* is analytical, rational, and verbal. This mind will *tell* you how to do something by using words and sentences. The operations of critical thinking and linear analysis are very important to this mind.

Your *intuitive mind* goes beyond the rational analysis; it is inspiring and nonverbal. This mind will *show* you how to do something by presenting pictures, symbols, and metaphors. This mind functions through creative thinking patterns, spatial arrangements, and visualization.

To help you isolate the respective functions of each mind, let me ask how you would respond if I came up to you and asked, "How are you today?" Your logical mind would respond with sentences like, "I feel very good and particularly noticed when I got up this morning that I had no aches or pains in my body. This is a day when I have a lot to do so I have to be careful not to get too stressed. I will make sure that I engage in some exercise today to offset the mental work." The intuitive mind would send a smile to your face, or perhaps briefly respond with a metaphor by saying, "like sunshine."

The contrasting styles of these two minds would also be evident if you were suddenly called upon to give a talk. If your logical mind were working overtime, you would be digging through many books and making extensive outlines. In contrast, your intuitive mind would encourage you to relax and be guided to know what to say when you get up to speak.

The introduction paved the way for us to open the intuitive doorway and walk through. By reading and completing the exercises in the next two chapters, you will become thoroughly familiar with the various facets of intuition.

As we explore your intuition, you will become more aware of which mind you tend to favor. Let's go back to our focus which is developing your intuition as the master key to success. The power of intuition can be used to help you "crack a tough case." This can be in the form of a *problem* to be solved, a *decision* to be made, a *perspective* to be gleaned, an *understanding* of the dynamics of a person or situation to be gained, or an elusive *creative or innovative idea* to be found.

OPEN YOUR MIND TO NEW IDEAS

When was the last time you used a "Post-It™ Note?" I certainly am grateful to Art Fry, the inventor of Post-It™ Notes, for his open mind. Fry sang in a church choir, where he marked the hymns selected for each service with slips of paper. The markers stayed put for the first service but usually fell out by the time the second service came. He needed a marker that would adhere to the page but not damage it when pulled off. One day, he found samples of unused adhesive that had been written off as defective by his employer, 3-M. His intuitive flash allowed him to combine his need for a better place marker with the existing adhesive product to come up with a most profitable invention. Where others initially saw only failure, Fry envisioned opportunity. He persisted, overcoming each difficulty until a marketable version of the Post-it™ Note was born.

A student slipped me a note one day in which she quoted Alexander Graham Bell when he described the "conquering force within you" with the following words: "What this power is, I cannot say. All I know is that it exists…and it becomes available only when you are in a state of mind in which you know exactly what you want…and are fully determined not to quit until you get it."

The men and women who did "get it" used their intuitive skills to innovate concepts, create methods, and invent conveniences that we all use and enjoy today. Imagine the excitement and sense of discovery surrounding the invention of things like your computer, fax machine, CD player, or VCR. Or how about the less high-tech but highly successful Frisbee or Cabbage Patch doll?

Look around the room you are sitting in now. Become aware of all the objects you cherish. How many were "inventions?" As I look at my office I am grateful for the intuitive "light bulb" that flashed in the minds of the people who invented the microchips and circuitry that have helped me share this book with you. Literally every man-made thing surrounding us was "born" as a vision or intuitive spark in the inventor's mind. Examining some of the bright ideas behind familiar inventions will introduce you to the dynamics of the intuitive process. Presented here are a few of my favorite inventors and their discoveries.

Every time you use a copier, think of Chester Carlson, who invented the Xerox process. By listening to his intuition, he invented a process that has yielded untold profits. He was never daunted by the "nay-sayers" who claimed something couldn't be done. He first had the idea of photocopy when he was a young patent lawyer, but his technical friends looked with scorn upon this "waste of time." The staff of the research department of a photographic company ridiculed and rejected his idea. Unfortunately, they were blinded to the inherent possibilities. They turned their backs on one of the most important and profitable inventions of the twentieth century.

Are you familiar with the name Clarence Saunders? You honor his discovery whenever you visit a supermarket. When he invented the self-serve market back in 1916, Clarence Saunders's "insane idea" of putting groceries on shelves, sticking a price tag in front of them, and letting shoppers pick what they wanted made him the village joke. The innovative feature at the time was having customers, rather than a clerk, select and take their groceries to the checkout counter. Despite discouraging words and ridicule, Saunders continued with his self-service idea. A few short months after the first store opened, Saunders had acquired 43 stores and significantly changed the way we shop.

Paradigm Shifts:
The Ability to Convert Old Patterns into New Ideas

Inventions come about because an *intuitive spark* ignites a new vision, helping the inventor change whatever model of reality he or she held. In other words, new times and changing circumstances lead to new discoveries. This is known as the *paradigm* concept, and it has become popular in recent years. As new paradigms, or models, evolve, inventors learn that necessity truly is the mother of invention.

Joel Barker, in his book, *Future Edge*,[1] and three excellent videos,[2] describes paradigms as a set of rules and regulations that we use to set boundaries for ourselves. Paradigms teach us how to behave within preset parameters in order to be successful. As an example of this, Barker cites what Federal Express did for overnight mail. At one time, everyone said it wasn't possible to deliver something overnight and maintain consistently perfect service. Now the paradigm has shifted with the expectation that "if you can't do it overnight (whatever your business is), something must be wrong with you. FedEx does it all the time."[3] What seemed impossible 10, 15, or 20 years ago is the expected way of doing things today.

Paradigm shifts occur as realignments in your thinking take place. You just read about the inventions of Chester Carlson, Art Fry, and Clarence Saunders. The common denominator? Each was subjected to ridicule and scorn when he tried to introduce a new way of doing things. When Albert Einstein said that "no problem is ever solved by the same consciousness that created it," he could have been referring to the paradigm shift. He suggests stepping outside the situation, looking at it through a different pair of eyes, and using intuition to shift your paradigm and perspective. So, to make a paradigm shift, you have to be open to a new vision, perspective, or insight into a situation.

Intuition, innovation, and paradigm shifts are all interrelated processes that require an inner knowing. I'm sure this is what Ralph Waldo Emerson meant when he said, "What lies behind us and lies before us are small matters compared to what lies within us." The intelligence that lies within us can invent or discover different ways of approaching our daily affairs. Making a paradigm shift means discovering new and different ways of doing things as we become open to the potential for change.

EXERCISE

How Open Are You?

Answering the following questions, borrowed from Joel Barker, will let you see how open you are to change.

How has your thinking or perspective about any issue changed in recent years?

_____

_____

_____

_____

_____

_____

Was it easy or difficult to change your perspective? Explain.

_____

_____

_____

_____

_____

_____

What would you like to see changed in your business affairs that would revolutionize the usual practices?

_____

_____

_____

_____

_____

WHAT IS INTUITION?

Defining intuition will be easier after you read the following examples.

Put yourself in Bob's shoes and identify with his *intuitive* moment. He relates, "This morning I was working on a cost justification for an $80,000 capital investment. All the data showed it was a good investment and that we should move ahead. In the middle of our approval meeting, I asked that it be tabled for eight hours because I felt that something wasn't right. Upon deeper analysis, I found that the database was incorrect, and the whole picture changed. This project is now canceled. Thanks to intuition, we saved $80,000 of bad investment."

Alicia told me about a tenant moving out of her rental property. Although her gut told her to ask if anything was broken or in need of repair, she pushed the feeling aside because this had been a model tenant. She assumed there would be no problem once the tenant departed, so she refunded the tenant's damage deposit. Later, when Alicia went to inspect the unit, she found over $200 damage to the bathroom. Because of the tenant's model behavior, she didn't listen to her intuition, or gut feeling, prodding her to inquire about any breakage before the tenant left. This is a very simple example. But listening to the intuitive voice speak can be simple. The challenge is to hear the voice within that speaks ever so gently in the silence.

One morning at work, Sandra was doing her stretching exercises as part of a program called "Corporate Athletes." While exercising, she suddenly *had a sense* that something was wrong and went to the area of the company where a new product was being displayed. She found a defect in the product that no one had caught, despite all the testing that had been done. As a result of this discovery, the company avoided liabilities that would have come from this product. Engineers were called in to fix the defect and, after five days, arrived at a very costly solution. On the sixth day, Sandra spent a few minutes looking at the problem again and came up with a very inexpensive fix that all the engineers had overlooked.

Brent had a hunch that a friend's deteriorating health was more serious than the friend realized. At Brent's insistence, the friend scheduled a doctor's appointment and found out that there was a serious heart problem. Further tests revealed a major blockage, but early attention to the problem prevented a major heart attack.

Bob, Alicia, Sandra, and Brent all received information from their intuitive mind. As a result, they were alert to a major error in a business plan, irresponsible behavior, a way to fix a costly product defect, and a significant health problem. To help you conceptualize your understanding of the intuitive process, reread each of these brief vignettes and then answer the following questions.

Defining Intuition

How do you define intuition?

_____

_____

_____

_____

What other words would you use to describe intuition?

_____

_____

_____

_____

Describe how you use intuition in your everyday business activities.

_____

_____

_____

_____

When do you rely on your hunches or gut feelings in your personal affairs?

_____

_____

_____

_____

The Logical Mind: The "Experts" Define Intuition

Frances Vaughan, a transpersonal psychologist, describes intuition in her book, *Awakening Intuition*,[4] as "a way of knowing…recognizing the possibilities in any situation."

The Swiss psychiatrist Carl Jung defined intuition as the function that "explores the unknown, and senses possibilities and implications which may not be readily apparent."[5]

And Noah Webster defines intuition as *direct knowing or learning of something without the conscious use of reasoning; immediate apprehension or understanding.*

Business people I have interviewed in my research describe intuition as

- Knowing what to do in any situation without thinking.

- The ability to arrive at a decision without any "logical" steps.

- Hunches or random thoughts moving to conviction.

- A "gut feeling" allowing them to make decisions that go against what the facts tell them.

- Knowing without conscious awareness.

- A question clearly answered by internal judgment, without reference to outside facts or sources.

- A sense of knowing through the subconscious, rather than through linear cognitive analysis.

The definitions I use are:

- Intuition is a clear knowing without being able to explain how one knows.

- Intuition is knowledge gained without logical or rational thought.

Go back to your definition of intuition on page 8 to see if it reflects your intuitive or logical mind. After determining which mind helped you define intuition, compare your response to those that have just been given.

EXERCISE

Comparing Your Responses to the Definitions

How did your ideas about intuition compare with these definitions?

_____

_____

_____

_____

_____

The Intuitive Mind: A Picture Is Worth a Thousand Words

You will discover how the intuitive mind communicates by sending you a picture, symbol, or metaphor.

EXERCISE

Let Your Intuitive Mind Define Intuition

Here are several pictures. Record your impressions of how each symbol represents intuition. When you finish, compare your responses to mine on page 11.

Lightning—Intuition comes spontaneously "in a flash" and strikes like a "bolt out of the blue."

Key—Gives you an answer. As something "clicks in place," intuition opens the door to further understanding.

Puzzle Piece—Intuition helps you put all the pieces together.

Light Bulb—A bright idea! Also, by using intuition you can become enlightened and resolve indecision.

Satellite Dish—Picks up signals from your intuitive mind in the form of images, ideas, and feelings and beams them onto the screen of your conscious awareness.[6]

We use several expressions to imply that intuition has been at work. Have you ever heard anyone say:

My **gut feeling** told me not to hire him.

I had a **hunch** the deal would go through.

I had a **premonition** that the market would crash.

My strong **business acumen** helped me make the right bid.

My **insight** helped me select the right people for the project.

I made an **educated guess** that the new product was a winner.

I always **fly by the seat of my pants** in making decisions like this.

Our group at work has a shared **vision** of where we are headed in the next few years.

I had a **sixth sense** that I would receive a raise next week.

Playing it by ear, I knew just what to say during my presentation.

As a good lawyer, I can **sniff out** what my opponent will do.

Shooting from the hip, I expressed myself during the sales meeting and hit the target.

I got the picture when I saw them working together.

A light suddenly went on and I found the solution.

Record any other symbols, metaphors, and images you can think of that are sent by the intuitive mind.

_____

_____

_____

_____

_____

Intuition can bypass logic and provide innovative leaps in new and untried situations. To isolate intuition, you have to clearly understand what it is and what it is not.

Intuition Is:	*Intuition Is Not:*
Nonrational	Logical
Nonlinear	Rational
Insightful	Common sensical
Nondata-based	An emotional state
An extension of the five basic senses	Based on experience

Many people confuse common sense and past experience with intuition. These processes emanate from the logical and rational mind and are integrated with intuition for effective decision making, but they are not the same as being intuitive. Although several researchers[7] call intuition a logical skill and blend both these processes, my view is that intuition is very distinct and separate from logic.

Leo Buscaglia, noted author and international speaker, emphasized one of the elements related to intuition that tends to be dismissed: what fun it is! A sense of discovery and a sense of joy can be realized when we tap into this source and say, like Einstein, "Don't sit here and wrack your brains. Go sit under a beautiful apple tree in a meadow" and wait for the apple of discovery to fall into your lap. How often we struggle at length to solve a problem, to come up with the right words to use, to make a decision, only to have the solution, clever phrase, or best choice present itself after we ourselves have given up. This ability to provide ourselves with the resolutions we seek is within us all, but we almost unconsciously fight against it or simply don't believe the answers when they come to us.

THE FIVE LEVELS
OF INTUITIVE EXPERIENCE

You can extend your understanding of the intuitive process by discovering the various ways you receive intuitive input. Frances Vaughan[8] described the first four levels of intuitive experience, and I have added a fifth level, the environmental, to underscore how intuitive input also comes from the things around you. Let's look at these five levels.

Physical (body)—Examples of physical intuitive cues include any of these physical sensations: the proverbial gut feeling, a stomachache, ears tingling, a tension headache, or adopting another's pain as your own (feeling someone's toothache).

Mental (mind)—Familiarly known as the "Eureka—I've found it!" or the "Ah'ha" effect. This happens when you put the separate pieces of a problem together into a coherent whole. The intuitive light bulb in your inner mind lights up to signal new theories, an instant illumination, or a sudden flash of understanding.

Emotional (heart)—Intuitive cues transmitted to or about another person in the form of a feeling. This can be an immediate like or dislike, sudden change of mood, or feeling extremely receptive or averse to someone without logical provocation.

Spiritual (soul)—An awareness that is connected with something greater than what is in the physical world. For example, an executive understands how the company's purpose is interlinked with all of humanity, or a woman, considering a career change, suddenly understands how a particular job will allow her to fulfill her true purpose in life.

Environmental (place)—Cues or signals from the environment send intuitive messages in many ways. A flat tire on your car may be telling you not to go to the meeting or take the trip; an electric outage causing your computer to go down is screaming out "take time off," or failing to reach someone by phone despite numerous tries is telling you now is not the time to connect with this person.

EXERCISE

How Does Your Intuition
Speak to You?

Discover how your intuition speaks to you by recording two examples for each level of intuitive experience.

Physical:

_____

_____

_____

Mental:

_____

_____

_____

Emotional:

_____

_____

_____

Spiritual:

_____

_____

_____

Environmental:

_____

_____

_____

DISCOVERING YOUR INTUITIVE QUOTIENT

What is your intuitive quotient? How would you answer this question? Could you assign a percentage such as 55% or 82% to your intuitive quotient? Would you reply high, average, or not so hot? Perhaps you wouldn't respond at all because you never took a "test" to measure your "intuitive quotient." While descriptive words and numerical indices might be helpful, more important, can you remember *using* your intuition in any situation? How do you use your intuitive mind? Many people think that intuition is a special gift that belongs to someone else. As you go through the exercises in this book, you will claim your right to use your intuitive gifts. You are now at the starting gate of your quest to unlock your power of intuition. At this juncture it is most important that you ask, "How Intuitive Am I?" You can answer that question after you complete the "Intuitive Quotient Checklist." Don't be surprised if you discover that you have been using your intuition all along.

What Is Your Intuitive Quotient?

Complete the "Intuitive Quotient Checklist" by going through and checking yes if you can identify with the situation posed. You may even be reminded of other times you used your intuitive input. Make a note of these other situations in the blank space following the checklist. When you have finished this checklist, you will be able to respond to anyone who asks you about your intuitive batting average.

Intuitive Quotient Checklist	*Yes*	*No*

1. Has a flash of insight ever helped you solve a problem?

2. Do creative ideas suddenly show you new ways to view a situation?

3. Do you ever know things about people without having advance information about them?

4. Do you ever sense when an accident is about to occur?

5. Do you ever know who is calling when the phone rings?

6. Have you ever had a compelling urge to call someone, only to have them say, "I was hoping you would call!"

7. Are your hunches about situations at work ever confirmed later?

8. When you first meet someone you've talked to but have never seen, do they match the image you had of them?

9. Can you fix machines or appliances without looking at the directions or manual?

10. When being introduced to someone new, do you have a feeling about how you will get along?

11. Do you instantly know where to find something that has been lost?

12. Do you have a strong feeling which candidate is best qualified for a job?

13. Do you know just what to say when you have to make a sudden speech?

14. If someone is late for an appointment, can you sense when they will arrive?

15. Do you clearly know if the automobile or appliance you are about to purchase is right?

16. Do you ever think of someone and have them call soon after?

17. Are your first impressions of people usually right?

18. Do you ever feel a strong desire to go someplace and later discover that you needed to be there?

19. Have you ever met someone for the first time, felt uncomfortable, and later heard "bad news" about them?

20. Have you ever applied for a job and known instantly you would be chosen out of all the applicants?

21. Can you "see" what your friend will wear to lunch?

22. Can you "hear" the boss's first words at the meeting?

23. Do you make snap decisions at work with limited facts available and know you are right?

24. Can you tell in advance if a meeting is going to be worthwhile?

25. Have you met someone and known instantly that you would be good friends?

Results: Number of YES Answers: _____   *Number of NO Answers:* _____

These "informal results" will help you answer the question, "How intuitive am I?" If you answered "yes" at least once, your intuition has been active at some time in your life. You have intuition and you can use this ability to manage any situation rapidly, effortlessly, and creatively. Each time you complete an exercise in this book, your intuition is being strengthened and you will be able to access this source of information more readily.

What other intuitive situations do you recall? Help yourself become more aware of your intuitive experiences by recording some of them in this space. Don't censor your notes or evaluate whether an experience was genuinely intuitive. After you complete the last page in this book you can return to this page to make that assessment.

_____

_____

_____

_____

_____

Perhaps you haven't used the term intuition to describe any of these experiences. If not, how did you account for them?

_____

_____

_____

_____

_____

YOUR SUBCONSCIOUS:
A RESERVOIR OF INTUITIVE WISDOM

Earlier, I mentioned that we all have access to a giant data bank containing all the information we could possibly need. This vast reservoir known as the subconscious contains stored memories, creativity, and wisdom. Wisdom in the form of an intuitive flash or insight comes from the subconscious. Your intuition operates to uncover the truth and wisdom of this world within you. There are times when I teach, lecture, or talk to clients when I allow myself to be spontaneous and I surprise myself with the pearls of wisdom that roll out of my mouth. I find I am most successful in these situations when I am not reading a talk or following an outline.

The logical mind, or thinker, would have a difficult time telling you exactly where the subconscious resides, but the intuitive mind can graphically show how the subconscious works.

Wilferd Peterson is a retired advertising executive.[9] For one of Mr. Peterson's presentations, he had an artist create for him a character called "Subby" to graphically represent the subconscious. He wanted to show his audience, all advertising folks, how the subconscious mind can come up with clever ideas and novel concepts that escape the grasp of the solely logical "thinker." For example, the artist showed the thinker hitting a stone wall while Subby jumped over it and went on with his work. Subby typed clever slogans while the thinker slept, providing him with the ad campaign focus the thinker needed. And Subby even presented a list of catch advertising phrases to the thinker.

EXERCISE

Find Your "Subby"

How is your Subby helping you be more innovative? At work? At home?

_____

_____

_____

_____

_____

Intuitive Tidbits

- Intuition or inner (in) teaching (tuition) comes from the Latin verb *intueri*, which means looking or knowing from within.

- Using your intuition will help you sense new possibilities and discover new alternatives. This gives you more flexibility and freedom of choice in decision making.

- To use intuition effectively, simply believe it works.

- The more you use intuition, the more available it becomes to you.

- Through repeated practice, you will improve your decision making and make powerful, early good decisions.

- Several culprits can impair intuition: you engage in wishful thinking, you may be acting out of fear, you are too embedded in a sense of ownership, or you are projecting your needs onto someone or something else.

- Keeping a journal will help you discover the internal signals that confirm your intuition is correct.

- Using intuition helps you discover your authentic self and special talents.

- Intuition will help you identify what you truly want. You are more likely to achieve success with this certainty than when you are unclear.

- Daily periods of stillness and quiet are vital components that help you develop and use your intuition consistently.

EXERCISE

Collect Your Intuitive Tidbits

Become immersed in the joy of intuitive discovery. What have you noticed about the intuitive process? What priceless gems have you discovered? Note them here. This list can be extended for pages. Add to it as you move along.

_____

_____

_____

_____

_____

TEN POWER KEYS FOR DEVELOPING YOUR INTUITION

These keys will help you open and walk through your intuitive doorway. Use them to become more balanced and integrated in your decision-making or problem-solving activities. These keys will help you understand other people better, improve your creative touch, and help you unlock the wisdom of your subconscious.

1. *Honor*—Respect your flashes and don't label any as silly or coincidental.

2. *Brevity and simplicity*—Express your hunches from the intuitive mind briefly in a word or two. Considerable talking belongs to the logical mind.

3. *Symbol, picture, and imagery*—The intuitive mind will turn on the images inside your head. Do you get the picture?

4. *Suspend assumptions*—Use intuitive input as naively as possible without entertaining any preconceived notions.

5. *First impressions*—Your first impressions are usually correct.

6. *Faint stirrings*—Respect the weakly articulated impressions as strongly as you do the loud raps of intuition.

7. *Active-passive*—Intuition can come passively, like a "flash out of the blue" or actively when you ask a question and wait for a reply.

8. *Relax for enhanced receptivity*—Letting go of tension or stress helps you relax and receive the pictures, images and symbols sent by the intuitive mind.

9. *Associate*—Freely associating to the imagery sent by the intuitive mind will help you unravel the underlying meaning of the symbols. If you see your new employee as a bear, perhaps he "speaks the bare truth."

10. *Playful moments*—Enjoy the intuitive process. Fun and levity weaken analysis and strengthen the intuitive flow.

EXERCISE

Searching for Keys

Record your experiences using the ten keys just introduced.

_____

_____

_____

_____

_____

Can you think of any other keys that will help you develop and strengthen your intuitive ability?

_____

_____

_____

_____

_____

In the next chapter, you will discover how to unlock your intuitive mind for more effective decision making and improved problem solving.

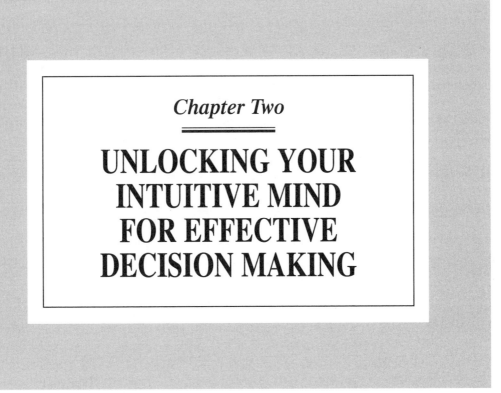

Chapter Two

UNLOCKING YOUR INTUITIVE MIND FOR EFFECTIVE DECISION MAKING

The intuitive mind will tell the thinking mind where to look next.

JONAS SALK, M.D.

INTUITION AND LOGIC: THE DECISION-MAKING TEAM

"Intuition" and "logic" are the key players on your decision-making team. Distortion can result when "emotion" tries to join this team effort.

To illustrate this, take the following situation. Your work unit is about to market a new product. You are presenting this product to a group attending a monthly club meeting. Your *intuitive mind* sends you a brilliant flash showing you how to demonstrate the time-saving aspects of this product. You then switch to your *logical mind* to determine what details, such as price and availability, need to be mentioned. You also need to check your *emotional* barometer to be sure that your audience's decision won't be affected by any negative associations they might have had to a similar product.

The distinction between the roles played by intuition and emotion in decision making is subtle. But I want to state simply that emotion is not intuitive, nor is intuition emotional.

Let me clarify this distinction by focusing on the newly divorced man who just married the woman of his dreams. Although this new union seems to fill a void and restores companionship to his life, it may not have been the best choice intuitively. The emotional factor—fears being alone—could have intruded, consciously or unconsciously, on his decision. If so, it will not be surprising if, months later, this perfect union begins to disintegrate. These two people were not really fated to be mated, but the emotional need, masquerading as intuition, unduly influenced the marriage decision.

The term "gut feeling" can further cloud this issue. Your "gut," located in the abdomen region or pit of your stomach, can act as an intuitive signal or alarm. This is the physical level of intuitive experience described on page 13. For example, a discomforting physical feeling can intuitively signal that something is wrong, in contrast to the peace that resonates throughout the body which can signal a correct intuitive choice. Emotion is also confused with intuition by those who say, "I have a feeling that something will happen." That feeling, too, is more of a *gut feeling*, or physical cue from the "stomach area" acting as an intuitive signal.

In making any decision or solving any problem, you truly have to recognize any emotions that are exerting an influence on the decision. These can be positive emotions such as love, happiness, and joy or negative emotions such as anger, anxiety, hate, or fear. The intuitive voice can be heard more clearly when you recognize that your emotions can color your decision. For example, suppose you are voting to select a president of your business or social club. First, you want to sort out your emotional feelings about each candidate; then you can go beyond the emotion to intuitively sense who the best person for the position would be.

To summarize, to maximize effective decision making, you can draw upon your logical mind, which becomes integrated with any intuitive input after you factor out any emotional influences. This simple formula for effective decision making can be expressed as

Intuition + Logic - Emotion = Effective decision making

EXERCISE

How Do You Make Decisions?

Over the next few days, notice which factors prevail when you are making a decision, solving a problem, being creative, or trying to understand someone's character. You will be able to scrutinize the role each factor plays in your decisions. Are you primarily logical, needing factual backup? Do new intuitive ideas prompt you to make changes in your usual plan? How do your emotions impact the decision? Record your observations here.

_____

_____

_____

_____

_____

INTUITIVE DECISION MAKING

The concept of intuitive decision making refers to the conscious use of intuition as one of the decision-making components. These discoveries about intuitive decision making spring from the research spearheaded by Dr. Douglas Dean. Over a ten-year period beginning in 1962, Dr. Dean, a noted chemist, physicist, and parapsychologist, conducted various laboratory investigations with his colleague, engineer John Mihalsky, to probe the intuitive decision-making process. According to Dr. Dean, intuition involved knowing, apart from logic, how something was going to work out in the future. The results of this research are summarized in their book, *Executive ESP*.[1]

After testing approximately 165 presidents and CEOs of American companies, they found that 80% of these company leaders who doubled (or more than doubled) their company profits in a five-year period had above-average predictive computer test scores.

The predictive computer score was a measure of their intuitive ability. It is interesting that "nondoublers" had much lower predictive test scores. These results led Dean and Mihalsky to conclude that "prophets make profits." In testing members of 100 professional organizations, they found that dynamic people, those who tend to get 25–30 things done in a day, had higher than average intuitive scores. The nondynamic people who put things off until tomorrow had lower scores than average.

Another major thrust for "intuitive explorations" came from Weston Agor. His work occurred ten years after Dean's concluded, and was published in his book, *Intuitive Management*.[2] After testing more than 3,000 managers nationwide, he found that top executives rated significantly higher in intuition than did middle- or lower-level managers. Agor interviewed 100 of the top scorers on his intuition scale to find out how they actually used their intuitive ability in decision making. These findings, described in detail in his book, *The Logic of Intuitive Decision Making*,[3] identified these circumstances in which intuition was most often used by the respondents. They include:

- where there is a high level of uncertainty
- where there is little precedent
- where variables are less scientifically predictable
- where facts are limited
- where facts do not clearly indicate the direction to take
- where analytical data are of little use (i.e., an emerging trend)
- where there are several plausible solutions
- where time is limited and there is pressure to be right
- where negotiations and personnel decisions are paramount.

Joel Barker pointed out several interesting applications of intuition in business during our phone interview. He referred to Peter F. Drucker's book, *Managing in Turbulent Times*.[4] Drucker talked about entrepreneurs. He was basically talking about paradigm pioneers, or the people who get in before everyone else gets in, and about how they never feel the risk. Everyone else is going "Oh my God, look at the risk you are taking" and these paradigm pioneers are saying, "What risk? It's obvious what I am doing."

Barker then elaborated on these innovative pioneers who arrive first on the scene and actually have a tremendous amount of knowledge. Their intuition lets them recognize patterns in new developments much earlier than other people with much less detail needed. They can make a good decision without much information, while many of the rest of us have to wait for enough information and say, "Oh there's the pattern." The intuitives pick it up very early. Barker emphasizes that decision making can be improved considerably by relying on intuition to give early good decisions. Using intuition, you will get to a much better decision earlier than you will if you wait for the numbers to come in.

EXERCISE

How Is Your Intuitive Decision Making?

Consider the decisions that you make at work or about your personal life. What situations are you in that are like those of Agor's "top executives"?

_____

_____

_____

_____

_____

What do you do when you have to make a quick decision without all the facts?

_____

_____

_____

_____

_____

What do you do when you are forging into a new area and making a decision without precedent?

_____

_____

_____

_____

_____

THE SIX FAMILIAR I's OF PROBLEM SOLVING

Incorporating intuitive decision making into a formula or process for resolving problems grows out of the work I just discussed that was initiated by Dean and Agor. The intuitive problem-solving (IPS) formula presented in this book is unique and came to me intuitively as I was teaching my graduate course, "Integrating Intuition and Logic for Managers." Although you haven't seen this formula before, you may recognize its different components. I doubt if you ever sat down at work and specifically said, "I am going to engage in intuitive problem solving," but you have probably used many facets of this process without even knowing it.

EXERCISE

The Familiar I's of Problem Solving

Here are the I's of the problem-solving process that you have used before. When you see these words or phrases, what thoughts come to mind? Write your associations to these words or phrases in the space provided.

In the silence: _____

_____

Introspection: _____

_____

Imagination: _____

_____

Illumination: _____

_____

Incubation: _____

_____

Implementation: _____

_____

Notice how these words or phrases are incorporated in the following familiar situations.

♦ Retreating from the noisy office, Susan just wanted to sit *in the silence* and clear her head. In doing so, she was becoming *centered* and more focused so she could complete the report that was due.

♦ Jane was going through an *introspective* period. During this *receptive* time, she wanted to go within herself and scrutinize her present patterns of behavior. For her, this was a time of slowing down and reducing activity to hear what the inner self has to say.

♦ Arnold taps his creative *imagination* to find new ways to market his products. He says the *images* that help him successfully sell his products just jump into his head.

♦ Joe found an *illuminating* way to gather his staff together from their various work sites for a monthly meeting. The image of a lot of fish swimming together from different directions came to him *in a flash* while he was taking a shower. *Interpreting this imagery*, he clearly knew that he had to organize an outing by the beach.

♦ Andrea mentioned how she puts a problem on hold during *incubation* to replenish the well of new ideas. This *taking time out* is necessary so the subconscious can work.

♦ Bill and Joyce wanted to have a better understanding of their 14-year-old son Chuck. They were often puzzled by his idiosyncratic behavior. One moment he was happy, and then he suddenly became uncommunicative. One night, these intuitive parents had a flash about how to *implement* more meaningful communication with their son. They knew that talking to him about his new-found interest in the school band and encouraging him to try out for music camps would bring them all closer. They *activated* the intuitive solution and gained instant rapport with him.

Go back to each of these examples. The first italicized phrase is probably more familiar to you than the second italicized phrase that represents the "new IPS" elements in this process. Let's see how the familiar I's translate to the IPS components:

Familiar I's	IPS
In the silence	Centering
Introspection	Receptivity
Imagination	Retrieving imagery
Illumination	Interpreting the imagery
Incubation	Resting period
Implementation	Activating the solution

DISCOVERING THE DYNAMICS OF INTUITIVE PROBLEM SOLVING

Let's study Mary to understand the dynamics of the intuitive problem-solving process. Mary is in charge of personnel in a company facing staff cutbacks. One of the employees she must let go has become a close friend. In fact, they live in the same neighborhood. Looking at her desk calendar, Mary realizes that tomorrow she must tell her friend that she is no longer needed.

Mary sits back in her chair, concentrates on the geometric shape embedded in the blossom of a plant sitting in front of her on the desk (centering). She takes several deep breaths (receptivity) and ponders her problem.

The image of a "weightlifter" comes to mind (retrieving imagery). As she begins freely associating (interpreting the imagery) with this word to unravel the meaning of this symbolism, she thinks of a weighty issue, an athlete, a workout, practice time, and muscles. None of these associations gives her a resolution to the problem.

After dinner that evening, Mary takes her usual walk around the block. During this time, she suspends all thoughts about this pressing concern (taking time out). As she passes her friend's house, the problem comes back into her thoughts. Suddenly, the "Ah'ha!" is reached when she thinks about the weightlifter and knows she must be strong when she approaches her friend (activating the solution). Though striking in its simplicity, the image sends a clear message to Mary that she will feel "strong" in delivering the dismissal message to her friend.

Now, let's translate Mary's decision-making process into the IPS formula. First, notice how Mary *became centered* by focusing on the natural pattern in the plant blossom on her desk. To become more relaxed, she used deep breathing to enter a *receptive* state. Her imagination allowed her to *elicit the imagery* of a weightlifter. Unable to successfully come up with a good interpretation, she took a *resting period* by letting go of the problem so the solution could incubate. Later, during her regular evening walk, the spontaneous insight occurred with little effort and helped her *interpret the imagery* showing how she would feel strong talking to her friend. The next day, she *activated the solution* by confidently confronting Mary about her dismissal.

Centering, receptivity, eliciting the imagery, and interpretation are the four main elements of IPS you will now begin using. Each will be discussed in subsequent chapters of Part Two. In the last chapter of Part Two, you will be introduced to the IPS formula again so you can practice "putting it all together."

An exciting facet of intuitive problem solving is that you can get to the core of a problem rapidly. This is when intuition comes to the rescue to help you present something new or make a decision before all the facts are available.

Darwin Clark, the vice president of sales, marketing, and aftersales for General Motors Europe, had many challenging experiences throughout his career at Buick. He told me about the time he was asked to facilitate a leadership conference for top Buick executives. He was originally told that a professional facilitator would preside at the meeting and use Clark's expertise for support. At the meeting, they proceeded with the process of developing, as a team, a customer vision of Buick. Soon after they started, Clark was told he would be conducting the entire meeting alone. As a neophyte, Clark wondered how he would facilitate others to create this important customer vision. His discomfort slipped away, he said, when he started listening and *intuitively* discovered what kind of questions he needed to ask.

When faced with several options, your intuitive mind will also highlight the right choice or even present new options. As you become more adept with IPS, you will be delighted to receive a renewed perspective or deeper understanding of any problem, person, or puzzling situation. When the solution is not evident, your intuitive mind will present the next step and help you move forward. At other times, you will be able to go right to the "light at the end of the tunnel" to discover the solution.

Any IPS process starts with a "problem" that needs a resolution or next step.

FOR EVERY PROBLEM THERE IS
AN INTUITIVE SOLUTION

You were given a set of keys on page 18 with which to unlock your intuitive mind. Use them to become more effective when you make decisions, solve problems, come up with an innovative idea, or try to understand someone's challenging personality. To use these keys and activate the IPS formula, you have to start with a problem or issue in need of resolution.

Perhaps you are one of those people who believe that you don't have any problems. Or, at the other extreme, you might think that your problems are too weighty to be solved. Think again! Everyone can benefit from using the *intuitive problem-solving* formula (IPS). I use the word *problem* loosely here to cover a variety of situations. For example, you might want to use the IPS method to

Resolve a personal issue.

Make an important decision at work or at home.

Understand an unpredictable personality.

Get a new perspective on a situation so you can take positive action.

Discover a creative or *innovative approach* to marketing a product or service.

When the word "problem" appears anywhere in this book, mentally substitute any of these words—resolution, decision, understanding, perspective, creative or innovative idea.

You Can Be Anywhere When a "Problem" Strikes!

In the office surrounded by coworkers or superiors.

At a professional meeting.

Attending a social gathering and wondering what to say next.

At home disciplining your 13-year-old.

On the athletic field.

Stuck in traffic wondering what to do.

At home with everyone competing for your time and attention.

In the card shop looking for the right invitation.

Do you get the picture? You can be anywhere when a fresh perspective on a seemingly insoluble dilemma is needed. IPS will come to the rescue with a resolution or elusive creative touch. You can solve any problem or issue with the IPS formula.

If, as Einstein said, *no problem is solved by the same consciousness that created it*, then the implication is that the answer is there all along, and you need to alter only your perspective to discover it. IPS is a unique process that can give you access to unlimited perspectives on any problem or situation.

During economically troubled times, many people are concerned about losing their jobs. Their "fear consciousness" is so strong that it implicitly reinforces the message "if I lose this job, I won't be able to get another one." This attitude can be changed by using IPS to discover other alternatives. For example, the "worried one" can let the intuitive mind reveal what new job avenues to pursue, or it can lead the person to a more suitable field of interest. A young man I know was one of several candidates being considered for a managerial position with an engineering firm. Though he was disappointed that he didn't get the job, he realized that what he really wanted to do was have adequate time to work on his inventions. He was eventually rewarded when the CEO of a large company decided to invest in his latest gadgetry, a product that eventually saved the company a tremendous amount of money.

And we are all familiar with the people who are afraid to part with the "dream" man or woman, when in reality the person has neglected and is mistreating them. They are afraid they will never find someone else. The intuitive mind can come to the rescue, if allowed, to show a more caring person also eager for a relationship waiting on the horizon.

Problems Come in All Shapes and Sizes

Paula, the director of the Medical Records Department at a hospital, supervises a staff of 20. One of the employees had been receiving a considerable number of personal phone calls at work. She was also frequently taking time out during her work shift to make calls. This was unusual for this individual, who had always been very conscientious. The situation was brought to Paula's attention by grumbling from the employee's peers. Resentment appeared to be mounting. Because this employee had also been very sensitive whenever Paula tried to correct even minor mistakes, Paula was at first uncertain about how to approach her. She knew she could use IPS to find the best way to resolve the matter.

First, she had to let go of all the emotion attached to the situation and clearly formulate the problem. Paula defined her problem in question form and asked, "How shall I approach this person about the disruption caused by the personal telephone calls?" In the final analysis, there was a reasonable explanation for the phone calls that might not have been uncovered if the emotional discomfort had escalated and prevented open communication. For now, notice how Paula began the intuitive problem-solving resolution by formulating a succinct question.

Defining Your Problem

To use IPS you must first clearly define the problem or situation you need to resolve. Are there some issues you would like to clarify or resolve? You will be listing five problems on page 31. Keep them in mind so you can practice applying each IPS step featured in the upcoming chapters to your problem(s).

In many ways, stating your problem clearly and concisely in the form of a question is the most important part of the IPS process. Clearly knowing what your search is about culminates in an illuminating resolution.

Here are some pointers to help you structure concise questions:

1. Separate the problem from the background.

   Do: Describe the background first and then pose the question in a separate section.

   Don't: State the background and include the question(s) in that narrative.

   Notice how the two questions are lodged in the following background description.

Background: At work, I am putting together our first ever annual report. I have been struggling with the problem of how to recognize the nearly 5,000 benefactors who have helped the organization become a successful entity in just a few short years. I have been undecided as to how I wanted to recognize the generosity of these wonderful people. Should I group these individuals according to their church parish or according to the amount of their contribution, the customary procedure in fund-raising organizations?

The two questions found in the background can be consolidated into one "problem" and then be resolved using IPS. The questions are

Should I group these individuals according to their church parish?

Should I group them according to the amount of their contribution?

The problem should be stated: "How should I recognize the generosity of our benefactors?"

2. Focus on only one part of the problem.

Do: Will I receive a promotion?

Don't: Will I receive a promotion and be transferred to another division?

These two questions can be explored independently.

3. If you make more than one inquiry, each must focus on a single facet.

Do: When shall I make the request? How shall I make the request?

Don't: When shall I make the request and in which office?
How shall I make the request and what shall I wear?

Your Turn to Define a Problem

Let me jog your mind by posing some problems or issues that might need to be clarified. Then, I would like to have you formulate five problems of your own that you will be solving as you work your way through this book and become adept using IPS.

Sample Problems in Need of Resolution

- ◆ How will the ongoing contract dispute be resolved at work?
- ◆ What is the appropriate way to express my dissatisfaction to a superior?
- ◆ Shall I offer the newly created position in my department to my assistant?
- ◆ Is this the right time to sell my house?
- ◆ How can I relieve the stress from the hiring and firing decisions I make?
- ◆ How will I prepare for new styles and policies at work?
- ◆ Will I ever understand my teenager?
- ◆ How can I resolve the misunderstanding with my neighbor?
- ◆ Do I want to keep my membership in the sailing club?
- ◆ How can my spouse and I compromise on how to spend money?

Problem Refinement

Formulate five problems of your own that you would like to resolve using IPS. This is your opportunity to write and rewrite until each of your five problems is clear and concisely formulated as a question to be answered.

Problem 1: _____

_____

_____

Problem 2: _____

_____

_____

Problem 3: _____

_____

_____

Problem 4: _____

_____

_____

Problem 5: _____

_____

_____

Now that you have begun to clearly state the problem, you can begin to put all the components of the IPS formula together. As you are learning how to use this process, I suggest keeping a copy of the formula in a handy place in your office and at home.

Here is the unique IPS formula that you will be using to resolve any problem.

THE INTUITIVE PROBLEM-SOLVING FORMULA (IPS)

1. *Define the problem*: What is your problem? Write it out as a concise and clear question.

2. *Center yourself*: Select one or all of the following techniques, to be discussed in Chapter Three:

   Use an affirmation: For example, "my intuitive signals are strong and reliable."

   Say a focusing phrase: For example, "peace be still."

   Focus visually on a geometric shape: For example, the leaf of a plant.

   Listen to recorded instrumental music.

3. *Make yourself receptive*: Sit quietly with your eyes closed. For optimal receptivity, use one of the four breathing techniques and then one of the six relaxation techniques from Chapter Four.

4. *Elicit imagery*: What imagery appears? You may see an image, hear a voice, have a feeling, taste the answer, sniff it out, or clearly know the direction to take. Remember that your intuitive flash can come *passively* or spontaneously as an impression, number, picture, metaphor, symbol, or a familiar word or phrase. Or you can *actively* elicit the imagery you need for problem solving by using techniques discussed in Chapter Five.

5. *Interpret the imagery*: Use amplification, word association, clustering, or mind mapping methods for unraveling the symbolism and deciphering the underlying meaning that will be explained in Chapter Six.

6. *Rest*: If the solution isn't clear, let the problem go. Let it incubate or rest until the right solution emerges spontaneously.

7. *Interpret further*: Be alert to any sudden flashes of insight illuminating the resolution.

8. *Activate the solution*: The intuitive mind has shown you what to do. Now, implement the solution.

You will be learning how to use each component of the IPS formula for success in Part Two. IPS is a handy tool or process that will speedily help you resolve any long-standing nagging dilemma. Repeatedly practice using the IPS steps so they become second nature.

After defining the problem, the next step or preparatory phase, presented in Chapter Three, is to learn how to *become centered*. During this step, you are shifting your attention from "out there" to the silent place within so you can hear the intuitive mind speak. Making this shift so you can access the intuitive mind and disengage the logical mind is vital.

Taking this step requires you to become more *receptive* to the intuitive mind. Using the proper breathing and receptivity techniques that you will learn in Chapter Four will help you "slow down" your brainwaves so you can enter this receptive state.

It is important to recognize how your intuitive mind speaks to you. In Chapter Five, on eliciting the intuitive imagery, for example, you may discover that you are not a visualizer but are better at "feeling" the solution. That will be the key to consistently retrieving your imagery.

You will learn several ways to interpret your imagery in Chapter Six. The primary method is through an association process called Amplification, but you might find you want to delve further into the imagery and prefer using some of the auxiliary methods.

Finally, as you begin to "put it all together" in Chapter Seven, you can begin resolving some of your basic troubling situations. After achieving that success, you can resolve some of the more dynamic issues in the work place or in your personal life.

In Part Two, you will learn how to use each component of the IPS formula. Now, let's go to the next chapter so you can begin to shift your perspective.

Part Two

THE FORMULA FOR SUCCESS

Chapter Three

CENTERING: HOW TO QUIET THE LOGICAL MIND AND AWAKEN THE INTUITIVE MIND

An affirmation is more than just words that are spoken. An affirmation is a belief, a dedication. It is a powerful statement of personal understanding.

WILFERD PETERSON
The Art of Creative Thinking

A QUIET MIND IS AN INTUITIVE MIND

Donald is a financial analyst for a large corporation. His responsibilities include all hiring and termination processes. He has just heard that one of his employees is very ill. As soon as he hears this, his mind starts swimming with a number of questions and details about how to handle this delicate situation. He has to make changes in this employee's work schedule to allow for the disability. Other employees, unaware of their coworker's deteriorating health situation, express concern about "unfair" treatment. Donald is in a quandary and wants to tell the others, knowing that they will understand and pull together to provide emotional support for the worker, but the person wants to keep the details private. Following a rule book isn't possible in this situation. Yet Donald has to act quickly before emotional pressures and negative feelings toward the afflicted person escalate. Can you feel Donald's pressure? What would you do?

The first thing Donald has to do is become quiet or centered to "silence his noisy and worrisome mind." As the noisy logical mind recedes, the intuitive mind is given the opportunity to emerge and be heard. Donald starts his centering process by repeatedly stating, "My intuitive mind will lead me to the right answer." Donald becomes calm enough to start the intuitive problem-solving (IPS) process and find an enlightening answer to his vexing problem.

In this chapter, you will discover several techniques for centering or quieting the mind so the IPS process can begin.

The need to silence the noisy logical mind to bring out your intuition is expressed in the graphics in this section. These pictures show that the optimal conditions for awakening your intuition occurs when you are centered and still.

 YOU *WON'T* AWAKEN INTUITION IF LOST IN A TENSE, NOISY WORLD

 YOU *WON'T* HAVE HUNCHES WHEN YOU ARE IN TURMOIL

 YOU *WON'T* BECOME INTUITIVE WHEN YOU ARE STRESSED

 YOU *WON'T* BECOME AWARE OF GUT FEELINGS WHEN YOU ARE ENGULFED IN WORDS

 YOU *WILL* AWAKEN YOUR INTUITION WHEN YOU ARE STILL, CENTERED, AND RECEPTIVE

You just read about how Donald retreated from an agonizing worry about his problem and became still. In the next exercise, you will find out whether becoming still is easy or difficult for you. Now, let's see how long you can be still.

EXERCISE

Can You Be Still?

Sit still for 3 minutes. Close your eyes and try to block out any interfering thoughts, bothersome emotions, and physical distractions. You can look at a clock before you start and then check the time when you sense 3 minutes have elapsed. Evaluate your present ability to be "still" by answering these questions:

What thoughts went through your mind?

_____

_____

_____

Did any emotions intrude?

_____

_____

_____

Were any bodily sensations distracting?

_____

_____

_____

Evaluate your "centering" experience.

_____

_____

_____

How did you do? Don't be surprised if you have difficulty concentrating even for a brief period. Our busy world rarely gives us the opportunity to "be still." The exercises in this chapter will help you learn to be still for at least 15 to 20 minutes, allowing you to become more relaxed and centered. Keep this goal in mind as you monitor your progress. Centering will become easier as you practice. On page 291, you will find a list of audiocassettes that will help you with these exercises.

You must learn to quiet your logical mind so your intuitive mind can emerge. To achieve maximum receptivity, you want to become as still as possible, disengaging from "the outer sensory world" and becoming attuned to your inner intuitive mind. You will actually alter your awareness by lowering your brainwave frequency.

Lowering Your Brainwaves Will Help You Become Still

Don't be afraid of the term "altering your awareness." You do it every day! During your normal activities, your brain functions at the *beta level*, which is measured at 13–25 cycles per second. In beta, you are fully alert and conscious of logical and analytical input that comes to you through your five senses.

As you begin to enter the *alpha level*, your brainwaves fall to 8–12 cycles per second. Your inner awareness actually expands as you begin accessing the 90% of your mind that is submerged in the subconscious. Intuitive receptivity is high at the alpha level. You can identify the alpha level, as that "drifty" feeling you experience just as you are falling asleep at night and the same feeling you often sense on awakening in the morning. Now, when you begin drifting off into a daydream, you will know you are entering the alpha level.

The brainwaves slow to 5–7 cycles per second at the *theta level*. This occurs during sleep and at a very deep level of meditation or hypnosis. Intuitive receptivity is also strong at the theta level.

At the *delta level*, the brainwaves are slowed to 1–4 cycles per second. Delta level occurs during deep or full sleep.

EXERCISE

Alpha Awareness

Can you recall how you felt falling asleep last night? What sensations did you feel? What thoughts were present in your mind?

_____

_____

_____

_____

_____

Describe how you felt awakening from the drifting "twilight zone" in the morning.

_____

_____

_____

_____

_____

Did any unusual or creative ideas come into your mind as you awoke?

_____

_____

_____

_____

_____

At what points during the day do you feel drowsy, distracted, and inattentive? During these unfocused moments your mind is shifting from the logical mind to your intuitive mind. Become aware of these times by writing them down and begin to honor the intuitive input coming into your awareness as you naturally access your intuitive mind.

_____

_____

_____

_____

_____

Create an alpha log by observing the onset of the alpha level. Keep a record of your unfocused moments for a week. How often do you find yourself taking an intuitive break? If this occurs about every hour and a half, you are validating research that shows we shift into this intuitive mode every 90 minutes.[1]

FOUR CENTERING TOOLS TO STRENGTHEN YOUR INTUITION

Now let's look at four preparatory tools that will help you become centered and still.

- ◆ Affirmations
- ◆ Verbal focusing
- ◆ Visual focusing
- ◆ Music

Condition Your Mind with an Affirmation

One of the best tools for helping you center and enter a receptive state is the *affirmation*. An affirmation can also be called a conditioning phrase or "self-programming." It is a brief statement that can put you in the "right frame of mind" for maximum receptivity.

An affirmation is most effective when stated in the present tense and repeated several times throughout the day. By making an affirmation, you are in fact sending a message to your brain. This is telling your brain that the desired result has already been achieved. What you state as an affirmation can easily become a reality. Post your affirmations on the refrigerator, mirror, or someplace you will see them regularly during the day. They work!

To begin, you can use an *affirmation* to strengthen your intuitive ability. For example,

- ◆ My intuitive ability grows more reliable each day.
- ◆ My intuitive ability is consistently accurate.
- ◆ My intuitive mind tells my thinking mind where to look for the best solution.
- ◆ My intuitive signals get clearer and stronger.
- ◆ I can easily distinguish intuition from wishful thinking, fear, and projection.
- ◆ My intuition is increasingly strengthened as I make the right choices.
- ◆ My intuition helps my logical mind proceed.
- ◆ I hear the faint intuitive taps as well as the loud raps.
- ◆ My intuition is always available.
- ◆ My intuition is simple and straightforward.

EXERCISE

Write Your Own Affirmations

Using the above examples just given as a guide, formulate your own affirmations.

_____

_____

_____

_____

Strengthen Your Intuition:
Practice Using Your Affirmations

Select an affirmation that you will faithfully repeat several times a day for one week. Record your observations each day. At the end of the week, see how repeating the affirmation has strengthened your intuition.

Example: To become centered easily, I am working on the affirmation, "I am clear and relaxed." The first day I repeat it for about 5 minutes and begin to feel the knot in my right calf relax. In the next couple of days I notice I can elicit imagery easier after saying the affirmation for several minutes.

The affirmation I want to practice is

_____

_____

_____

My observations:

Sunday: _____

_____

Monday: _____

_____

Tuesday: _____

_____

Wednesday: _____

_____

Thursday: _____

_____

Friday: _____

_____

Saturday: _____

_____

ADDED AFFIRMATIONS: Some affirmations you might practice along with those previously suggested are

- I honor and use my special skills and abilities.
- I have a unique and special contribution to make.
- I accept prosperity and abundance into my life.
- I trust that everything comes at the perfect time and in the perfect way.
- I am open to receive with every breath I breathe.
- I am peaceful, relaxed, and centered.
- I trust myself.

Condition Your Mind with Verbal Focusing

Have you ever felt harassed because of overlapping time commitments? For example, you have a business meeting with an important client. At the same time your boss has scheduled another meeting he says you just can't miss. Stop!

As the anxiety mounts while you try to determine which commitment has priority, you can repeat a focusing phrase to restore balance so you can decide calmly which function to attend. Take a moment to be still, repeat the phrase several times, and you will gain the focus you need to make the decision. Once the necessary peace, accompanied by inner stillness, is achieved, you will feel clearer and intuitively know which function to attend.

Notice how the focusing word or phrase helps improve your intuitive receptivity. You can select any meaningful word or use several words as your personal *focusing phrase*. For example, I use the word "peace" to restore balance after I have been working hard to meet a deadline. Or I sometimes use the phrase, "peace, be still," or remind myself to "be still and know."

Other suggestions for effective focusing are positive words that you can say one at a time or in combination: love, joy, strength, courage, freedom, power, and happiness.

EXERCISE

Discover Your Focusing Phrase

What words or phrases make you feel still and receptive?

_____

_____

_____

_____

_____

Strengthen Your Intuition:
Use Your Focusing Phrase

You can use your focusing phrase in any situation to restore internal balance and serenity. Record any situation when you think a focusing phrase can provide the necessary centering.

_____

_____

_____

_____

_____

How did you feel after saying the focusing phrase?

_____

_____

_____

_____

_____

Which focusing phrase was most effective during your practice sessions?

_____

_____

_____

_____

_____

Condition Your Mind with Visual Focusing

Focusing on a geometrically shaped object or picture will help you quiet the talkative logical mind so you can focus on the pictures, images, and symbols presented by the intuitive mind.

The basic function of this technique is to shift perception to an inner mode, halt your talking mind, and let your intuitive mind through.

Use Visual Focusing

Gaze at this picture for a few minutes.

Do you notice your consciousness shifting? What do you feel?

_____

_____

_____

_____

_____

How do you recognize this shift?

_____

_____

_____

_____

_____

Do you feel yourself becoming centered?

_____

_____

_____

_____

_____

Discover Your Visual Focus

You are surrounded by objects, shapes, and designs perfect for visual focusing, for example, the leaf of a plant on your desk, a flower in your home. Look around outdoors in any natural setting and focus on the beautiful symmetry nature has given us in the blossoms and leaf patterns. What do you see outside?

_____

_____

_____

_____

_____

Look around your office or home at the symmetrical patterns on the wallpaper, the woodwork, the ceiling, the floor covering, or even on the face of a clock. What patterns or pictures do you see?

_____

_____

_____

_____

_____

What object or picture helps you focus best? I like to hold and focus on a special shell that was "tossed to me" from the sea.

_____

_____

_____

_____

_____

When you focus on your object, how do you feel shifting to the nonverbal mode? Staring at my shell, I start feeling joy as I "smell" the ocean and "hear" the roar of the wave.

_____

_____

_____

_____

_____

Condition Your Mind Using Music as a Facilitator

Music can be relaxing and soothing. It can help you become centered and receptive to your intuitive mind. The best music for achieving maximum intuitive receptivity at the alpha or theta levels is gentle and instrumental. If possible, have a cassette or CD player or radio at your office or home.

Some of the best pieces of instrumental music for this purpose come from natural environmental sounds. You can relax to the sounds of a babbling brook, rhythmic ocean surf, or birds chirping in the forest. I have suggested some audio programs on page 291; your local music store can also help you select appropriate music.

EXERCISE

Discover Your Musical Focus

What type of music helps you relax best and become centered and receptive?

_____

_____

_____

List three of your favorite cassette tapes or CDs that have a calming effect on you.

1. _____

2. _____

3. _____

How do you feel after listening to any of this music?

_____

_____

_____

_____

_____

Which tape is most effective for you?

_____

_____

_____

_____

_____

Can you close your eyes and recall a favorite melody to help you relax? What is it?

_____

_____

_____

_____

_____

How can you bring any of your favorite music into a noisy setting? I can close my eyes and hear the *Missa Luba*, an African mass that is one my favorite calming pieces.

_____

_____

_____

_____

_____

Let's Review How You Become Centered

How do you become inwardly still? There are many ways you can alter your awareness and become still. You can

- Say an affirmation such as "my intuitive mind knows the right answer."
- Use verbal focusing by repeating a word such as courage, freedom, or strength or a phrase such as "peace, be still."
- Focus visually on a pattern in the carpet, a painting on the wall, or an object on your desk to help you become still.
- Play your favorite nonlyrical musical cassette.

What do you do to center yourself so you can hear the intuitive mind speak?

_____

_____

_____

_____

Practicing the exercises in this chapter will help you become still and centered whenever you wish. You are now ready to enter into a deeper level of receptivity for the IPS process.

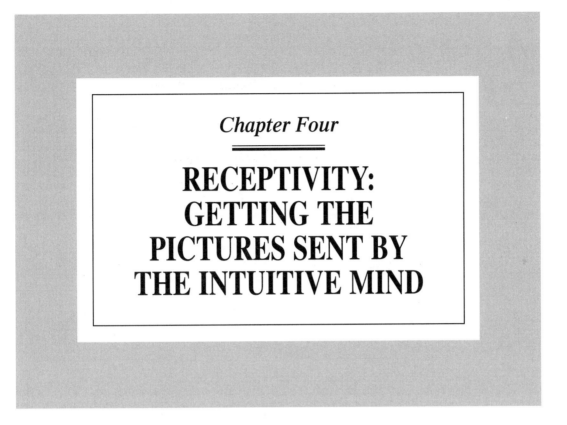

Chapter Four

RECEPTIVITY: GETTING THE PICTURES SENT BY THE INTUITIVE MIND

I am happy because I want nothing from anyone. I do not care for money; decorations, titles, or distinction mean nothing to me. I do not crave praise. The only thing that gives me pleasure apart from my work, my violin, and my sailboat is the appreciation of my fellow workers.

DR. ALBERT EINSTEIN

Albert Einstein valued his periods of relaxation to balance the strenuous mental demands of his work. He loved to play his violin and relax on his sailboat. When I read that he liked to drift aimlessly about in his canoe while in residence at Princeton University, I conjured up a wonderful image of Einstein totally relaxed as the canoe slowly meandered through the water. I have no doubt that during these times he became receptive to the profound discoveries that came from his intuitive mind.

Breathing and relaxation are two activities you can do to become receptive. When you centered, you verbalized, watched an object, or listened to music. Now, to slow down your brainwaves even more so that you can enter the alpha level of awareness, you are going to learn proper breathing and relaxation techniques. The intuitive mind is sparked when you enter the alpha level, so the time you spend practicing to become more receptive is particularly important.

This is how four people took the intuitive problem-solving (IPS) steps of centering and receptivity, so they could use the IPS process to resolve some of their concerns. Bruce

Nyenhuis, director of admissions at Alternative Directions, a nonprofit corporation that operates a 70-bed residential program for circuit court probationers, wanted to discover the answer to a simple personal question. He became *centered* by sitting in his favorite chair and listening to environmental music that had the sounds of whales in the background. He stared at a flowery vase and focused on a particular flower that had a pleasing symmetrical shape. Then, to become *more receptive*, he closed his eyes, took several deep breaths and repeated to himself, "Relax and let the tension out." On the final three deep breaths, he raised his shoulders high on the inhale and dropped them on the exhale. This action, along with the soothing music, helped him alleviate the tension in his shoulders.

Tom Carnegie, district director of Michigan's Office of Civil Rights, uses a different approach to become centered. He becomes centered by repeating the affirmation, "You have the intuitive ability to find the answer." After several repetitions of this phrase, he plays the Ray Lynch tape, *Deep Breakfast*. With no one around to interfere, Tom continues by taking three "total" breaths (discussed later in this chapter) and listening to the tape.

At times the centering and receptivity activities are combined. Ken, for example, begins to relax by taking a series of "hang-sah" breaths. Focusing on a thick bunch of day lilies, he used the "count down" technique to achieve an alpha state. John prepares for his IPS program by taking five deep breaths. He then shut his eyes loosely so he can sense the sunlight warming his face and hear birds chirping in the trees surrounding the pool. The pool's pump emits a soothing hum as water trickled into the filter basket. It doesn't take long for him to enter the alpha level.

In this chapter you will learn *breathing* and *relaxation* techniques that will help you become more *receptive* to your intuitive mind.

BREATHING AND RELAXATION:
RECEPTIVITY TOOLS TO STRENGTHEN YOUR INTUITION

When you are completely receptive, the outer noise that is created by your conscious thoughts, feelings, and other preoccupations will fade. Your brainwaves slow down as you relax and become more receptive to the images of your intuitive mind.

The receptivity techniques in this chapter are an integral part of the IPS process and will be used repeatedly throughout this book. It is best not to go through all these techniques at once. Stay with one until you feel comfortable. Then, move on to master the next.

Since the "breath of life" precedes everything we do, it is appropriate that I introduce you to the breathing exercises first.

BREATHING:
THE VITAL KEY TO YOUR INTUITIVE MIND

We all know that without breathing we would not live long. We take for granted that we know how. Have you ever been *taught* to breathe? Unless you have taken singing lessons, had a baby, or attended a stress reduction class, you probably haven't. In addition to inducing the alpha level of consciousness for increased receptivity to your intuitive mind, using specific breathing techniques will *increase your stamina, help you become mentally alert, reduce stress*, and *reenergize your body*.

Obviously, learning to breathe properly has many benefits. It is important that you learn and practice these breathing techniques, which will improve the depth and quality of your breathing, so you can become more receptive to your intuitive mind. Deep breathing is a vital key for both increasing body energy and relaxing deeply. As you learn the various techniques, you will select the ones with which you feel most comfortable. I do suggest you learn to vary the breathing techniques used to help you sustain your interest.

First, familiarize yourself with the content of each exercise. In many cases, reading the directions once or twice may be sufficient, or you can record the directions onto a cassette tape and play them back whenever you like. Or you can have someone read the exercise to you. Another alternative is purchasing one of the tapes listed on page 291.

Before trying any of these new breathing techniques, take the time to find out how you presently breathe.

EXERCISE

Observe Your Breathing

Follow the directions and record your observations in the spaces provided.

Begin by taking two deep breaths.

Did your chest rise on the inhale or did your stomach expand?

_____

_____

Did you breathe through your nose or through your mouth?

_____

_____

How did your body feel?

_____

_____

Did you feel anything inside your head?

_____

_____

What did your throat feel like during the breathing process?

_____

_____

What were you thinking?

_____

_____

Repeat this breathing process.

Take two breaths, but this time feel your breath and concentrate on *how* you are doing the breathing—into your chest or into your stomach? Are you breathing through your nose or through your mouth? At the end of the two breaths, close your eyes and experience how you feel from the inside out. I usually feel like my head is clearing as the oxygen rushes in.

Ready—Begin, take a deep inhale (1..2..3), hold (1..2..3), Exhale.

Again—Inhale (1..2..3), hold (1..2..3), exhale.

Now, close your eyes and become aware of how you feel at this moment. Notice how this experience is different compared to the first two breaths. Record your observations about the second breathing experience.

Did you breathe into your chest or into your stomach?

_____

_____

Did you breathe through your nose or through your mouth?

_____

_____

How did your body feel?

_____

_____

Did you feel anything in your head?

_____

_____

How did your throat feel?

_____

_____

What were you thinking about?

_____

_____

Record anything else you recall.

_____

_____

EXERCISE

Breathing Awareness: Clearing the Air

Before introducing you to the *four* breathing techniques in this chapter, I'd like you to do another exercise to become aware of your breathing.

Inhale and be aware of your breath. Mentally, follow the stream of air as it courses through your chest. What other body parts are touched? Imagine your breath flowing throughout the body to your toes, arms, stomach, and head. As you inhale, realize how the life force enters your body and creates renewed energy. When you exhale, imagine you are letting go of accumulated waste and fatigue. Imagine you are breathing in quiet and breathing out tension. On the next breath, see yourself breathing in "life" and then breathing out stress.

As you inhale, mentally count to five and then hold your breath for five counts as the oxygen is distributed throughout your body. Finally, exhale to five counts. Repeat this two times. Next, try inhaling and holding it to a count of six, then slowly release your breath to a count of nine. Repeat this two times.

When you have finished, you might feel somewhat "lightheaded." This can happen to people performing these breathing exercises for the first time. Don't be alarmed. Your brain may not be accustomed to the amount of oxygen it is suddenly receiving. Notice how the fresh air circulating freely throughout your body is making you feel more energized.

Write down your experiences each time you complete this exercise. Do you feel more energized; clearer?

_____

_____

_____

_____

_____

Four Breathing Techniques to Enhance Receptivity

The four breathing techniques that follow have their unique properties. After practicing each for a reasonable amount of time, you can determine which appeals to you most.

FIRST BREATH: THE "TOTAL" BREATH. The "total" breath is an excellent breathing technique to help increase your breathing stamina and enhance mental alertness. The best time to do the "total" breath is in the morning after you get out of bed. It only takes one or two minutes to do three to five "total" breaths and will have a tremendous positive impact on your day.

Another good time to practice the "total" breath is just before you go to bed. It's also a good practice to take two or three "total" breaths several times during the day.

Because you take more oxygen into your body with this breathing technique, you may find you need less sleep at night. Many people gain an hour or more of active work time during the day by using this breath. *Whenever you remember to...try it!*

EXERCISE

Experience the "Total" Breath

Preparation: Before you begin, make certain that you are sitting in an upright position with your feet flat on the floor and hands uncrossed in your lap.

Practice: As you inhale, pretend that you are blowing up a balloon inside your stomach. When you feel you have filled the balloon, raise your arms so that your elbows are even with your shoulders and inhale even more air into your lungs. Hold your breath for a slow count of three and then exhale as you lower your arms and let the imaginary balloon deflate. Experience this breathing technique by repeating three "total" breaths in succession. Inhale and fill the balloon in your stomach, raise your arms as you continue to inhale, hold your breath, exhale as you lower your arms and let the air slowly escape from the imaginary balloon. Do this two more times.

Now, close your eyes, and experience how you feel throughout your body at this moment.

Open your eyes and write down any observations that this experience of "total" breath brings to mind.

_____

_____

_____

_____

Do you feel more alert?

_____

_____

_____

_____

Observe the objects around you. Do they seem to be sharper and clearer?

_____

_____

_____

_____

Did you feel a tingling sensation in any part of your body?

_____

_____

_____

_____

SECOND BREATH: THE "REENERGIZING" BREATH. This is a *power boost* for your mind and body. The "reenergizing" breath helps create mental alertness and reenergizes your body. Whenever you become unproductive, dull, sluggish, or blocked, try using the "reenergizing" breath to carry you through your IPS with greater vigor. Use this breathing technique whenever your energy is low.

Experiencing the "Reenergizing" Breath

Preparation: Sit up straight in a chair with your feet flat on the floor, arms uncrossed in your lap.

Practice: Experience three "reenergizing" breaths. Begin by exhaling all the air from your lungs. Then, take six short inhales in quick succession through your nose:

1—(sniff) 2—(sniff) 3—(sniff) 4—(sniff) 5 —(sniff) 6—(sniff).

Hold…take a seventh inhale (sniff).

Hold…then exhale completely.

Repeat this two more times.

Now, close your eyes, and experience how you feel throughout your body at this moment. Open your eyes and write down any observations of your experience from the "reenergizing" breath.

_____

_____

_____

Look at the colors in the objects around you. Do they seem brighter?

_____

_____

_____

Do you feel reenergized?

_____

_____

_____

What sensations do you feel throughout your body?

_____

_____

_____

THIRD BREATH: THE "HA!" BREATH. Another breathing technique that gives a *quick boost* to both mind and body is the "ha!" breath. This technique is also particularly useful in reducing built up stress.

By removing built-up stress, you can become more receptive to your intuitive mind.

EXERCISE

Experience the "Ha!" Breath

Preparation: The most effective posture for this breath is either standing or sitting upright. It helps to place your hands on the stomach just above the waist with your fingertips meeting near your navel.

Practice: Begin by inhaling and inflating the imaginary balloon and then exhaling with an explosion of air as you say out loud, "ha!" When first practicing this breath, you can push your stomach in with your fingertips as you exhale.

Repeat this sequence five more times.

Close your eyes now and observe how you feel in mind and body. Open your eyes and write down any observations from your experience with the "ha!" breath. For example, you may feel a warm tingling in the center of your body. This is common when the deep stress is released from the pit of your stomach. Many people feel like laughing when first doing the "ha!" breath, and some people actually do break down in spontaneous laughter, which is perfectly normal. Laughter in fact is a form of the "ha!" breath done in rapid succession. Laughter also reduces our stress.

How do you feel inside your head?

_____

_____

_____

How does the rest of your body feel?

_____

_____

_____

Another place to do the "ha!" breath is in a parked car with all the windows closed. If you do it at home or in any public setting, make sure that you inform those around you before you begin. You don't want to startle or disturb them. (You don't want them to think you are mentally disturbed, either.) Try this breathing technique the next time you are extremely agitated and filled with stress. It will help.

FOURTH BREATH: THE "HANG-SAH" BREATH.   All the breathing techniques have the dual function of helping you enter a receptive state as well as combating stress. This last technique is most important for helping you slow down your brainwaves to help you easily enter the alpha level of awareness. In fact, soft music and the "hang-sah" breath used together can be used very effectively for the centering and receptivity steps in the IPS process. As you inhale and whisper "hang," it lifts the diphthong in back of your throat just like when you are yawning. And as you exhale and whisper "sah," it's like sighing, which will quickly put you into a relaxed state.

EXERCISE

Experience the "Hang-Sah" Breath

Preparation: Sit upright in a chair with your feet flat on the floor and your arms uncrossed. Since this breathing technique can also aid people who have difficulty falling asleep, it is advisable that you say a mental affirmation before using it.

Before beginning the "hang-sah" breath, you can avoid falling asleep by affirming, "I will stay awake and mentally alert while using the 'hang-sah' breath." Repeat that affirmation three times.

Practice: The breath is simple. Whisper aloud the word "hang" as you inhale and "sah" as you exhale.

Continue inhaling and whispering "hang," exhale whispering "sah" for ten more repetitions.

With your eyes closed, be aware of how and what you are feeling at this moment. Then open your eyes and write down any observations from your experience with the "hang sah" breath.

Do you feel more relaxed?

_____

_____

_____

_____

Could you feel yourself becoming sleepy and drifting into alpha?

_____

_____

_____

_____

RELAXATION:
THE KEY TO RELEASING YOUR CREATIVE POTENTIAL

My favorite "relaxation story" concerns how J. P. Morgan retreated from his active and noisy environment.[1] Whenever J.P. had to make a decision and the answer would not come to him, he would put the problem entirely out of his mind by getting a deck of cards and playing solitaire for an hour. After finishing the game, the right decision would always be crystal clear to him. With this simple relaxation technique, he was unlocking his mind and opening the lines to his creative potential.

I also like the perspective shared by Carole Valade Smith, an editor in a publishing corporation that produces both a monthly magazine and a weekly business journal. With her days consumed by editorial responsibilities, she values relaxation activities that give her logical mind a rest. For Carole, a wonderful way to relax is with her 7-year-old son. She can become "a kid with her kid" and stop to look at the ants, become immersed in a storybook, or play simple children's games with him.

Many people find that their most productive and innovative thoughts come to them when they are relaxed and not forced to attend to a particular problem. Even during dull and boring tasks, you can "alter your consciousness" and retreat to a more enjoyable setting to let ideas and breakthroughs occur.

You will see from the various relaxation exercises we cover in this chapter that there are many ways to relax. If you make time to do these exercises, the reward for you and anyone you encounter will be evident. Decide which exercise(s) is most suitable and effective for you, and use it (them).

Six Relaxation Techniques to Enhance Receptivity

You will now be introduced to *six* relaxation techniques. By relaxing the physical body, the logical mind also relaxes, allowing the intuitive mind to speak. Practice each exercise until you are familiar with the technique. In time, you will identify the relaxation technique(s) that work(s) best for you. In the resource section you will find a list of audiocassettes that can help you with these exercises. Of course you can also make your own tape or have someone read the directions to you.

EXERCISE

The Two-Minute Tune-up

To do this exercise, you can be standing up, sitting, or lying down. Tune in and listen to your body. Identify the aching areas.

Where do you feel tension?

_____

_____

_____

Do you feel pain in any particular area?

_____

_____

_____

Record the parts of your body that require immediate attention. Then be sure to give special attention to these areas during the relaxation exercises.

_____

_____

_____

FIRST RELAXATION: THE "AUTOGENIC" TECHNIQUE. In this exercise, you "create" the imagery by "seeing" or "feeling" or "knowing" that your tension is being released while you quietly tell yourself what effect you want to achieve. Your body is very intelligent. If you repeatedly tell it that it is relaxing, it will indeed relax.

EXERCISE

Experience the "Autogenic" Technique

Preparation: As each part of your body is identified, I want you to picture steam or hot air rising out of that part until it becomes relaxed. For example, imagine the steam blowing out of a boiling tea kettle and "hear" the hissing sound effects. Your goal is to release the tension residing in each part of your body so that area will feel wonderfully refreshed.

You can either sit or recline when you do this exercise. Begin with your toes and work your way up through the body until you have completed the head. As you send the message to each part of your body, elicit the imagery as you "see" or "feel" or "know" what is happening:

Practice: Send these messages from your mind to each part of your body:

I am relaxing my toes. My toes are relaxing.

I am relaxing my feet. My feet are relaxing.

I am relaxing my ankles. My ankles are relaxing.

Continue by focusing on your knees, thighs, pelvis, buttocks, back, abdomen, stomach, chest, shoulders, arms, hands, neck, back of the head, forehead, eyes, nose, mouth, jaw, and head.

When you are finished say: I am allowing myself to be completely relaxed. If any tension is left, return to that area and gently tell that part of your body to relax. It will!

Do you feel more peaceful and balanced now that you have completed this exercise? As you become more practiced at this technique, it will become even more effective.

SECOND RELAXATION: THE EXTENDED "AUTOGENIC RELAXER." This "autogenic" relaxer does not go through every part of your body but focuses on specific areas. The technique is combined with the "hang-sah" breath and an affirmation to help you eliminate any remaining tension in your body.

EXERCISE

Experience the Extended "Autogenic Relaxer"

Preparation: Use the "hang-sah" breath to get into the alpha level of consciousness where you will then tell yourself to relax each part of your entire body. Begin as you inhale whispering "hang" and exhale while whispering "sah." Continue this for nine repetitions.

Practice: Send these messages from your mind to each part of your body:

My feet feel warm and relaxed. My feet feel warm and relaxed. My feet are warm and relaxed.

My legs feel warm and relaxed. My legs feel warm and relaxed. My legs are warm and relaxed.

My midsection feels warm and relaxed. My midsection feels warm and relaxed. My midsection is warm and relaxed.

My chest and back feel warm and relaxed. My chest and back feel warm and relaxed. My chest and back are warm and relaxed.

My arms feel warm and relaxed. My arms feel warm and relaxed. My arms are warm and relaxed.

My shoulders feel warm and relaxed. My shoulders feel warm and relaxed. My shoulders are warm and relaxed.

My neck feels warm and relaxed. My neck feels warm and relaxed. My neck is warm and relaxed.

My face and head feel cool and clear. My face and head feel cool and clear. My face and head are cool and clear.

Affirm:

Every cell in my body feels relaxed and comfortable.

Every cell in my body feels relaxed and comfortable.

Every cell in my body is relaxed and comfortable.

I am now totally relaxed.

Are you feeling more relaxed? You should be feeling peaceful and less tense.

THIRD RELAXATION: THE "STRETCHING AND BREATHING" TECHNIQUE. This technique combines breathing with stretching parts of your body to help you enter a more relaxed state. This is a good exercise to do the first thing in the morning. It is also helpful when you come home from work or return from any activity from which you feel stressed and need a quick battery recharge. You can breathe in through your nose and exhale through your nose or your mouth.

EXERCISE

Experience the "Stretching and Breathing" Technique

Preparation: To start with your "stretching and breathing," sit upright in a chair, feet flat on the floor and arms at your sides.

Practice:

Shrug your shoulders, inhale through your nose, and raise your shoulders toward your ears. Hold a moment.

Let your shoulders drop as you exhale through your mouth with a sigh of relief.

Repeat this three more times.

Inhale as you straighten your spine and hold your head upright.

Exhale and let your neck bend forward as your chin rests on your chest.

Inhale as you bring your head upright.

Exhale as you bend your neck backward letting your jaw relax as you open your mouth and say "aaah!"

Inhale as you bring your head up stretching your neck.

Repeat these neck stretches three more times.

Inhale as you straighten your spine and hold your head upright.

Bend your neck to the left as you exhale, letting your left ear attempt to rest on your shoulder.

Inhale as you bring your head up.

Bend your neck to the right as you exhale letting your right ear attempt to rest on your shoulder.

Inhale as you bring your head up.

Repeat this three times.

Roll your head around on your neck three times to the right and three times to the left.

Close your eyes and feel what part of your body is relaxed.

Write down your observations. What parts of your body are still tense?

_____

_____

_____

_____

Fourth Relaxation: The "Tense and Release" Technique. Can you imagine making a body area more tense in order to create a relaxed state? It works! This technique helps you relax by *tensing and releasing* your muscles. That is how you are going to relax the tense or painful areas you identified in your "body tune-up."

EXERCISE

Experience the "Tense and Release" Technique

Preparation: Start by sitting in a comfortable position or lying down. Breathe in deeply through your nose and be aware of your chest rising and falling. Follow the current of air as it comes in through your nose. Be aware of the areas in your body touched by this breath of life. Hold the air and note how you feel. Finally, let the air come together from the various body parts to unite in a large current of air that will be expelled from your nose or mouth.

Practice:

First, inhale and curl your toes as tightly as you can as you hold your breath.

Exhale and release the tension from your toes and feet. Repeat once more.

Now extend your legs straight out as you inhale and tighten your leg muscles.

Hold for a moment and then exhale and release the tension from your legs. Do that again.

Inhale again as you tighten your stomach and buttocks muscles. Hold, then exhale, and let these muscles relax. Repeat once more.

Inhale, making a fist with both hands, as you tighten the muscles in your arms. Hold for a moment and then exhale as you let your arms relax. Do that once again.

Inhale as you tighten your shoulder and neck muscles. Hold, then exhale and relax your neck and shoulders. Repeat once more.

Inhale as you tighten all the muscles in your face, clenching your teeth. Hold, and then exhale as you let these muscles relax. Do that again.

Take a deep breath as you inhale. Then hold for a moment and exhale.

Close your eyes and be aware of how your body feels at this moment.

Open your eyes and write down your observations.

What parts of your body still feel tense?

_____

_____

_____

Do you feel warmth in any particular areas?

_____

_____

_____

If any spot is stubbornly hanging on to the tension, tell it to *"relax and be still."* It will listen to you. As you practice your body will listen more easily.

FIFTH RELAXATION: THE "PROGRESSIVE RELAXATION" TECHNIQUE. Now "directed" breathing is used in a "progressive relaxation."

Experience the "Progressive Relaxation" Technique

Preparation: Close your eyes and imagine energy coming into your body each time you inhale. It helps to visualize the energy as colored light, like rays of sunshine.
   Practice:

Then, as you exhale imagine the tension flowing out through the soles of your feet, like the tide of the ocean as it is going out. Inhale the energy in and exhale the tension out.

Now, inhale and direct the rays of energy to your legs. Exhale and imagine the tension flowing down your legs and out through the soles of your feet. Inhale the energy in and exhale the tension out.

Inhale, bringing the golden rays of energy into your chest and upper back.

Exhale and let the tension flow down your spine, through your legs, and out through the soles of your feet. Again, like the outgoing tide. Repeat.

Inhale and direct the rays of energy into your arms and hands.

Exhale and imagine the tension flowing down your arms and out through your fingertips. Do this again.

Inhale and direct the golden rays of energy into your shoulders.

Exhale as you imagine the tension flowing down both arms and out through your fingertips. Repeat this and imagine the tension flowing down your spine, down through your legs, and out through the soles of your feet.

Inhale and direct the energy into your head and neck. Exhale, and let the tension flow down your spine, down your legs, and out through the soles of your feet. Do this once again.

Take a deep inhale and then hold momentarily before you exhale. Open your eyes and record your reactions.

How are you feeling now? Are you feeling more relaxed?

_____

_____

_____

Are you aware of any remaining tension in your body?

_____

_____

_____

Sixth Relaxation: The "Countdown" Technique. This exercise can be used in conjunction with any one of the other relaxation techniques, since it is so easy to remember. This is also suitable when you want to enter an even deeper relaxed state.

Strong clear imagery affects the speed with which relaxation is accomplished. Picture yourself standing at the top step; walk down stairs until you arrive at the bottom step. With each step you are becoming increasingly relaxed. You can use your imagery to count off each step by seeing the step light up with a number. The countdown and affirmation for each step is given in the following exercise.

EXERCISE

Experience the "Countdown" Technique

10	9	8	I am beginning to feel relaxed
7	6	5	I am feeling more and more relaxed
	4	3	I am feeling very relaxed
	2	1	I am feeling completely relaxed

Write down how you feel with this brief relaxation.

_____

_____

_____

_____

_____

Do you feel lighter? Freer? More open?

_____

_____

_____

_____

_____

USE YOUR IMAGINATION

To help you relax you can also imagine a peaceful scene. Take yourself to a mountaintop, far above the rest of the world, or walk on a beautiful stretch of beach and hear the ocean waves gently lapping on the shore. Or perhaps you will want to walk through a rain forest and listen to the chirping of the birds. If you find it difficult to imagine such a setting, simply look at a picture on the wall that you find relaxing.

EXERCISE

Select Your Receptivity Technique

Which technique worked best for you?

_____

_____

_____

What receptivity setting, if any, do you imagine?

_____

_____

_____

Any other helpful hints for practice can be noted here.

_____

_____

_____

_____

After practicing the receptivity exercises for a week, do you enter the alpha level more readily? You will find that "feeling lighter" or more relaxed takes less time. You might even notice a weightlessness in the body as you become more relaxed.

_____

_____

As you begin to enter a receptive state more easily, you will take the next step of eliciting the imagery. The exercises in the next chapter will show you how to consistently retrieve the images you need to resolve your IPS problems.

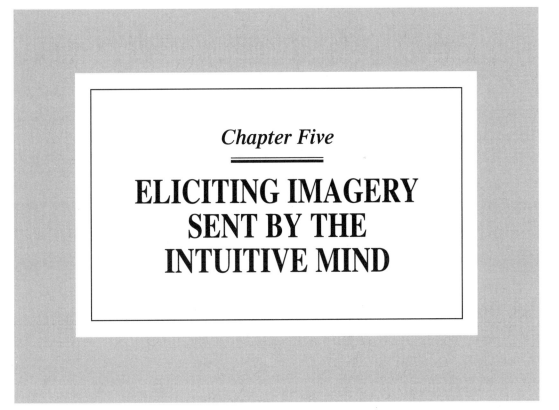

Chapter Five

ELICITING IMAGERY SENT BY THE INTUITIVE MIND

But now visualization has entered the domain of business. CEOs are forming new images of their businesses and where they ought to be going and are bringing those visions into reality. The leader who would create a vision sufficiently compelling to motivate associates to superior performances must draw on the intuitive mind.

J. NAISBITT AND P. ABURDENE
Re-Inventing the Corporation

HOW DOES YOUR INTUITIVE MIND SPEAK TO YOU?

Awareness of your senses is the key to understanding and knowing how *your* intuitive mind will communicate. You can experience imagery through all your senses. This chapter on imagery will help you discover how *your* intuitive mind speaks to you, not only by "seeing" things, but also by hearing, smelling, tasting, and touching them in your mind. In the receptive alpha level of awareness, you can go beyond these five senses to experience related affective states that reflect your inner emotions, such as "feeling" happy or sad, and the kinesthetic state or inner awareness of body movement, such as the sensation that you are floating on a cloud or falling through space. Notice how you sense the imagery as you read John's account of a breakfast "training meeting."

I walked into a crowded lobby and felt very annoyed when I was knocked off balance as someone quickly ran past me. My agitation was further increased by everyone's chatter. I easily found the meeting room by following the aroma of bacon and eggs. I joined several people I knew who were also attending this meeting. The juice was refreshing and tasted like the oranges had just been squeezed. I felt very excited when the meeting started, since I wanted to learn some of the new concepts that were to be presented. The trainer used brightly colored markers to highlight the main ideas. Since we were learning how to sell our new shoe line, they handed out samples, which were very smooth to the touch. I was happy to receive good pointers about the new line. Now, I'll know how to make a better sales pitch.

EXERCISE

Arousing Your Senses

As I said, becoming aware of your senses is the key to unlocking your intuitive mind's communication. Notice what senses John activated at the meeting:

Visual—Saw the bright colored markers used to highlight the ideas.

Auditory—Heard all the chatter surrounding him.

Olfactory—Smelled the bacon and eggs.

Gustatory—Tasted the orange juice.

Tactile—Touched the smooth shoes.

Affective—Emotionally felt annoyance and agitation initially and then excitement when the meeting began.

Kinesthetic—Moved by being knocked off balance.

Which of your senses were aroused as you read about John's experience?

_____

_____

_____

_____

How a Carmaker Used Intuitive Imagery to Change Its Image

Several years ago, top management at Buick wanted their employees to develop a strong image of the *essence of Buick* which they could then communicate to their organization, dealers, and customers.

This campaign was mounted during a period when the image of a Buick had become somewhat blurred. The goal of the conference was to make Buick personnel intuitively understand what Buick really represented by the time they left. The challenge was to create a conference to teach employees to communicate the Buick image *without speaking a word*.

After the executive team decided that Buick was going to represent the premium American motor car, their strategists suggested these four words to underscore what the product division was trying to convey: "substantive," "distinctive," "powerful," and "mature." Additional characteristics were added, such as muscular grace, rich detail, comfort, accommodation, and image-enhancing technology. The image conference was designed to help people identify what those words really meant and how they related to Buick.

To do this, they used sight, sound, touch, music, and videos to help the attendees see, hear, and feel the image of Buick.

To get an idea of the impact this image conference had on all the attendees, I will highlight two concepts—muscular grace and rich detail, to show how the images were presented. Imagine yourself standing in the middle of a large conference hall. Everywhere you look in the enormous hall, you discover an image on the huge video screen, on the wall, or on any of the standing displays throughout the room. At one end of the hall, you pause to watch the video projected upon a screen. You focus on the ballerina swirling around and gracefully moving her body with agility and strength. The words muscular grace once again become etched in your mind as you watch thoroughbred horses in action, resplendent with grace and strength during their run. The images are very different—one a human and the other an animal—yet each strongly conveys the image of muscular grace.

The Buick imagineers were equally adroit in reinforcing the concept that Buick is rich in detail. The display included many examples of fine crafted objects like a finely detailed western saddle that reflected this rich detail. The objects emphasized Buick as American and stressed the rich detail. The connection was made between the attention to detail behind every Buick automobile and these finely crafted products. Without saying a word or using a chart or graph, these images and the others displayed at the conference strongly and easily communicated the Buick image to any customer or employee. It was just sensed or felt!

Do You Get the Picture?

You have now learned the first three IPS steps of identifying the problem, centering, and receptivity. Now we'll focus on retrieving the imagery sent to you by your intuitive mind—how you can become attuned to the language of intuition through mental pictures, images, and symbols. The intuitive mind communicates by *showing* what you are thinking and feeling. Whenever I use the word "imagery," I am talking about the "pictures inside your head."

Imagine, for example, that you have just won two round-trip tickets to anywhere in the world. Where would you go? Personally, I would choose the Bahamas. When I think of the Bahamas, I imagine the sandy beaches and the clear blue-green water with the little fishes swimming around; I can see the tall palm trees blowing and hear the strains of merengue music playing in the background. No picture of that area is complete for me without a recollection of eating conch salad and cracked conch. As I described these images, "did you get the picture?" Did you see, hear, feel, or sense any of the Bahamian images I just mentioned?

EXERCISE

Picture a Getaway

Choose a destination that for you would serve as a welcome retreat. Write a paragraph or two describing the sensory images that come into your mind about this locale. What do you see? What do you hear? What do you feel? What do you smell? What do you taste?

_____

_____

_____

_____

_____

Have you ever tried to communicate a difficult concept to a workmate? After paragraphs pour forth, do you finally say, "Do you get the picture?" You are trying to "paint a picture" to describe your thoughts. Imagine a marketing group describing the sales campaign for the new product to the rest of the company. The first words out of the group leader's mouth are "let me paint you a picture." How about trying to get the attention of a young child. As they restlessly fidget around, do you drop an image in front of them, like being "quiet as a mouse," to get their attention? Do you entice them with images of ice cream, a video game, or a fishing trip?

One of my favorite cartoons shows a little boy saying, as he reads a book, "I like reading because it turns on the pictures inside my head." And people often prefer a book to the movie version of it because the latter rarely conforms to the "pictures inside their head" that the book created.

I give you *four* challenges in this chapter. The first challenge is to realize and acknowledge that your intuitive mind does in fact send images to you. The second challenge is to find out how your intuitive mind speaks to you and through which of your senses. The artist Gauguin said, "I close my eyes in order to see." Not everyone can retrieve a clear image and "see" after they close their eyes. Suppose I said, "Close your eyes and imagine you are looking at a tree." Some people will actually see the tree, but others may hear the leaves rustling in the wind or smell the scent of the pine needles. All are imagining they are looking at the tree, but not all are actually seeing it. So rather than asking, "Get the picture?" I might say, "How does this sound to you?" Or "Are you getting in touch with what I am saying?"

The third challenge has to do with the way in which intuition comes to you—actively or passively. Are you aware of these pictures or images when they are presented to you? Often, imagery is fleeting and forgotten. Imagery can also be somewhat faint, especially when drowned out in a sea of words. The following examples reflect the passive or spontaneous side of intuition, although intuition can come to you more actively or deliberately when you ask a direct question and get a reply. In this chapter, you will learn how to actively access the pictures and images showing intuitive replies and creative directions, and how to become more attentive to the spontaneous imagery presented by your intuitive mind.

The fourth challenge is to learn how to test the progress of your imagery by rating the quality of your intuitive pictures, symbols, or images.

HOW TO "SEE" THE IMAGERY

If you think you can never see or picture anything, you're mistaken. You just don't know how. But since your intuition is already working, your challenge is to strengthen the pictures and images you receive so you can consistently gain access to the solutions your intuitive mind presents to you.

To activate your imagination, let's take a guided imagery trip so you can see that your intuitive mind does in fact speak to you. As the word "guided" implies, I will be leading you with my words and directions to elicit specific imagery. This exercise is most effective if you read the directions into a tape recorder and then play them back to yourself, or having someone read them to you.

EXERCISE

A Guided Imagery Trip

Preparation: To ease into the receptive alpha level, take five "ha!" breaths followed by the "progressive" relaxation technique. Start the "ha!" breath by either standing or sitting upright. It helps to place your hands on your stomach just above the waist with your fingertips meeting near your navel. You begin by inhaling and inflating an imaginary balloon, then exhaling with an explosion of air as you say out loud, "ha!" Repeat this sequence five more times.

Begin to "progressively" relax your body as you close your eyes and imagine energy coming into your body on the inhale breath. It helps to visualize the energy as colored light, like rays of sunshine for example.

First, as you exhale imagine the tension flowing out through the soles of your feet, like the tide of the ocean as it is going out. Inhale the energy in and exhale the tension out.

Now, inhale and direct the rays of energy to your legs. Exhale and imagine the tension flowing down your legs and out through the soles of your feet. Inhale the energy in and exhale the tension out.

Inhale, bringing the golden rays of energy into your chest and upper back.

Exhale and let the tension flow down your spine, through your legs, and out through the soles of your feet. Again, like the outgoing tide. Repeat.

Inhale and direct the rays of energy into your arms and hands.

Exhale and imagine the tension flowing down your arms and out through your fingertips. Do this again.

Inhale and direct the golden rays of energy into your shoulders.

Exhale as you imagine the tension flowing down both arms and out through your fingertips. Repeat this and imagine the tension flowing down your arms, through your hands, and out through your fingertips.

Inhale and direct the energy into your head and neck. Exhale, and let the tension flow down your spine, down your legs, and out through the soles of your feet. Do this once again.

Now you are ready to take a guided trip to the woods.

Directions: It is a beautiful day for a hike in the woods. The sun is shining and the trees are in full foliage. As you walk, you are sensitive to the fragrant aromas released from the flowers. Surrounded by nature's sound and color, you feel delighted. Walking through the woods, you notice animals scurrying across the path and even see squirrels running up the trees. They seem to run to the opposite side of the tree so you can't see them, but you know they are there. Chickadees and other birds fly from tree to tree. Listen to the beautiful call of the cardinal as it sings in the trees.

Walking along your path you hear running water in the distance. You come across a small stream and begin to walk alongside it, glancing occasionally at the gravel and rocks beneath the stream. The water is very clear. You notice a fish darting from rock to rock. Continue walking along the stream. After walking for an hour, you feel the warmth of the sun on your head. You stop by a place in the stream where the water has been diverted into a small pond. It is about eight feet across and may be three or four feet deep in the middle. The water trickles in at one end and then out the other end, going back into the stream and finally down the river. You sit down by the side of the pond and lean against a tree. After taking your shoes and socks off, you put both feet in the cool water and feel them relax.

Leaning against the tree, you look up at the sky to see the cloud formations. You are fascinated by the different forms and shapes. Some are shaped like animals. Others seem to look like numbers. A familiar object or person may appear.

The clouds contain a clue that will help you solve a recent problem, make a decision, or provide an innovative touch to a project. Pose your problem or decision to the clouds. The solution could even come in the shapes of the clouds!

Is a special person on your mind? Can you see them in the clouds? What are they doing?

Observe these clouds for a while. In back of your mind, record everything you are seeing so you can easily recollect the details.

After a while you know it is time to leave and return to your current surroundings. You wave good-bye to the clouds, stand up, and take in a wonderful stretch. Going back, you follow the stream and eventually come to your starting point.

Return your awareness to your room as you stretch and look around. You feel refreshed and revitalized. Answer the following questions to help you achieve clarity about anything that happened during this experience.

How do you feel?

_____

_____

_____

How clear was your imagery?

_____

_____

_____

Record any intuitive solution, decision or innovation you received.

_____

_____

_____

Discovering Your Dominant Sense

You will reinforce the connection between sensory input and your intuitive mind by discovering your *dominant sense*. As a teacher, I am fortunate to meet many students who in turn become my teachers. One such experience came from Jim Stark, the circulation sales and marketing manager for the *Muskegon Chronicle* in Michigan.

At the beginning of the course, Jim admitted that he was skeptical of this "intuitive area" since he was quite secure wearing his "logical cap." He selected this class simply because it fit his scheduling needs. This brief background will help you appreciate the importance of the discovery he made about intuition. Jim writes,

> What is the sixth sense? Is it really intuition? If it is, what is intuition? As a class assignment, we were required to conduct interviews to find out what others in the business world thought about the use of intuition. We were encouraged to examine others' use of this sense, even if they weren't aware they used it. What I noticed was how they answered the questions once they were required to internalize the thought process before answering.
>
> Each candidate "processed" the questions and arrived at answers by heightening one of their existing senses before responding. In other words, they went to a natural sense (sight, sound, taste, smell, touch) and concentrated the processing of the information through their strongest sense. This proved especially true when they were requested to "intuit" their answer.
>
> Each time the candidate "thought" he was ready to give an answer, he would "process" the information through an existing sense. If it didn't taste, smell, feel, sound, or look correct, back into the processing chambers the data went for another go at it.
>
> Some would swirl it around in their mouth until it tasted good, and then spit it out in the form of an answer. Those who heightened their sense of smell would change their breathing routine as if to search for the correct smelling answer. Listeners would tilt their heads to one side or the other as if they could "hear" a soft answer that would instruct them as to how to respond. The visuals would squint, alternate squinting between eyes, look to the corners of their visual parameters, and then focus straight ahead when they "saw" their answer to the asked questions. The touchers would rub their thumbs and middle fingers together to "feel" the answer before responding. Some would bounce their response between several of their natural senses prior to answering as if they were searching for the best "sense" to weigh their response.

Intuition seems to include a heightened awareness of the senses that we naturally possess. After this experience, Jim Stark felt that "Intuition is what one tastes, smells, sees, hears, or feels in their natural state of awareness." If we can find a person's "dominant natural sense," we should be able to teach him how to intuit through that natural sense so he can see, smell, taste, touch, or hear intuitively.

When the intuitive mind is activated, each of your five senses becomes extended and requires that you "reach in" before "reaching out" to one of your natural senses. The uncomfortable feeling "in the pit of one's stomach" is clearly as important as the input we receive from the five senses. Perhaps more so.

The implication of Jim Stark's intuitive discovery is fascinating. We often talk about these senses as if we were conscious of them actually giving us information. For example, I've talked to many lawyers who mention "sniffing out" the clues. Richard Antonini, president and CEO of the Foremost Insurance Company mentioned that you can *smell* or you can *feel* if it's not right. He mentioned that his senior staff often talks like that by saying, "This doesn't smell good; it doesn't feel right." I also recall a policewoman telling me after a life-threatening incident that the only thing that saved her life was listening to a little voice inside her head telling her to wait.

A person's dominant sense can sometimes be detected in the way he or she responds to an angry or emotional moment:

Don't talk to me!

Don't look at me!

Don't touch me!

You leave a bad taste in my mouth!

You smell bad!

You make me sick!

Observing how the dominant sense works in other people is illuminating. For example, I asked Leo Buscaglia if he was aware of the role the senses played in his writing. He said, "Well, a lot of my work depends on memory, and my memories are so vivid that when I speak of Mama's kitchen, I can see the foods, I can smell them simmering in pots. I can visualize the activity, I can hear the movement. All the senses are always in use. It is the same way when I am walking through a beautiful forest. Everything works on me. I don't allow myself to interfere with the experience, so everything comes out and presents itself like the ripe apple."

James Adamson, the CEO of Burger King, made an interesting observation regarding his dominant sense. He said, "When I think about my decisions, I always need to paint a picture. Pictures come to me when I don't expect them most of the time. What I find myself doing, even when someone is talking to me, is painting a picture in my mind related to some decision or change I am in the process of making. I don't listen well. In fact, I've told everyone who works for me to please, if they see me start to wander, bring me back to what we are talking about. I am already thinking about something we are going to want to talk about later, and I am already painting a picture."

Discovering Your Dominant Sense

With continued practice you will clearly discover your dominant sense and know how this sense communicates intuitive information to you. The next exercise will help you identify which imagery is strongest as you "sample" the various senses.

EXERCISE

Combining the Senses

Preparation: Close your eyes and relax. Take seven "hang-sah" breaths to relax. Inhale as you whisper "hang," and exhale by whispering "sah."

Direction: Picture yourself in your kitchen. There is a bowl of fruit sitting on a kitchen counter or table in front of you. Reach out with your left hand and pick up an orange from the bowl. Look closely at the orange and "see" the various colors of the skin. "Touch" the orange with your right hand and feel the texture of the skin. Scratch the surface of the orange with the index finger of your right hand, hold it up to your nose, and "smell" the orange.

There's a knife sitting next to the bowl of fruit. Pick up the knife and cut a cross-section of the orange. Bring the cross-section up to your mouth and "taste" the orange. As you set the orange down next to the knife, you "hear" the doorbell ring.

At the door someone hands you a bouquet of flowers. You take one of the flowers with your left hand and "see" the colors that are in it. Bring the flower up to your nose and "smell" its fragrance. Hold a petal of the flower between the thumb and forefinger of your right hand and "feel" the texture of the flower's petal. Experience this flower any other way you would like to help you bring the image of the flower into your intuitive mind.

Open your eyes and record the results.

Were you able to see the orange and/or the flower?

_____

_____

_____

Were you able to use your touch to feel the texture of the orange and/or flower?

_____

_____

_____

Could you recreate the smell of the orange and/or flower?

_____

_____

_____

Could you taste the orange?

_____

_____

_____

Could you hear the bell ring?

_____

_____

_____

What affective feeling was aroused? What are your favorite memories of eating an orange?

_____

_____

_____

Can you imagine throwing an orange to someone? What is this sensation like?

_____

_____

_____

EXERCISE

Continue to Discover
Your Dominant Sense

Observe each of your senses and note how you process information. Can you identify your dominant sense?

_____

_____

_____

Can you see how others process information? Record your observations showing how they use their five senses.

_____

_____

_____

You will continue discovering which sensory modes you use in the next exercise. Though you can activate several, you will find that one sense tends to predominate.

Evaluate Your Senses

To evaluate how you respond to your inner imagery, check any item you can experience.

Visual: Inner Vision—Can You "See"?

____ An apple

____ A tulip

____ A house

____ A banana

____ A book

Auditory: Inner Sounds—Can You "Hear"?

____ A doorbell ringing

____ A musical melody

____ A phone ringing

____ Someone laughing

____ A buzzer

Olfactory: Inner Smell—Can You "Smell"?

____ A rose

____ A pie baking

____ Fresh cut grass

____ Perfume

____ Gasoline

Gustatory: Inner Taste—Can You "Taste"?

____ Lemonade

____ Cup of tea

____ A potato chip

____ Barbecue chicken

Tactile: Inner Touch—Can You "Feel"?

____ A cat or dog

____ A satin shirt or blouse

____ Sand on the beach

____ The nap of a thick carpet

____ A large rock

Affective: Inner Emotion—Can You "Feel"?

_____ Joy from a recent event

_____ Happiness from hearing good news

_____ Love sent to a family member

_____ Anger resulting from a recent disagreement

_____ Sadness from something you heard

Kinesthetic: Inner Movement—Can You "Recall"?*

_____ Walking up the stairs

_____ Running

_____ Imagining you were floating on a cloud

_____ Swimming

_____ Dancing

Which sensory expression mode is the strongest?

_____

_____

_____

_____

Is that mode activated when the intuitive mind speaks?

_____

_____

_____

_____

We will find the answer to this question with the following exercise.

---

* Neurolinguistic programmers include olfactory, gustatory, tactile, emotional, and this kinesthetic sense under the "kinesthetic" heading. Just be aware that here we are pulling apart these separate senses before we condense them under any heading.

> **EXERCISE**

Retrieving Imagery

This is an exercise to help you retrieve images from your intuitive mind. You can be anywhere when you do this exercise—in your office or home. Before you begin, select an object that can be held in your hand and put it in front of you. Place a pen or pencil next to that object. Close your eyes and take four "hang-sah" breaths to relax.

Open your eyes and hold the object you selected in your hand for 1 minute. Study it carefully as you rotate it to view it from various angles. Put it down and close your eyes. Recreate the image of the object in your mind.

Can you "see" the object with your mind's eye? What do you see? Is your impression strong, moderate, or faint?

_____

_____

_____

Pick up the pen or pencil and hold it in your hand. Sit comfortably in your chair, inhale deeply, hold momentarily, and exhale. Try that deep breathing sequence again. Look at this writing object closely. Notice the color, the design, and any writing on it. Now, close your eyes and recreate a picture of the pen or pencil with your inner mind. If you can't retrieve a clear image, open your eyes, look at the pen or pencil again, close your eyes, and see the image of the pen or pencil with your mind. Describe the image that you see.

_____

_____

_____

You can strengthen your ability to "see" an image by practicing with other objects. Try this exercise again. Select a coin from your wallet or pocket or use some other objects in the room. Is your imagery clear?

_____

_____

_____

Which sensory mode was dominant?

_____

_____

_____

Do you see it, relate through your other senses, or simply know it is there?

_____

_____

_____

Be conscious of the sensory mode you have isolated. This is one of the windows your intuitive mind uses to communicate with you. Continue to practice retrieving imagery as you are guided on a journey to the beach.

EXERCISE

Guided Journey to the Beach

Preparation: To ease into a receptive state, do the "total" breath followed by the "stretching and breathing" technique. You can practice imagery with your eyes open or closed.

Directions: See yourself lying on the white sand of a beautiful beach. The sand has a tinge of pink left by the traces of coral. You look at the clear blue sky and hear someone singing the title song from a classic Broadway show, *On a Clear Day You Can See Forever*. You lie on the beach with your eyes closed and feel the sun's rays caress your face. As the breeze blows, you inhale the salty sea air.

In the distance, you hear the cry of a lone gull. You continue to rest on the beach and listen to the roar of the ocean waves. The rays coming from the sun bathe your entire body, making you feel totally regenerated. These rays help melt any tension and calm your thoughts.

Finally, you glow all over, emanating peace and love. The waves are louder as they come crashing down on the jetty rocks. You lie still, listening to the surf as it draws back and washes in again.

You continue to bask in the sun's warmth and listen to the music produced by the ocean waves. In the distance, you can hear some people talking. New sounds come forth as you hear familiar tunes playing on their stereo. Although you are no longer alone on the beach, you still relish basking in the sun's warmth. You'd like to stay here, listening to the rhythms of the waves, forever. Finally, though, it is time to leave the beach. You gently rise to your feet, brush the sand from your body, and walk slowly away.

Now, return your awareness to the room, feeling deeply refreshed and relaxed.

Evaluating Your Imagery

Recall the images of the beach, sun, water, gull's cry, sounds of the surf, distant voices, and music on the stereo. Indicate how you used each of your extended senses on this journey:

Visual   _____

_____

Auditory _____

_____

Olfactory _____

_____

Gustatory _____

_____

Tactile _____

_____

Affective _____

_____

Kinesthetic: _____

_____

EXERCISE

Further Imagery Practice—Working Out the Senses

Sit still as you practice your breathing and relaxation. Elicit the imagery of a house. See the house from outside. Enter the front door. Walk through and observe each room.

Experience this house from as many sensory experiences as possible. Afterward, record your imagery. Then, you can compare your responses to my associations of the house imagery.

Indicate how you have used each of the senses to experience a house.

Visual _____

_____

Auditory _____

_____

Olfactory _____

_____

Gustatory _____

_____

Tactile _____

_____

Affective _____

_____

Kinesthetic _____

_____

Some of my associations to the house include

Visual—Saw the house I lived in as a youngster

Auditory—Heard the buzzing of flies

Olfactory—Smelled the food Mom was cooking

Gustatory—Tasted a glass of cold lemonade

Tactile—Felt the grass on my bare feet outside the house

Affective—Experienced nostalgia for the old times

Kinesthetic—Swayed to hearing music played

How are you doing with your imagery retrieval? Record any observations here.

_____

_____

_____

_____

Practice makes perfect. Here are some additional imagery exercises to work with:

Next time you are hungry, try picturing a piece of fruit or another piece of food. Record your experiences of this "food" as you practice using all the senses.

_____

_____

_____

_____

Do you have an upcoming meeting to attend? Before you attend, close your eyes and picture the room. How many people are attending? What is the mix of males and females? What is the mood in the room? Record as many impressions as possible. If you have trouble creating imagery, first elicit the imagery of a recent meeting, and then you can "switch the screen" to the future mode.

_____

_____

_____

Do you have a speech or presentation to give at work, to a class, or for your club? First, see someone you admire giving a talk. What do you notice about the surroundings and audience reaction? Now, see your face imposed on the speaker's as you see, feel or sense yourself successfully giving the talk. Record as many impressions as possible.

_____

_____

_____

_____

You want to motivate your child, partner, or friend and are still searching for the right words to say. See yourself approaching them and note the positive reaction coming from the other person. They are truly pleased you have reached out to them. If this is difficult, recall the time someone approached you with advice that you were pleased to receive. When this image is fixed, transfer it to your interaction with the individual you want to motivate. Note your experiences with this in the space provided.

_____

_____

_____

_____

What sport do you enjoy? Do you walk, jog, swim, or fish? Is there a particular athletic event you like to watch? What else do you enjoy recreationally? Write your experiences as you retrieve the imagery of yourself happily engaged in this activity.

_____

_____

_____

_____

When you feel distressed for any reason, you can create any imagery you want to transport you to more enjoyable surroundings. Close your eyes as you silently count backward from ten to one. Take a deep breath and heave a sigh, knowing that relief is in sight. Imagine that you are taking a walk through a lovely wooded area. Imagine how beautiful the trees and flowers appear, hear the birds, and simply feel good as you breathe in the fresh air. Do this for 3 to 5 minutes. When you finish, write down your inner experiences. Also, note any memories or feelings that were aroused.

_____

_____

_____

_____

Another way to take a "getaway" when immersed in a stressful situation at work or anywhere else is to re-create a pleasurable past experience. For example, can you recall going on a family picnic, a hunting trip, or a company outing? What did you experience? Write your recollections in this space.

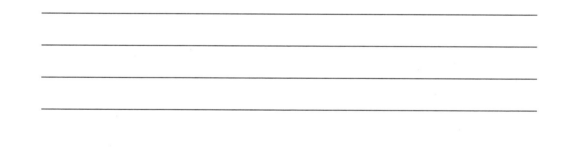

HOW TO ACTIVELY ACCESS YOUR INTUITIVE IMAGES

I know you have had the experience of listening to someone when a brilliant flash strikes. By the time it is your turn to talk, the brilliant idea that flashed into your mind has been forgotten. How about that time you dozed off and a brilliant idea seemed to leap into your consciousness. Or even the time you were just going about your normal work when an intuitive flash popped into your mind presenting a new perspective or innovative look at an old problem. These are good examples of the intuitive mind speaking to you when you are not actively searching for an idea or trying to retrieve the solution.

On the other hand, there are many times when you have actively tried to retrieve intuitive information. You have experienced the active mode in earlier exercises as you were guided to the beach or the woods. That is actively working your imagination. Other examples include rehearsing in your mind a letter you are going to write or planning something you are going to say to someone. As you actively rehearse the words, the imagery of where and how you will be saying them comes to you.

This is where a creative facet of IPS comes in as you decide how to actively retrieve the imagery that will answer your question. Here are some examples that will show you how you can actively retrieve imagery. Eventually, you will find it exciting to exercise your creativity, mold imagery, and answer questions. Start with relatively simple imagery.

EXERCISE

"Pull Up" an Image

Actively create an image to answer each of these questions.

Are you going to the meeting?

Image: Two neon lights—one has "Yes" on it and the other has "No." Which neon light is illuminated after you ask the question?

Should I change careers?

Image: Two banners hanging out a window. One says "Yes" and the other says "No." Which banner is accentuated?

Is this the time to ask for a raise?

Image: A stoplight with red, yellow, and green lights. Which light comes on? Red tells you "not now" while green signals a go-ahead; the yellow light indicates caution.

How do you feel?

Image: Mimic the images in the weather report. Is the sun shining? Do you see rain or clouds? Which image lights up to reflect how you feel about a specific person or decision?

On what day of the month will I receive good news?

Image: Watch the pages of a calendar being torn off. When do you stop tearing?

Will I get a promotion?

Image: Picture doors opening and closing. Do the doors open or close?

Can I mend the relationship with my distant coworker?

Image: You and the coworker face each other. Are you standing close or far apart? Are you shaking hands or looking the other way? How are you interacting with each other?

It is quite acceptable if your images are simple. Don't let their simplicity mislead you into ignoring important intuitive insights.

Activate Your Imagery

Pose three questions and "design" the imagery you will create to answer your question.

Question 1. _____

Image: _____

_____

Question 2. _____

Image: _____

_____

Question 3. _____

Image: _____

_____

Now that you have become aware of communication by the various sensory modes, are you noticing how each of the senses impacts you differently? Continue monitoring how your intuitive voice communicates with you and remember that, in addition to inwardly seeing, you can activate any of the other senses, which include feeling emotion or movement. Let's see, for example, how a question can be answered through each of the sensory channels.

Question: Should I change jobs?

- Spontaneously "see" doors opening or closing using visual imagery.
- "Touch" a piece of paper in front of you to see if the surface is rough or smooth.
- Take a deep breath to "smell" whether the odor surrounding the job is pleasant or putrid.
- Get a "taste" for the situation to see if it is sweet or sour.
- "Hear" familiar words or a phrase telling you "sooner than you think."
- Feel the "excitement" of a forthcoming offer.
- Feel yourself "being pushed" toward a new opportunity.

EXERCISE

Actively Eliciting Imagery Through Your Senses

Sit quietly as you silently pose three questions that can have a simple "Yes" or "No" answer. Write your questions here.

1. _____

   _____

2. _____

   _____

3. _____

   _____

How does the intuitive mind communicate its response? Do you see, hear, or get information through any other senses? Do you feel any inner emotion or movement about the right answer?

_____

_____

_____

_____

_____

Fantasize or Daydream

You are actively and passively eliciting imagery when you fantasize or daydream. Many people don't like to admit to these practices because they suggest that work responsibilities are being neglected while the mind plays. The truth is, you can use the daydream and fantasy as a wonderful stress buster that brings the opportunity to shift modes and relax.

The next time you are trying to escape from boring or tedious work, notice how your inner mind retreats into a fantasy or daydream. As a fisherman, for example, you may feel excited recalling the opening of the trout season when you "reeled in the big one." This imagery was retrieved spontaneously as you daydreamed about that moment; yet, if I directed you to "see" or "imagine" a man fishing, you might have difficulty.

I have found that people attending my classes and seminars become very concerned if they can't retrieve any imagery. *Hint*: When you are having difficulty, shift to familiar experiences you know and love so you can retrieve the imagery more easily.

You can elicit imagery! I have already suggested some circumstances where you have retrieved imagery. With these examples, I am adding to that list. For example, can you recall any time during the day when your mind drifted? Were you thinking of a work problem? Wondering how to sell the new product? Are thoughts of the dream house or car you want to buy intruding into your consciousness? Deciding how to confront one of your employees about a disciplinary problem? Were you trying to think of the opening lines for your talk? Perhaps your mind drifted from work issues as you mentally wrote a letter to someone, went to the woods during hunting season, visited your favorite hideaway, or relived the last family outing. These imaginary retreats can be called a daydream or fantasy. While daydreams tend to be more passive, fantasies are actively created. Both utilize the pictures, images, and symbols sent by the intuitive mind.

EXERCISE

An Excursion into Fantasy and Daydream

Notice the next time your mind spontaneously drifts into a daydream and record your images. Pay particular attention to the sensory experiences such as sights, sounds, smells, touch, and taste. You can write your daydreams on a scratch pad while at work and transfer them to this page later.

_____

_____

_____

_____

_____

Perhaps you are angry at someone and mentally rehearse a confrontation. Consciously change this negative drift by actively creating a pleasant fantasy to counteract the negativity. Does any fantasy image help you change the reality?

_____

_____

_____

_____

_____

THE ALPHA TO OMEGA TECHNIQUE

More imagery exercises will be presented as we continue. This next exercise will let you create your own guided fantasy imagery. One day a student came in and thanked me for helping her lose weight. Doing this had long eluded me personally, so I was quite puzzled. I asked how I had helped her. She replied, "I just followed the *alpha to omega* exercise in the book and have had wonderful results losing 12 pounds in a couple weeks." With that encouraging introduction, I present the *alpha to omega technique.*

With the alpha to omega technique, you will be creating your own guided fantasy. The script for this fantasy will start with the current status of the problem, which is the alpha, or beginning, and continue until you reach the desired outcome or ending, which is the omega.

You can create a scene where you actively counteract any unproductive tendencies or attitudes. This is similar to erasing an old cassette tape so you can record new ideas. Likewise, you can tear up an old script and write a more productive scenario. For example, if you struggle in search of a compelling introduction to your talk, you can visualize yourself confidently introducing the topic before your audience. If you can't hear the words spoken, perhaps you can see yourself productively writing the beginning. As the time for the talk comes, you will watch the words flow readily out of your mouth.

This technique can be extremely effective in all problem solving, especially since you are the author of the script. Your logical mind will help you write or create the basic outline of the script. Then, you can close your eyes while your intuitive mind "previews" this outline and adds the necessary images while you are in the alpha level. Additions to the original script may come *passively*. At other times, you will *actively* continue to create the imagery until you come to the desired end result.

Start by confronting the problem; then watch the imagery "dance before your eyes." Continue with the script as you give yourself some perks or positive reinforcement for making the changes or making the necessary confrontations.

Warning: Be alert to what you create with this visualization, since you will undoubtedly get it! When you get your script clearly in mind, play it out several times a day, giving full reign to your inner imagery. Bombarding your senses will powerfully convey the message to your intuitive mind, which will receive it and help you find the most productive solution or conclusion.

You can create any reality you want using the alpha to omega technique. If you are in poor health, create a healthy body. If you want to get out of an unsatisfactory situation, imagine that change taking place.

How to Lose Weight with the Alpha to Omega Technique

Here is how the technique works for the weight loss mentioned earlier. At the beginning of your script (alpha), see yourself looking into the mirror. Notice your distressed, sad face as you bemoan the tight fit of your clothing. Throughout the script, see yourself exercising, getting on the scale several times, and finally showing a significant weight loss. The last time you get on the scale, see the weight you want to achieve registering as you continue to picture yourself at your goal weight. With a huge smile, and wearing clothing to show off your trim body, you go forth to greet friends who are hugging you and shaking your hand. The omega, or script ending, shows you receiving praise and congratulations for the weight loss.

Turn a Negative into a Positive with the Alpha to Omega Technique

Let's take this alpha to omega technique into the business and home setting to see how you can turn a negative into a positive.

Problem: Turn a disagreeable situation with someone around by using the alpha to omega technique.

Problem: Learn to master the new computer system that is giving you difficulty.

Problem: Feel comfortable leading the new study group at work even though the initial appointment to be the leader brought discomfort.

Problem: See how you are helping a child or friend learn something new. *What problems of yours* can be changed with the alpha to omega technique?

_____

_____

_____

PRACTICE SHARPENING YOUR IMAGERY

By now you are beginning to do well with your imagery practice. This next exercise will show you how to test your progress by rating the quality of your imagery.

Evaluate Your Progress in Creating Imagery

Practice 1: This exercise will show what level of imagery—basic, intermediate, or advanced—you are currently using. We will start very simply. First, close your eyes, then take a deep breath and relax. With your intuitive mind, imagine a ball. Continue to observe how this nonverbal mode speaks to you. Do you see the ball, feel it, observe it in any other sensory way, or simply know it is there? How does the ball appear to you?

_____

_____

_____

Which of the following classifications match your imagery?

♦ *Basic Level (B)*: The image of the ball is a round object of any color.

♦ *Intermediate Level (I)*: Your imagery can show the ball from all sides as you turn it around in your inner mind. You might note that it is decorated in different colors or has writing on one side.

◆ *Advanced Level (A):* The imagery of the ball is presented in a context, such as an "ornament" hanging on a Christmas tree or a ball used in a game you are playing with others.

Basic _____   Intermediate _____   Advanced _____

Can you elevate your visualization until your image of the ball is at the highest level? Make any notes here about the quality of your imagery.

_____

_____

_____

_____

Practice 2: Close your eyes, take a deep breath, relax, and elicit the imagery of a flower. Open your eyes and write down what you have experienced.

_____

_____

_____

_____

How would you rate your imagery?

Basic _____   Intermediate _____   Advanced _____

Please note that these criteria are not fixed but suggested so you can have some guidelines to help you evaluate your progress in retrieving imagery.

◆ At the *basic level,* the imagery reflects just one dimension, like a red flower.

◆ At the *intermediate level,* you might imagine the flower from different angles. Look inside to be aware of other colors, or notice the stem or any added observations.

◆ At the *advanced level,* the flower might be presented as part of a centerpiece on a table, or part of a group of flowers in the woods or garden. There might be a bug sitting on one of the petals.

How can you upgrade your imagery to the next level?

_____

_____

_____

Practice 3: Close your eyes. Take a deep breath. Create the image of a piece of fruit.

♦ *Basic Level*: Do you see it in terms of just one dimension, such as size or color?

♦ *Intermediate Level*: Does the fruit have rotting spots or is it still attached to the stem?

♦ *Advanced Level*: Is the fruit in a centerpiece on the table? Is an apple being cut up for apple pie?

Where does your image rate?

Basic _____   Intermediate _____   Advanced _____

Practice 4: Close your eyes, take two deep breaths, and relax. Elicit the imagery of a boat. Open your eyes and write down some details about your image.

_____

_____

_____

_____

How would you rate your imagery?

Basic _____   Intermediate _____   Advanced _____

How can you upgrade your image?

_____

_____

_____

_____

Practice 5: Practice retrieving imagery by recalling something from your office, such as the typewriter, telephone, or copy machine. Remember, there are no right or wrong images. With continuing practice you will receive clear, complex, and detailed pictures or images from the intuitive mind.

The image I have chosen is   _____

Describe in detail the image you have retrieved.

_____

_____

_____

_____

This image is at the

Basic Level _____   Intermediate Level _____   Advanced Level _____

In the next exercise you will be actively creating imagery on a guided journey so you can become more able to communicate with the intuitive mind.

Are there any weighty concerns on your mind right now, or important decisions needed? If so, you will find that taking a guided or fantasy journey is a wonderful way to retreat from all such concerns and lighten your pressures. Sure, the sights and sounds on these journeys may seem trivial compared to the heavier pressures in your life. But here is the reason you are doing this. These "fantasy adventures" are the starting point and training ground so you can activate your intuition easily and effortlessly to solve those "weightier problems."

EXERCISE

Taking a Nature Walk

Let's take a nature walk one more time so you can have additional practice retrieving and creating imagery.

Preparation: Get up from where you are sitting and stretch your arms over your head, inhaling deeply. As you exhale, bend forward at your waist and let your upper body relax as you reach toward your toes. Inhale again as you straighten up and exhale as you sit down again in your chair. Let's take seven "hang-sah" breaths to relax. Inhale as you whisper "hang" and exhale as you whisper "sah."

Send the following message from your mind to your body:

♦ Every cell in my body feels relaxed and comfortable.

♦ Every cell in my mind feels relaxed and comfortable.

♦ Every cell in my body is relaxed and comfortable.

Directions: This guided journey begins as you imagine that you are walking along a path in the woods. It is a beautiful cool morning and the sun is shining brightly from a vibrant blue sky. As you touch some ferns by the side of the path, you notice that they are still wet with the morning dew. Suddenly, you hear a noise off to your right and you spot a squirrel quickly running through the rustling leaves to a nearby oak tree, which he hides behind so you can no longer see him. You hear the piercing call of a bird and look up to see a blue jay giving his warning call to others in the forest.

Then you notice the chattering chickadees as they flit from one branch to the next, trying to see who is invading their forest. As your attention turns back to the trail ahead of you, a rabbit bounds across the path and runs down a hill to your left into an area lined with cedar trees. The aroma of cedar and pine drifts on the breeze toward you. You notice several rows of pine trees that were neatly planted next to the right side of the trail. After passing by the pines, the trail begins to ascend a steep hill. You can feel the pull on the muscles of your legs as you continue to climb.

At the top of the hill you go to a small field filled with wild blackberry vines. In your haste to pick one of the tasty-looking berries, you prick your finger on the thorny vine. Quickly recoiling your arm and hand, you put the injured finger in your mouth to ease the pain. Then, carefully, you pick a juicy berry and pop it into your mouth, discovering to your delight that it is very sweet. Picking several more berries, enough to fill your cupped hand, you continue walking down the trail, eating them as you go.

The sound of a gurgling stream catches your ear and you begin to run in the direction from which it is coming. The path leads right to the water's edge, turns, and follows the bank upstream. The water is so clear that it is easy to see the fish darting from the rapids behind the rocks to the slow clear pools near the sandy bank. Since you have been walking for some time, you decide to sit down next to a big oak tree not far from the water's edge to rest.

The sun is higher in the sky now and its rays are streaming down on your face as you lean back against the tree. The warmth of the sun feels ever so good as you close your eyes and enjoy this moment of peace and tranquility. The sun feels wonderful on your legs and arms, as if its penetrating rays are massaging your muscles.

As you open your eyes, you look up into the blue sky and see a hawk majestically circling round and round as he comes ever closer to the treetops, searching the ground for his next meal. You close your eyes again and suddenly feel the rough ridges in the bark of the big tree that you are leaning against.

Just as you begin to shift your weight to get into a more comfortable position, a splashing noise upstream startles you. As you glance up, you catch a fleeting glimpse of a deer crossing the stream and dashing into the woods.

The time has passed quickly and you realize that soon you must walk back to your starting point. As you stand up and stretch, a smile comes to your face. You are thinking how wonderful it feels to take this time today to take a walk through the woods and enjoy all the beauty of nature. You start back on the path, humming a favorite tune as you go. As you come down the hill and pass next to the pines, you take a deep breath to capture that wonderful smell of pine and cedar in your memory. Soon you are back to the road where you started.

Return your conscious awareness to where you are sitting. Stand up and stretch.

Now sit down and begin to write down whatever you can recall from this guided fantasy trip.

_____

_____

_____

_____

_____

EXERCISE

Evaluate Your Imagery

How was your imagery recall? Write down how you used each of the senses on this guided journey:

Visual: _____

Auditory: _____

Olfactory: _____

Gustatory: _____

Tactile: _____

Affective: _____

Kinesthetic: _____

Now compare your imagery examples with mine:

Visual: Seeing the trees, sun, animals, and stream

Auditory: Hearing the rustle in the trees, sounds of the stream (gurgling and splash)

Olfactory: Smelling the cedar and pine

Gustatory: Tasting the berries

Tactile: Feeling the warmth of the sun on the body and the roughness of the tree

Affective: Feeling happy

Kinesthetic: Feeling your muscles being tugged as you climbed the tree

Which of these levels describes your imagery recall?

- *Basic Level*: How was nature presented? How many senses were activated? If only a few, you are still at this level.

- *Intermediate Level*: Did you recall any of the details of the animals or the natural setting? Did you roughly describe the animals, the setting, and any of the other directions without giving specific details?

- *Advanced Level*: Detailed and complete recall of the concepts would place you at this level.

Basic _____   Intermediate _____   Advanced _____

EXERCISE

Another Look at Imagery

This next exercise provides additional practice to help you activate the inner senses emanating from your intuitive mind. Sit comfortably in your chair and close your eyes. Let's take seven "hang-sah" breaths to relax. Inhale as you whisper "hang" and exhale as you whisper "sah." Be sure to do seven.

Recreate in your inner mind one highlight of a memorable vacation. What scenery surrounds you?

_____

_____

_____

_____

What activity are you involved in?

_____

_____

_____

_____

_____

Who are the other people around you?

_____

_____

_____

_____

_____

Does any unusual event occur in that setting?

_____

_____

_____

_____

_____

You can continue to activate your inner senses by eliciting images of

The most "unforgettable work associate" I ever met.

A highlight from my present work position.

A significant contribution I have made at work.

Something I recently purchased for my home.

ASSEMBLING THE FIRST FOUR INTUITIVE PROBLEM-SOLVING STEPS

You have now learned the first four steps of the IPS process: stating the problem, centering, receptivity, and eliciting imagery. Let's put it all together so you walk right into the next chapter and have some imagery ready to interpret.

First, you need to decide if you want to solve a problem, make a decision, get a perspective on a situation, understand someone's personality more clearly, or discover a creative or innovative idea. Remember, I am using the word "problem" to represent any of these situations. Write your problem in the form of a question. You may choose to use one of the problems you listed on page 31.

Problem: _____

_____

_____

EXERCISE

Going to the House of Intuition to Solve a "Problem"

Preparation: It would be helpful to hear these directions on a cassette tape. You have several alternatives for this. You can make a tape from the script, purchase a tape from our catalog in the resource section, or have someone else read the directions to you.

Find a quiet place where you can practice this exercise completely undisturbed for 15 minutes. If necessary, take the phone off the hook. When any background noise intrudes, let it be incorporated into your exercise. On the next page, you will complete the exercise by recording your intuitive discoveries. Sit in a comfortable chair with your back straight and supported. Do not cross your hands or legs.

Directions: Become centered as you affirm, "My intuitive mind will lead me to the correct answer." Say that again, "My intuitive mind will lead me to the correct answer."

Relax to release all tension and stress from your body. To help you drift into a deeper relaxed state, focus your awareness on each part of your body as it is mentioned. Start by saying to yourself

My feet are relaxing…My feet are relaxing…My feet are now relaxed.

My legs and thighs are relaxing…My legs and thighs are relaxing…My legs and thighs are now relaxed.

My midsection is relaxing…My midsection is relaxing…My midsection is now relaxed.

My arms and hands are relaxing…My arms and hands are relaxing…My arms and hands are now relaxed.

My back and chest are relaxing…My back and chest are relaxing…My back and chest are now relaxed.

My shoulders and neck are relaxing…My shoulders and neck are relaxing…My shoulders and neck are now relaxed.

My head and face are relaxing…my head and face are relaxing…my head and face are now relaxed.

Take an inventory throughout your body to see where any tension or nagging sensations still reside. If any spot is stubbornly hanging on to the tension, take another deep breath and again exhale the tension out.

To heighten your receptivity, do some deep breathing. Take a deep inhale to the count of seven, hold for one count and then release to a count of seven. Do that once again and count:

INHALE 2 3 4 5 6 7 HOLD EXHALE 2 3 4 5 6 7

Feel the charge you are receiving from this breath.

Remember, this takes seven counts to come in, one count to hold and seven counts to release and expel the air.

Again,

INHALE 2 3 4 5 6 7 HOLD EXHALE 2 3 4 5 6 7

On the next inhale, send the incoming air to the top of your head and feel a tingle

INHALE 2 3 4 5 6 7 HOLD EXHALE 2 3 4 5 6 7

Inhale as you let the air come to the space between your eyes

INHALE 2 3 4 5 6 7 HOLD EXHALE 2 3 4 5 6 7

Inhale directing the next breath to your heart center

INHALE 2 3 4 5 6 7 HOLD EXHALE 2 3 4 5 6 7

Imagine that you are being charged by a light beam coming down from the sky, entering your head and going right down your spine. Feel that light spreading throughout your body.

Are any environmental noises interfering with your concentration?

Are any distracting thoughts or feelings intruding? To minimize these distractions, recall a peaceful scene like a lake where someone is fishing from a boat. Get in touch with the stillness of the lake and peacefulness of the fisherman.

To heighten your relaxation, repeat this simple phrase: "Peace, be still."

Say that again. "Peace, be still."

Use your imagination to go to your favorite natural setting. Where might this be? You might go to the ocean, climb high into the mountains, or find yourself walking through the woods. Walk undisturbed in this setting. Ambling along, you suddenly notice a large house ahead. Unlike most houses, you have to walk down ten steps to get to the front door. Count down as you walk from the top, down each step until you reach the bottom.

10 9 8 7 6 5 4 3 2 1

Enter eagerly, knowing that you can freely explore the rooms in the house. Initially, you remain on the first level and find the excitement mounting as your discovery continues. Sit down on a nearby chair and recall any past intuitive experiences when you simply knew what was about to happen. (PAUSE) Store these impressions in your subconscious and know you can retrieve them at any time you wish.

As you are sitting, your eyes focus on steps going to an upper level of the house. Walk up the steps and notice the library at the far end of the hall. You are fascinated by the books lining the wall from floor to ceiling. Sit down on the chair in the corner and close your eyes.

Think of the problem you have selected and envision what steps you want to take to resolve this vexing situation. The answer to this dilemma can be found in one of the books. As you stand up, a book from the shelf draws your attention. Take it and turn to a particular page. There in a word, phrase, or sentence is the information you need to resolve your problem.

Continue searching for additional clues that show you how this particular problem can be solved. Turning around, you notice a closed box. Open the box and see an object inside. This is another clue to help you resolve this vexing problem.

You know these two clues will help you find a solution, since the intuitive meaning is stored in your subconscious and can be retrieved whenever you wish.

Walk down the steps to the first level of the house. Before you leave this house, take a last look around. Go out the door and once again find yourself in your favorite natural setting. Complete your fantasy trip by going up the ten steps, returning to the wooded area, or mountainside, or beach.

To bring your awareness back to the current reality, count to five. One, two, three (touch your fingers together), four (move your head from side to side), five (look around the room and stretch.)

Centering: How did the affirmation help you shift your focus from "outside concerns" to focusing on your problem?

_____

_____

_____

Receptivity: Describe how you felt doing your breathing?

_____

_____

_____

How did the "autogenic relaxation" technique help you feel more receptive?

_____

_____

_____

Imagery: What intuitive experiences did you recall from the past?

_____

_____

_____

What message did you find in the book? Was it helpful?

_____

_____

_____

What object did you find in the box? Does it hold any meaning for you?

_____

_____

_____

Now that you have developed the imagery you need to help your intuition resolve the problem, you are ready to move on to the next chapter, where you will learn how to interpret the images themselves. Since this is your personal workout, you can always come back and complete this exercise. After working with the exercises in the next chapter on interpreting the imagery, you will become more adept at unraveling the symbolism sent by the intuitive mind.

Chapter Six

INTERPRETING THE IMAGES FROM THE INTUITIVE MIND

It probably is only the intuitive leap that will let us solve problems in this complex world. This is a major advantage of man over computer.

THOMAS PETERS AND ROBERT WATERMAN
In Search of Excellence

HOW TO GET A "HOT FLASH"

Actually that is what you are learning to do as you go through the pages of this book to discover how to access your intuitive mind. A most interesting description of intuition was given to me by an administrator of a college. She said, "What else could intuition be but a *hot flash*!" As you explore your own intuition, you too will see the word *intuition* used in many different contexts and go on to collect your favorite sayings.

Let's go back to the hot flash that leaps into your awareness quite unexpectedly or passively to help you suddenly become aware of a new perspective or a creative direction your work needs to take. Often, the symbol sent by your intuitive mind is enigmatic and needs to be unveiled. This is when you put on your detective cap to solve the "case of the puzzling symbolism." In this chapter, I will show you how to decipher and interpret the images and symbols sent from your intuitive mind.

Another characteristic of imagery is that each symbol is unique and custom designed for you. To illustrate this point, I often ask the members of my class to visualize a tree. As we go around the room I ask them what kind of tree they visualized. I always get a variety of responses, like maple, pine, dogwood, Japanese maple, cherry, oak, and magnolia. So you see, these symbols are personal. You can't assume that "your tree" is the same as "my tree."

Cracking the Golden Egg

I sense you will be like many "initiates" I have helped to develop their intuitive ability. Once they feel comfortable closing their eyes and "letting go," they drift into the receptive alpha level and easily elicit imagery. The excitement of receiving a symbol is often short lived though, and is soon replaced by the puzzlement of trying to figure out what this symbol really means.

Right now, my intuitive mind is showing me that, symbolically, you are like the goose that laid "a golden egg." Is this puzzling? Are you wondering what this means? The interpretation tools highlighted in this chapter will help you determine what the object you found in the box in the last exercise really means, as well as discover "the secret of the golden egg." Do you recall the message in the book and the items in the box in the last exercise? Interpretation entails penetrating the outer appearance of any picture or image to truly understand the underlying meaning of the symbol. So you need to go through the outer layer or representation to find out what the symbol really means.

Sometimes the answer will be very clear and literal. If you ask a yes or no question, the answer will not require interpretation. However, many times you will have to interpret the symbolic message so the underlying intuitive meaning can come forth. Be alert when interpreting so that you might have fun as you retrieve very "punny" associations. The "cherry tree" image might be telling you that your idea is "the pits." Imagining "a man with a gun" may symbolically suggest a holdup or delay. Or seeing a naked person may be a reminder to speak the "bare truth."

In the first exercise, let your "mind flow" as you try to unravel a puzzling image.

EXERCISE

Interpret This Puzzling Image

Someone attending one of my workshops posed the question, "Should I make a job change?" Her intuitive mind sent her a symbol of a burned piece of wood. This was puzzling and she had no idea what it meant. If this symbol was sent to you in response to that question, how would you interpret its meaning? In the following space, I'd like you to write as many associations as possible to this burned piece of wood symbol.

_____

_____

_____

_____

_____

If that were my symbol, a possible association to the burned piece of wood would be "burn out." This connection suggests I'm quite tired and need to take time for renewal and repair before trotting off to a new job.

Return to any of the symbols you received when doing the last exercise in Chapter Five. Let your associations flow to the object in the box or message in the book.

How do you interpret these symbols?

_____

_____

_____

_____

_____

MASTERING FOUR INTERPRETATION TECHNIQUES

There are *four* interpretation techniques in this chapter: amplification, word association, clustering, and mind mapping. As you become conversant with them, you might find that you prefer one over the others. When you are looking for a "single lead" to a problem, you can use either amplification or word association. Clustering will give you two or three paths to follow. And the mind map, as implied, diagrams all the roads or options to follow. Be alert while doing these techniques. The associations and connections you are looking for are not always what you think! This means you have to consciously turn off any analytical tendencies emanating from your thinking or logical mind so you can elicit the true associations from the intuitive mind. Interpretation takes time and patience, especially at first. Approach this IPS facet playfully as you unravel the wonderful and insightful associations sent by your intuitive mind.

It is difficult to interpret an isolated symbol without having some glimmer of knowledge about the person who retrieved it and his or her underlying concern. The associations I elicit, for example, reflect my life experiences and concerns. Therefore, my interpretations of any symbol might differ from yours. That is why you must pose the question or problem first, so the meaningful interpretation of that symbol refers back to that specific problem. There are no right or wrong answers to the associations that are made; they simply have to strike a responsive chord in the questioner's life experience. The first technique, amplification, is the most useful for rapidly eliciting an intuitive insight.

Amplification—Let the Connecting Thoughts Flow

The amplification process originally came from the Swiss psychiatrist Carl Jung. To use the amplification method, you will start with a central image and add connecting thoughts as they come to you. Each time a connecting thought pops into your head, write it down. Then, go back to the central image and retrieve another connecting thought. Repeat this process until you have no more connections to the central image and the final or intuitive association to the central image occurs.

It is important to

- ◆ Let the ideas flow freely to you.

- ◆ Use a circle, square, or other shapes around the concept.

- ◆ Draw lines between concepts.

- ◆ Use different colors for representation.

- ◆ Vary the style of print, such as all capitals for some things and script for others.

Don't censor any ideas that come forth. Capture as many ideas or associations as you can. As you do, the real underlying meaning may suddenly burst forth.

Make Associations with Amplification

Let's say you raise the question, "Should I start a business?" and receive a symbol showing a tree in full bloom.

How would you amplify or associate to this central concept? When you have finished amplifying, you can compare your associations to mine.

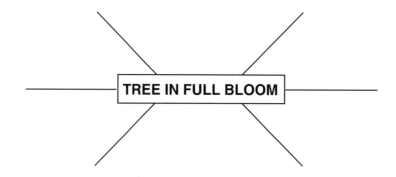

Problem: Should I start a business?
Here is how I amplify to the symbol showing a tree in full bloom.

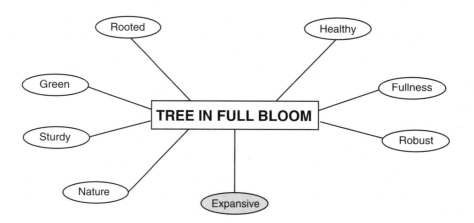

As you can see, my associations are sturdy, healthy, nature, green, rooted, fullness, robust, and expansive. The intuitive "Ah'ha!" comes to me after the word "expansive." I know the answer to my question, "Should I go into business?" is positive.

My answer came from my intuitive mind just as your associations will be tailor-made for you. You, too, will clearly know when the intuitive association fits. For example, suppose you inquired about a health condition and received an image showing a "tree in bloom." Look at the associations I just made to the business question. Can you see that a positive outcome suggested by the word "healthy" leads me to intuit that you can anticipate robust health?

Can you see how the "right association" is contingent upon the questioner's inquiry? Suppose that same tree symbol is elicited in response to your question, "What is the future of the economy?" The full-bodied tree could elicit the "green" association, which intuitively suggests a "prosperous future." We'll take a look at color interpretation in a few pages, but first, let's go back and find out the secret of the golden egg.

The problem I posed to myself when I started writing this chapter was, "How can I help the reader understand the amplification technique?" After I posed that question, my intuitive mind sent me "a golden egg." I'd like to share my association to the "golden egg" imagery with the following amplification diagram.

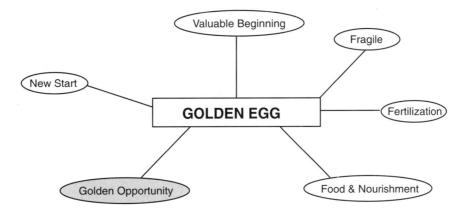

Among the many associations, the one that "jumped out intuitively" was the phrase golden opportunity. This showed me that my readers were being given a "golden opportunity" to learn this intuitive skill. More broadly, it told me that it would help readers achieve the many benefits of IPS that were identified in Chapter One, which would certainly open the door to golden opportunities. As you proceed in this book and develop your intuitive skills, you will equate the value of using your intuition to that of possessing a "golden" egg.

This technique looks so simple because the intuitive response comes so easily. In fact, I have repeatedly seen people retrieve instant, meaningful insights to problems when logical solutions have eluded them. That is what happened to John, a former student, who used IPS to find the answer to the following query: "What is the most economical design for our first church building in order to maximize space and provide for the needs of our congregation?"

Before using the amplification technique, he first became *centered* by focusing on a picture of a sunset over Hawaii. Then, to become *receptive*, he used the "total breath" exercise from page 54. At the point of total relaxation, he started to imagine that he was walking the beach in Hawaii, which brought back good memories of his visit to the Islands. While walking this imaginary beach, he focused on a box that had washed ashore. In the box was *a blank piece of paper.*

When amplifying to the *paper* imagery, John elicited the following associations: unwritten, white, clean, new, simple, flat, and square. For John, the blank piece of paper suggested that the solution to his problem was to design a building that resembled a "square." This would maximize space and provide the "best value" for the money. It became evident that other plans were just not cost-effective. The building committee had been struggling with this decision for about six months, but when John presented his "square" suggestion to them, it became obvious to them as well. They, too, realized the simplicity of the answer. The builders, too, said the "square" was the most economical design. John was amused that what seemed so simple and obvious had plagued his group for many months.

The following examples of eliciting intuitive input through amplification demonstrate how this process works. One of my former students, Mary Kay Russell, is a nurse by profession as well as a mother of three children. She and her husband wondered about the feasibility of bringing a fourth child into their lives. Using the IPS technique, she retrieved a puzzling symbol showing "the sun coming up over the horizon." Some of her associations to the sun coming up over the horizon were bright, warm, heat, and future. I immediately saw the pun sent by the intuitive mind and told her that a "son was on the horizon." I clearly knew that the intuitive mind was substituting "son" for "sun." And coming up over the horizon signalled a future event.Ten months later, she wrote to tell me that Alex Steven was just born and added, "I'll never forget that piece of intuition!"

A personnel manager is in a staff meeting with her boss sitting directly across from her. She has a great idea about hiring practices she wants to present to him, but for some reason she is afraid to bring it up in this meeting. As she looks across the table at her boss, an image of a bear comes to her mind. She writes the word "bear" down on her scratch pad and draws a square around it. She then begins to associate other words to her bear symbol, such as ferocious, huge, scavenging, furry, honey, cuddly, and huggable. The "Ah'ha!" strikes her when the words cuddly and huggable are written, and she realizes that her boss is really approachable to her new idea. She raises her hand, explains the idea, and is relieved when he accepts her suggestion and agrees to implement it into the company policy. Here is a diagram of her amplification.

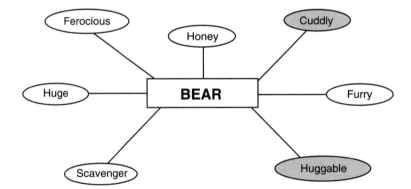

Another example involves a student who is having difficulty finding time for family, work, and school. He asks the question, "Shall I finish my master's degree?" After playing some soft music and taking a few "hang-sah" breaths, he gazes at a plant on his desk, which serves as a focus to lull the logical mind to sleep. Soon the intuitive mind sends him a hammer symbol. After drawing a picture of the hammer within a square, the student makes the following associations: nails, tool, carpentry, pound, and work. The "Ah'ha!" comes with "pound" as he realizes, "I have to pound away until I finish."

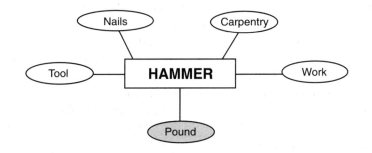

Your Turn to Amplify to the Hammer Symbol

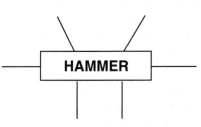

Additional Amplification Practice

Use amplification to find the answer to each question that applies to you. Create an amplification diagram to at least one of these questions.

1. Should I change jobs?
2. Will I be recognized with a career promotion or raise?
3. How will I learn a new skill on the job?
4. Will my new friendship endure?
5. How can I manage my time more effectively?
6. What type of hobby or activity should I pursue to relax?

Word Association—An Association Chain

A related technique for deciphering the hidden meaning of any symbol is word association. Initially introduced by Sigmund Freud to unearth the hidden meaning of dreams, this technique can also help you unravel the latent meaning underlying any symbol. You might want to use this to supplement any insight provided by the other interpretation techniques. In this linear process, one word or thought triggers another until the "real meaning" stands out.

Instead of responding to the central symbol, you react to each word as it is presented, forming a train or line of associations.

Let me go back to the tree in full-bloom symbol to show you how a series of associations triggers ideas until the final "intuitive hit" is reached. As before, it is important to ask a question first so the intuitive input will relate in a meaningful way to the initial problem or concern. Let's say I want some additional insight about my concern, "Is this a good time to start a business?" I receive an image of a "tree in full bloom" and then do a word association.

TREE IN FULL BLOOM→Extensive→Great→Magnanimous →Prosperous

The tree in full bloom reminds me of the word extensive, which leads me to think of the word great and then magnanimous comes to mind. When the word "prosperous" came to mind, I knew intuitively I have the right answer. Notice how the train of associations to each word was triggered until I arrived at the final "Ah'ha!" showing me that starting a new business would b e prosperous.

EXERCISE

Your Turn to Word Associate

Pose six questions and elicit an image or symbol in response to each. Let the train of word associations flow until you come to the "true meaning" of the initial symbol. State the question and then proceed with the associations.

1. Question: _____

   Associations: _____

   _____

   _____

2. Question: _____

   Associations: _____

   _____

   _____

3. Question: _____

   Associations: _____

   _____

   _____

4. Question: _____

   Associations: _____

   _____

   _____

5. Question: _____

   Associations: _____

   _____

   _____

6. Question: _____

   Associations: _____

   _____

   _____

Clustering—Make Clusters of Answers

The third technique, clustering, was introduced by Gabriele Lusser Rico in her book, *Writing the Natural Way.*[1] This is a combination of the word association and amplification techniques. But, unlike those techniques, you don't elicit a single answer. Instead, you will receive several intuitive responses that come from the clusters you will be forming.

Basically, you begin a cluster with a nucleus word that is put in a square or circled. Like the amplification, you fully associate to the nucleus word or central concept until you want to branch off and form a chain of word associations to another word. In the following example, the nucleus word is "manager." Notice how two clusters were formed to the words "liaison" and "director."

Forming a Cluster

What problem would you like to clarify through using the clustering technique? Put your nucleus term in the center and fill in the blanks by letting your associations flow. You can go off in any direction or several to form one or more clusters.

Mind Mapping—Creating a Map

Mind mapping is the fourth technique that can spark the intuitive flow. Tony Buzan first outlined this approach in his book, *Use Both Sides of Your Brain*.[2] There are many recent applications, including Joyce Wycoff's book called *Mindmapping*.[3]

With amplification, word association, and clustering, the intuitive flash is presented in one or just a few words. That is not the case with the mind map, where a schematic diagram showing many options or possibilities results. Intuition comes into play as options are elicited that may have been overlooked in planning by the logical mind.

The mind map includes all the thoughts, ideas, feelings, qualities, details, and elements of a "problem." Mind mapping allows your thoughts to flow. Record them as they enter your mind. You can organize them later.

The elements of the mind mapping process are

- ◆ A word (or words) representing the central focus of an image or a graphic representation of the problem is centrally placed on the page.
- ◆ Ideas should flow without analysis or evaluation.
- ◆ Key words are used to represent ideas.
- ◆ One key word or phrase is printed per line.
- ◆ Key word ideas are connected to the central focus with lines.

◆ Color is used to highlight and emphasize ideas.

◆ Symbols and images are used to highlight ideas. These symbols stimulate the mind to make other associations.

Here is a problem to illustrate this mind map technique. You are an independent contractor and would like to have others contract your services. You want to let them know you are available. You want to find out how to best represent yourself. You can use a mind map to do this.

Here is a mind map developed in response to the central focus of "ideal advertiser."

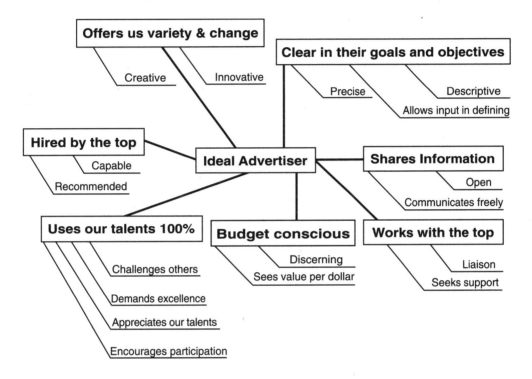

As you can see, sometimes an idea (shown in **bold face type**) spawns additional considerations (shown in regular type). The contractor now knows how to represent himself as an *ideal advertiser*. One look at the mind map shows hm that being *clear in his goals and objectives* requires him to be "Descriptive," "Precise," and "Allow input in defining the goals." Another glance at the map reinforces that as an ideal advertiser, *information has to be shared* with his clients "openly" and "communicated freely." The other facets of his being an ideal advertiser for his clients are spelled out in the remaining five categories in the mind map. These categories describe how to: *offer variety and change, be hired by the top, work with the top, be budget conscious and use talents 100%.*

Can you see how the amplification, clustering, and mind map are graphically related? Let us return to the "hammer" on page 106. Using amplification, the word "pound" provided the intuitive insight. Using that same example, notice that if you elicited such associations as perseverance and fun to the word "work," you would have a cluster to that word as well as hammer. Suppose you decided to make several associations to each of the five words (nails, tool, pound, carpentry, and work). Then you would have a mind map. The interrelation of all these techniques will become clearer as you get more experienced with these interpretation techniques.

Create Your Own Mind Map

Some projects or themes you can explore with this method are

- ◆ Business goals
- ◆ Business plan
- ◆ Communication skills
- ◆ My perfect partner

Pick one and make a mind map after you put your nucleus word or central concept in the center.

DECIPHERING YOUR COLOR IMAGES

The color of any symbol is very meaningful and intuitively gives you information about the object or person. For example, one of the associations to the "tree in full bloom" on page 104 was green. Intuitively, what does this mean? To answer that, first consider how you use color in your life. Is your language colorful? Do you "see red" when you are agitated, "feel blue" when sad, or find yourself "in the pink" of condition? Colors have a wealth of information symbolically attached to them. As you become sensitized to these connections, you will see how color can vitally impact your life. In this section, I will suggest some commonly accepted interpretations of color. You can then validate these connections by discovering the intuitive cues embedded in each color, and see how they work for you. You might also want to read some books that have been written about color interpretation.[4]

Use These Clues for Color Associations

Red—Physical: Recharging and energizing, action, physical and sexual energy, anger, fear, anxiety.

Orange—Balance: Symmetry between emotions and intellect, consideration, harmony.

Yellow—Mental: Logical and linear thinking, outgoing, investigative, communicative, cheerful.

Green—Emotion: Love, growth, life force, healing, prosperity.

Light Blue—Conceptual: Acquires wisdom and deeper knowledge, inner peace, serenity, introspection.

Indigo—Intuitive: Sixth sense, extended sense perception, insight, clear understanding, future-oriented.

Violet—Transformative: Imagination, fantasy, spiritual, divine order, deeply introspective, higher mind communication.

Let's weave these colored threads together. Do you recall the tree in full bloom that we amplified earlier? Now, can you see how I connected seeing the full-bodied tree to a feeling of robust health? Implicit was the sense that the full-bodied tree was green, which in turn was associated with a feeling of healing and well-being. I also related the full-bodied green tree to a prosperous future.

Using Color Intuitively

The following examples show how color can be intuitively coordinated to meet your needs at work, in the home, or in a social setting. Actual research has been conducted to validate these colorful connections.[5]

♦ You are scheduled to present a major report but physically feel quite fatigued. Changing to a red shirt may help you feel energized.

♦ Work pressures have you feeling very stressed. You go home and set the table with an orange tablecloth to invite balance and ease into the setting.

♦ You are having tremendous difficulty composing your acceptance speech. After changing into a yellow dress, the words flow readily.

♦ A long day is ahead of you and you simply don't feel well. Something green will act as a healing balm. Since green clothing is not available, you go outside and focus on the trees to bring the color green into your consciousness.

♦ You have a strong desire to paint your bedroom light blue. This correlates to your need for peace and serenity.

♦ You are taunted by a relationship problem and ponder what to do about this troublesome situation by contemplating the indigo sky.

♦ The job situation has presented a quandary and you wonder how to apply your talents usefully. Staring at the violet flowers on your desk helps you find a perspective to this puzzling situation.

EXERCISE

How Does Color Speak to You?

Look at the colors you are wearing. What messages are intuitively conveyed about your disposition? Anything else?

_____

_____

_____

Look around your office. What messages come forth from the colors in your work environment?

_____

_____

_____

What colors predominate in your home? What is this saying to you?

_____

_____

_____

EXERCISE

Understanding the Colors in the Candle Flame

Practicing this candle flame imagery will help you become more attuned to the intuitive link between color choice and your personal needs. You can intuit anything about your current mood or future expectations from the color of the candle flame.

Preparation: Use any of the breathing and relaxation exercises.

Directions: Close your eyes and imagine a brightly burning candle.

What color is the flame? _____

Think about last night's activities. Does the color of the flame change?

What color is it now? _____

As you think about tomorrow, notice what happens to the color of the flame.

Does it change or remain the same? _____

What color is it now? _____

Write your evaluation of each candle flame color:

Now? _____

Last night? _____

Tomorrow? _____

How are you relating the colors chosen to intuitive information about yesterday, today, and tomorrow? Record your observations here. To make these connections, refer back to page 113 for the color meanings.

_____

_____

_____

_____

_____

_____

_____

I'll share my own color evaluation exercise with you. My orange flame of yesterday is a reminder to get more balance between my work and play activities. Tomorrow's candle has a pale blue flame, suggesting that rest and repair are in sight. Today's bright red candle flame suggests I need more energy to get through the day's activities.

DON'T LET YOUR EMOTIONS MISLEAD YOU

Inevitably, someone will say to me, "I used my intuition, but it didn't work." I can only smile and point out that perhaps intuition wasn't operating because an emotional culprit intervened.

Let's look at an example to help you understand the distorting influence of these culprits. For example, I have had many CEOs talk to me about their hiring dilemmas. In one instance, someone was hired to fill a gaping hole in the organization. Though the people responsible for hiring had doubts about the potential applicant, the "hiring committee" feared that the position would remain vacant for a long time and quickly hired someone on the spot. Two weeks later, when the recruit abruptly left the company, the leaders of the company acknowledged that a major mistake had been made. Everyone had been led to make a decision that could have been prevented if they had allowed themselves to be guided more intuitively and had not fallen prey to the culprits of fear, wishful thinking, or projection.

There are several culprits that will limit and distort intuitive input. As you read about these distracting positive and negative emotional influences, I'm sure you will recall instances where these very culprits have led you astray. If you recall such a situation, you will realize the difficulty of receiving a clear signal from your intuitive antenna when these distracting factors are confounding the issue.

Emotional culprits can be positive or negative. Both can distort your intuition.
Positive emotional influences include

Wishful Thinking: Erroneous results occur when your hopes and dreams cloud the intuitive truth. For example, I always try to intuit how many people will attend my seminars so I can prepare sufficient materials. Wishful thinking has occasionally intruded, leading me to estimate that 55 will attend when in reality only 20 participants appear.

Self-fulfilling Prophecy: Related to wishful thinking, this is an attachment to knowing exactly what the outcome of a situation will be. Being told you will be a high-level manager leads you to "know" you can fulfill this prophecy even though blaring signals are telling you otherwise.

Pride of Authorship or Ownership: This leads us to unrealistically claim deeds, accomplishments, possessions, and friends, for example, that really are not ours.

Negative emotional influences include:

Fear: Fearful responses distort intuitive input. If someone is late for an appointment, you might automatically assume that she has had an accident. Actually, she has been looking forward to the upcoming meeting and simply is stuck in traffic. Another example is the rejection a person feels when a call isn't returned and the rejected one fears there is a lack of interest on the other party's part. Unfortunately, this fear cloaks the reality that the other person truly has a strong desire to call, but unexpected circumstances are preventing this from happening.

Anxiety, Fatigue, and Depression: These "drains" are other negative deterrents and blur the intuitive signal. As bothersome emotional states, they are detrimental and prevent us from attracting the inner balance and centering so necessary for intuitive receptivity.

Projection is another culprit. When this culprit is operating, you tend to project your needs and wants onto someone else. Reminding your workmate to "watch the budget" might reflect your delicate financial situation, which *you* should be tending to rather than projecting onto him. As another example, have you ever insisted that someone needed a "getaway" when in reality *you* needed the retreat? You have projected your weariness onto someone else.

Identifying Your Emotional Culprits

Can you show how these culprits distort *your* intuitive input? List several examples of how these culprits—positive emotional influences, negative emotional influences and/or projection—have distorted your intuitive process.

_____

_____

_____

_____

_____

How to Interpret Intuitive Signals Correctly

Confirmation or validation is the answer to knowing if you really received intuitive input. This confirmation process has two phases: immediate and eventual. Let's return to the hiring puzzlement of wondering if the new recruit will work out. Of course, eventually, the wisdom of your hiring decision is confirmed if the person remains on the job. But, when the person is hired, you can also make an immediate confirmation. How do you feel? Do you have a gut feeling that you have made the right decision? Do you "know" this is the right person for the job and feel very peaceful about the decision? If so, you are receiving immediate validation.

Here is another example. Suppose you want to approach your superior at work to explore your chances for promotion. You receive immediate physical confirmation from the warm and reassuring inner feeling telling you that the time is right to proceed with your request, so you can go ahead and approach the boss. You can confirm your actions eventually, when your boss approves of your promotion two weeks later. But, by relying on your intuitive barometer, you don't have to wait two weeks to find out about getting the promotion. You already know!

Through practice you will learn to separate the "real flash" from the "false alarm" so you will know immediately if you had the right impression, took the correct action, or made the best choice. Through continued practice you will become sensitized to the signals and cues saying that your intuition is truly operating. As you become more confident knowing how your dominant sense is sending you the intuitive input, you will respect those signals. Then, you will agree with me unequivocally that your intuition is always right.

You may want to review the levels of intuitive experience (Chapter One) to remind yourself of the variety of ways intuition communicates. For example, the physical feeling in the pit of your stomach or sudden "Ah'ha!" of discovery clearly signals a correct intuitive input. Does your body vibrate all over and provide a cue on the physical level to underscore the thought, "I strongly knew that would happen"? The parts of my body affirming the correctness of my intuition are my throat, solar plexus, and chest. It is difficult to explain the subtle physical changes that I feel in those areas, but there is a clear knowing. Intuition operates on all five levels (physical, emotional, mental, spiritual, and environmental) to send cues.

You will become more aware in time of how intuitive cues from these levels provide instant confirmation that the hunch you are acting on is correct.

Steve Bernard, an international business consultant, is aware of a strong physical cue, which is his hair standing up on the back of his neck, to signal difficulty. This physical barometer is so sensitive that he can walk into a room where 20 conversations are taking place and instantly "read" almost everything that is going on. Sally Rypkema, a clinical social worker, talks about her detector, or inner radar, that filters impressions of people to let her know when she needs to be careful. When this inner warning sounds, it tells her, for example, that she needs to protect herself around a particular person or that she shouldn't rush to trust this person.

Weston Agor[6] interviewed top executives and managers about their decision-making practices. Many described the feelings they experience at the critical decision-making point as "a sense of excitement, almost euphoric" or "a bolt of lightning or sudden flash that this is the solution." When an impending decision feels incorrect, the respondents report "a sense of anxiety," "mixed signals," "sleepless nights," or an "upset stomach." All this feedback provides immediate confirmation.

Recording your intuitive impressions in a journal will also help you become more attuned to the signals and cues that are immediately confirming or validating your intuitive accuracy. The way to keep a journal will be discussed in the next unit.

EXERCISE

Recording When Your Intuition Is Correct

Can you isolate any sensation that helps you separate the "real hunch" from the false pretender? Record all the emotional, physical, and other sensations you experience when you are in the middle of a decision-making process.

_____

_____

_____

_____

_____

Stifling Influences

Everyone has access to intuitive information! Unfortunately, many have their intuitive pipeline clogged by extraneous circumstances. Making you aware of some of these influences will, I hope, clear the way for consistent and accurate intuitive input.

Academia or any situation that emphasizes verbal, logical, and analytical skills stifles intuitive thinking. You can counteract any overload by taking courses to develop innovative responses and creative input. In school, at work, and at home, rewards should be given for imaginative responses in addition to verbal agility.

In an active society where people are constantly "on the go," stillness is rarely prized. Physical activity and fitness are extremely important and can comfortably be balanced with periods of stillness to develop the inner intuitive muscle. In my research,[7] I have noted that relatively few respondents take the time to be still. They may at best, grab quiet moments when they are traveling by car or in the air.

Is risk taking discouraged? Do you feel a sky diver or bungee jumper is taking a foolish risk? This is risk-taking behavior and can be compared in some ways to the investor putting reserve money into a new, unproved project. Does your family or peer group encourage you to take risks? Risk-taking activity stimulates listening to hunches. Do you recall Dr. Douglas Dean's description of successful executives, the "prophets who made profits"?

How dependent are you on structure for your daily operations at work? The extent of your need for structure will reveal how free you are to be spontaneous and explore new parameters.

When you are rigidly structured and strongly conditioned by time constraints, it is difficult to act spontaneously and retrieve intuitive responses. When you are trying to develop new and innovative solutions, watching the clock and being tightly regimented can be inhibiting. Racing from one chore to another without sufficient introspective time suppresses the intuitive response. What you need to do when that happens is take "time out." When your intuition becomes clouded from too much "noise" in the environment, it is time to retreat to quieter surroundings so the intuitive voice can be clearly heard.

EXERCISE

Examining Limiting Influences

What influences have stifled your intuition? In what ways are you structured? In what ways are you spontaneous? Try to be as honest and open as possible when examining the influences that limit your intuitive input. Awareness is the first and most important step in eliminating these distorting offenders. You can come back to this page and continue to add to this list as your practice continues and you become more aware of these intuitive deterrents. Write down the limiting factors.

_____

_____

_____

_____

_____

You should now be familiar with the four main IPS components. They are centering, receptivity, eliciting the imagery, and interpretation. In the next chapter, you will see how they are assembled into the intuitive formula and then applied to some sample problems.

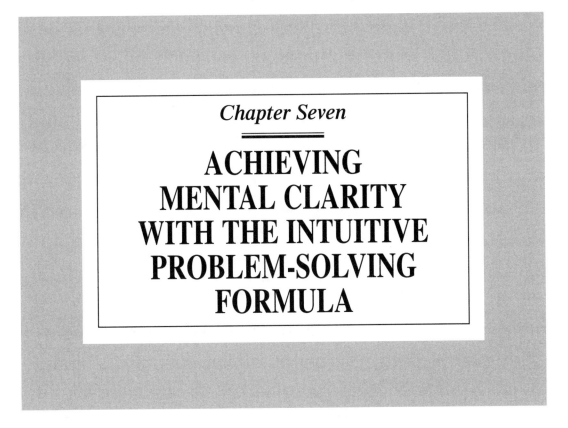

Chapter Seven

ACHIEVING MENTAL CLARITY WITH THE INTUITIVE PROBLEM-SOLVING FORMULA

What lies behind us and before us are small matters compared to what lies within us.

RALPH WALDO EMERSON

PUTTING INTUITIVE PROBLEM-SOLVING TO WORK FOR YOU

Have you ever felt like Bob? He is weary from trying to execute the perfect balancing act between work, family, and social responsibilities. Many people feel tired just thinking about how to address all these needs. At one time, Bob would have agonized over this, but now, armed with the IPS process, he knows how to engage his intuitive mind to help him find the best resolution to his dilemma.

One night when he is on the road traveling, he ponders his "time management" dilemma and sets out to find a solution using the IPS process. He reviews the background, which is that his new job requires a lot of traveling. He wants to know how to bring balance into his life, so he puts his *problem* in a question format and asks, "How can I balance my work life with my family life?"

To become *centered*, he sits in his hotel room and concentrates on the geometric patterns on the curtain. Then, to become *receptive*, he uses the "hang-sah" breath and imagines he is walking through a forest, down a hill to a house, and up a staircase to a room that is similar to the one he entered when he did the IPS exercise on page 98. Just as in that exercise, he sees a box on the table and a special book sitting on the shelf. The *imagery* is vivid. He sees a salamander in the box and the word "poison" written on the inside of the book.

He uses the amplification *interpretation* technique to interpret the imagery of the poison. There are several associations he makes to the word "poison," like toxic, venom, death, and antidote. The word "antidote" feels significant, so he amplifies further and gets the word "tonic." He is a bit confused about the salamander image, so he takes a *resting period* by walking around the hotel courtyard. While he is walking, the solution comes to him like a flash of lightning.

Further interpretation comes as he remembers reading that salamanders are very sensitive to subtle changes in the environment, especially increases of temperature. Like the canary in the coal mine, they are good indicators of the earth's well-being. Bob realizes that he must maintain a proper environment and balance in his life. He realizes that his family and social life act as a *tonic* to balance his work life. The demands of his work will *poison* him if he does not balance them with friends and family. "Ah'ha!" He will *activate the solution* by doing more activities with friends and family. He also wants to look for a tennis partner and to work on improving his golf game.

Each step of the IPS process is written in italic type. Let's review these steps so we can put all that you have learned in this unit together to discover how IPS can take you from mental chaos to clarity.

1. *Problem*: Succinctly put problem in question form.

2. *Centering*: Say an affirmation, use visual or verbal focusing, listen to music.

3. *Receptivity*: Use one of the four breathing and/or six relaxation techniques to become receptive to the intuitive mind.

4. *Imagery*: The flash will flow spontaneously or you may have to elicit the imagery more actively.

5. *Interpretation*: Use one of the four techniques—amplification, word association, clustering, and mind mapping—to decipher the underlying meaning of the imagery. If you actively elicit imagery and intuitively know the "right response," you won't need to use one of the interpretation techniques.

6. *Resting Period*: Take time out from the problem.

7. *Further Interpretation*: Elicit new flashes of insight.

8. *Activating the Solution*: Implement the solution shown.

HOW TO USE THESE VARIATIONS ON THE INTUITIVE PROBLEM-SOLVING THEME TO SOLVE PROBLEMS

These examples will show you the many ways of working with intuitive problem-solving (IPS). Sometimes, the intuitive answer comes after the first image is presented. This is the case with the first two problems, one a personal matter and the other a work concern. The third example shows how the symbol has been further interpreted to arrive at the correct resolution to the problem posed. The fourth and fifth examples show variations on the IPS theme as a number of questions are posed to elicit imagery so clarity about the problem can be achieved.

Example 1: A Family Communication Problem

Background: Brian's oldest daughter has just turned 14. She seems to be at odds with her mother, and they do not communicate well. He is concerned and would like to do what he can to help them through this difficult time in their relationship.

This is how he uses IPS to find a way to help them bridge the communication gap.

1. *Problem*: How do I help my daughter and wife improve their communication?

2. *Centering*: My home is a very busy place, and it is not easy to find any quiet time for myself. I steal away to my room early one evening and relax on my bed. From our second story window I can look out at the sky and trees of the woods behind the house while resting in bed. The house is quiet, as everyone is outdoors.

3. *Receptivity*: I do some "hang-sah" breaths. I feel the tension drain with each breath as I become enchanted by the pattern of the tree branches against the evening sky. When I feel sufficiently relaxed, I ask myself the question of how to improve the communication between my wife and daughter.

4. *Imagery*: The image I elicit is of my wife's new white Reebok shoes. She has just bought them for walking, which she does every evening for exercise. I see them very clearly and distinctly.

5. *Interpretation*: I use the amplification technique to the word Reebok and make the following associations: walk, run, "walk all over you," white, and aerobics. The answer I am looking for is walk, since my wife walks in the evening and likes to have someone go along to talk with her. Usually she asks me or the neighbor, but what if she were to ask our daughter? I decide to wait for the right opportunity to discuss it with her.

6. *Resting Period*: The next day my wife mentions that she has no one to walk with her that evening, so I go along. I mention that she should ask our daughter the next time and that it would do them both good. She agrees and says she will.

7. *Further Interpretation*: Notice that this step was not needed here.

8. *Activating the Solution*: My wife has agreed to ask our daughter, in a nonchalant and off-handed way, to walk with her. The nonthreatening evening walks together may enable mother and daughter to communicate more easily.

Example 2: An Engaging Work Concern

1. *Problem*: Should I hire a new general foreman?

2. *Centering*: I am sitting out on my patio late one evening. By watching the reflection of the moon on the rippling water, I have a natural focusing object. I listen to the crickets making their own music.

3. *Receptivity*: I do some deep breathing and become more relaxed. Then, I imagine myself walking down ten steps.

4. *Imagery*: I "see" a new penny surrounded by other, older coins.

5. *Interpretation*: Using amplification I find the following associations:

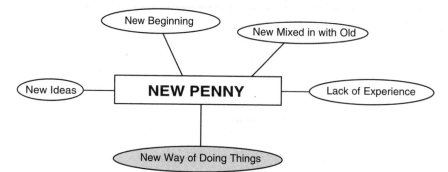

The new penny represents someone new from the outside and a new way of doing things. It is a penny among more worn coins of larger denominations. This new person is coming into an environment of people who have been there longer and have a good deal of experience in their current job.

6. *Resting Period*: I watch TV and temporarily forget about my question.

7. *Further Interpretation*: Before going to sleep, I have a sensation of motion, as of a car moving in the fast lane. I sense that the new general foreman needs to move into the position quickly and learn his job from there.

8. *Activating the Solution*: I interview someone who is a perfect fit for this position. I will recommend that he be hired immediately.

Example 3: A Moving Decision

Background: My wife has been looking at moving into a larger home. I've resisted her suggestions because moving is something I absolutely despise doing and feel would be a waste of time. Yet my wife persists and continues to look at house listings and stop at houses that have "for sale" signs. Lately, I have started noticing all the little things that are wrong with our house and I begin thinking that perhaps it's not such a bad idea to look around.

1. *Problem*: Is this the right time to move?

2. *Centering*: I find a bench close to the river and take in the sights and sounds of the area. I particularly focus on the leaves of a nearby plant.

3. *Receptivity*: The river water flowing over the dam is a very comforting sound. I do some deep breathing and the "autogenic relaxation" technique.

4. *Imagery*: I see someone in the bed—resting, not sleeping. I relax some more and continue to see this peaceful, restful bed.

5. *Interpretation*: Using amplification I make the following associations:

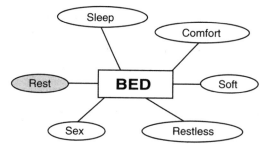

I repeat these words over and over. Sleep is a word you can associate to a bed, but the person I see in the bed isn't sleeping. A bed can be soft, but that and comfort do not feel right. Sleep can be restless and, even though this decision is a major one, I'm not losing sleep over it. Sex doesn't ring a bell yet. Rest—the word strikes an intuitive chord. My interpretation of the word "rest" is that we should not consider moving at this time and that we should rest and wait awhile before making such a decision.

6. *Resting Period*: I let the problem go for a few days.

7. *Further Interpretation*: A dam appears and I continue to amplify. Associations to the dam are water, pretty, fish, power, and hold back. I get the "Ah'ha!" when I repeat the words "hold back." A dam is used to hold back water. This confirms my first impression that we should wait and relax about buying a new house and "hold back" on any plans.

8. *Activating the Solution*: The next step is for me to sit down with my wife, discuss how I feel about buying a new house, and share my opinion that we should hold off for now.

EXPLORE AND DISCOVER THESE INTUITIVE PROBLEM-SOLVING VARIATIONS

As you become involved with IPS, you will note that the "Ah'ha!" resolution does not always come after the imagery is interpreted. Often, it is necessary to go back and forth for several repetitions with the logical mind posing the question and the intuitive mind responding. This follows the advice of Jonas Salk that the intuitive mind tells the thinking mind where to look next. So you ask, get the image, and, after interpreting, another question emerges. Don't be concerned about the logistics of how this specifically fits into the formula. As you will see in Examples 4 and 5, I include this "extended interchange" under the imagery section, then summarize what I receive in the interpretation, and finally go on to "rest" or implement the "Ah'ha!" solution. There will also be times when the clarification you get in the interpretation phase creates the need for another question, so the intuitive and thinking mind can go back and forth in the interpretation section.

I want to share another variation in Example 6, which shows that you can be involved in an IPS activity and "solve a problem" without using one of the four interpretation techniques. In this example, the imagery that was actively retrieved to solve the problem was clear enough to provide the resolution.

Example 4: Asking a Coworker to Participate in a Project

Background: Joan is known as "good old reliable" at work. People often ask her to do things because they know she finds it difficult to say no. The spring fund-raising event for the office is approaching and Joan once again is tapped to coordinate this event. She doesn't want to become overly involved, especially since many weighty personal responsibilities consume her time outside the office. Joan knows that she can probably handle this if she has the help of a coworker and is determined to find someone to assist her. She is faced with the dilemma of how to secure this needed help.

1. *Problem(s)*: Two separate problems are isolated: When shall I approach my coworkers with this request? And how shall this request be presented?

2. *Centering*: Joan closes her eyes and imagines she is at her favorite spot on a beautiful lake. To become more centered, she repeats the phrase, "peace, be still" several times.

3. *Receptivity*: Joan uses the "total" breath and "progressive relaxation" technique to help her become inwardly still. She takes the cassette player out of the desk drawer and listens to her *kitaro* tape.

4. *Imagery*: Joan creates the following imagery to answer the first problem:

    ◆ *On what date should I make the request for assistance?*

    Joan pictures a calendar in front of her that has tear-off pages for each day of the month. Starting with the present day, she sees herself ripping off one page at a time until she feels compelled to stop. Since the date for making the request is now clearly established as two weeks later, she realizes that patience is needed.

    ◆ *What time is best on the chosen day?*

    Joan pictures a clock on the wall across from where she is sitting. The hands on the clock are spinning around rapidly and suddenly come to a stop. The time highlighted is 10:20, but she wonders if this is morning or evening. Creating imagery once again, she notices the bright yellow sun appearing high in the sky, which suggests the time is morning.

    The following imagery is created for her second problem:

    ◆ *And how shall I present my request?*

    With eyes closed, Joan watches herself approaching the coworker to ask for help. She noticed herself limping as though she is lame. Her intuitive mind is showing a very weak presentation of self.

5. *Interpretation*: Joan asks for a symbol to help her understand the implicit dynamics of the situation. She doesn't understand why the image of an egg is presented. The amplification technique helps her clarify the underlying meaning of this symbol. Her associations reveal the following:

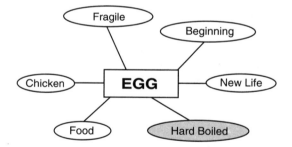

Several associations come with the amplification, but the big "Ah'ha!" comes when she realizes the egg is hard boiled. Joan then knows she has to take a hard line and not appear lame or limp.

6. *Resting Period*: Joan automatically has a resting period since she can't make the request until two weeks have elapsed. During that time she stops feeling sorry for herself. Joan also realizes she has other inner strengths, one of which is finding time to be very still in a natural setting so the right answers can come. Joan becomes more involved in her work without experiencing inner discontent and knows she will find the right way to make the approach in two weeks.

7. *Further Interpretation*: A flash now shows her wearing a bright red dress when making the request, enforcing the image of being firmer and more forceful.

8. *Activating the Solution*: On the planned day, Joan assertively approaches the coworker with her request for assistance.

EXERCISE

Finding the Best Time to Request a Favor

Can you identify with Joan's dilemma? You might want to request a favor. You clearly know that the outcome of this request will depend on your timing and approach. Think about a favor that you would like, and the person that you will be asking. After formulating your problem(s), follow the IPS steps and record your experiences.

1. My problem is _____

   _____

2. I become centered by _____

   _____

3. I practice relaxation by _____

   _____

4. Imagery is created to determine _____

   _____

5. The imagery is interpreted to mean _____

   _____

6. A rest period is used to _____

   _____

7. Further interpretation reveals _____

   _____

8. I activate the solution by _____

   _____

Example 5: Fostering a Harmonious Atmosphere at Work

In this example, notice how Lisa, a middle manager at a bank, continues to probe and elicit imagery until the intuitive flash satisfactorily answers the initial question. Throughout this process, the intuitive and logical minds are interacting, repeatedly raising questions and retrieving imagery until clarity is achieved. Here is Lisa's story.

Background: One of my current staff members is Korean and has been with us for 12 years. Although she has been in this country over 20 years, her English is not good, and it is difficult to understand her. This has caused problems between her and the rest of the staff, as well as with her customers. We recently had an incident at work from which there are still repercussions. I realistically see no improvements in Jena's ability to communicate unless she takes steps to improve her vocabulary.

1. *Problem*: How do I help facilitate a harmonious, cohesive atmosphere between Jena and my staff?

2. *Centering*: I repeat the focusing word "relax" until I start feeling a wonderful sense of relaxation coming over me.

3. *Receptivity*: I sit back in my chair and begin "tensing and releasing" all my muscles. I take some deep breaths followed by several repetitions of the "total" breath.

4. *Imagery*: I pose a few questions to myself, knowing that I may not be able to completely solve this problem by my own actions.

   ◆ *Should I approach Jena directly about her poor language skills to improve the work situation?*

   I imagine a stoplight on a deserted street. The lights remain dark and then the red light becomes illuminated and remains that way. It then begins blinking.

   ◆ *Should I approach the staff as a whole regarding this problem in a staff meeting?*

   I imagine the same stoplight. The yellow light begins flashing and the green light follows until they are both flashing simultaneously. I wonder if this means the light is broken and what significance that might have to my problem. I decide that perhaps our group is broken and take the flashing signs to mean that I should approach the group cautiously.

   ◆ *When should I approach my staff on this issue?*

   I "see" a calendar on the wall that is turned to August. I focus on the wall and try to get an image as to what day will be best. The calendar suddenly rips apart into long shredded pieces. I am confused. I decide to ask the next question.

   ◆ *Should I confront the group in a serious, straightforward manner?*

   I look to my traffic light again. It immediately turns red. I try to think of an alternative approach to the situation.

   ◆ *Should I perform some type of group exercise or relaxed discussion instead?*

   I continue to focus on the traffic light and it turns bright green.

   ◆ *What type of group exercise?*

   I pose this question to myself and imagine a movie screen. A picture appears showing a bunch of eggs with a variety of different faces on them. This is confusing and the picture leaves me perplexed.

5. *Interpretation*: Using amplification, the following associations are revealed:

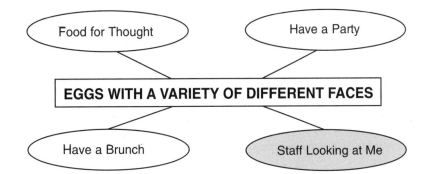

The eggs represent my staff looking at me. I will bring them together soon and, fortunately, we already have a meeting scheduled in two days. The picture of the calendar ripping up stresses the urgency of the situation.

6. *Resting Period*: Not needed in this situation.

7. *Implementation*: I can point out that our staff, like the world at large, is composed of a variety of individuals with differences in personalities and work styles.

By reminding the staff that we each have our own strengths and weaknesses, I am able to encourage everyone to work as a team.

Example 6: Requesting a Special Favor from the Builder

Background: Along with buying a new house, we also purchased the lot behind ours from our builder. This lot is very uneven and a lot of dirt has been dumped at this site. We would like to use this lot, but to do so we have to grade it first. Our builder has a man who grades his lots for him. I would like our builder to ask this man to grade our lot for us free of charge.

1. *Problem*: When should I approach our builder with this request?

2. *Centering*: I sit in the middle of the empty lot listening to the birds and the wind.

3. *Receptivity*: I use the "total" breath and "progressive relaxation" technique to help me become more receptive.

4. *Imagery*: I create imagery to find out the following:

   ◆ *On what day should I make the request?*

   I picture a calendar in front of me with the days flipping by. The pages stop flipping on Saturday, August 7.

   ◆ *What is the best time for this request?*

   I picture a clock with spinning hands. The hands stop at 2:20. I glance out a window and the daylight indicates an afternoon request.

5. *Interpretation*: I need to talk to our builder on August 7 at 2:20 P.M. This is a good time, because every Saturday from noon to 4:00 they hold open houses in our subdivision so I know he'll be in his office. And if he has had a lot of potential customers, then he'll be in a good mood.

6. *Resting Period*: I wait a few days and then use the same techniques to relax myself.

7. *Further Interpretation*: This time I imagine myself posing my request to him. His reactions to the request are favorable.

8. *Activating the Solution*: After doing the IPS, I will be going to the builder on August 7 at 2:20 P.M. to make my request, which I anticipate he will honor.

EXERCISE

Using the IPS Formula

After sampling these six situations, your own issues must be uppermost in your thoughts. This is a good time to practice applying the IPS formula to elicit an intuitive resolution to one of the problems that you identified on page 31. Select any concern, dilemma, or weighty situation revolving around a work, home, or personal issue and record your IPS resolution to each step.

1. My problem is _____

_____

2. I become centered by _____

_____

3. I practice relaxation by _____

_____

4. Imagery is created to determine _____

_____

5. The imagery is interpreted to mean _____

_____

6. A rest period is used to _____

_____

7. Further interpretation reveals _____

_____

8. I activate the solution by _____

_____

USING INTUITIVE PROBLEM-SOLVING
IN A CRISIS SITUATION FOR QUICK RESULTS

This next section is extremely important! How can IPS be implemented when you want to make a rapid and accurate decision in a crisis situation? Engaging in deep breathing and relaxation can take 15 or 20 minutes. However, when the crisis alarm sounds and time is precious, instant receptivity is needed. The following short form is suggested:

1. *Pose the question*: Be succinct.

2. *Centering*: Quiet the talkative logical mind and shift to the intuitive mind by finding a visual focus. You can pause to look at the wallpaper, grains of wood, patterns in the ceiling, floor covering, or even the face of a clock.

3. *Receptivity*: Heave a hearty sigh of relief and take a deep breath. Make a fist and release, point your toes and release, and shrug your shoulders and release. Then, roll your head around on your shoulders to help the body relax. Use your inner imagery and allow yourself to be transported to your favorite retreat.

4. *Imagery*: The intuitive flash may come spontaneously as an impression, picture, metaphor, symbol, familiar word, or phrase. You may hear a voice, have a feeling, or clearly sense the answer. You can actively elicit the imagery by creating symbols to help you answer your question. You can see a stoplight, for example, with the red, yellow, and green lights telling you to stop, pause, or go.

5. *Interpretation*: Quickly and readily let the associations flow from your symbolism by using the amplification method.

EXERCISE

*Using the Short Form
for a Quick Response*

Use this short form the next time you have to make a quick decision at work or in any situation when an immediate response is needed. Write down how you proceed through the IPS steps to receive clarification for your crisis.

1. *Posing the question*: _____

_____

2. *Centering*: _____

_____

3. *Receptivity*: _____

_____

4. *Imagery*: _____

_____

5. *Interpretation*: _____

_____

YOU CAN RETRIEVE IMAGERY IN A VARIETY OF WAYS

You can see that eliciting the imagery is a vital part of the IPS process. Here are three additional methods you can use to actively retrieve intuitive imagery to help with problem solving. I will present each of these techniques in the remainder of this chapter. They are

- Take a guided fantasy journey.
- Do an internal brainstorming.
- Use the metaphor process.

Take a Guided Fantasy Journey to Retrieve Imagery

Although you have had quite a few examples of guided imagery, I want to take you on one more journey to show how this guided fantasy can be used to help you with problem solving. First, think of a problem or question that is in need of resolution. State your problem clearly and concisely in this space.

Problem: _____

_____

Preparation: As I suggested with previous exercises, you can record this on tape or have someone read the script to you. When you are comfortable and know you will not be disturbed for a brief period of time, ease into the receptive alpha level by taking three "reenergizing" breaths, followed by the "tense and release" relaxation.

Directions: Take a trip to the park. As you walk, notice the trees in full foliage and feel the rays of the bright shining sun. On occasion, you will see a squirrel running from tree to tree or notice the birds flying overhead.

In the distance you hear running water. Walking, you come to the edge of the stream and see crystal-clear water. Many things have been bothering you lately and you feel relieved that you can sit down by a tree and reflect on these events. Leaning against the tree and looking at the water helps you reflect on the problem you just wrote down. Going over this problem is particularly easy now because you feel very relaxed.

Your thoughts are interrupted when your eye is drawn to the water. The sun is reflecting off something at the stream's bottom. You get up from where you are sitting and walk to the edge of the water. You find a stick and use it to reach into the water to pull the object toward you. Reaching down, you pick out the object and hold it up in the sunlight. This object is very significant and holds an important clue toward the resolution of your problem. This may signify the next step you are to take.

You have another clue for the solution since there is writing on this object. You read these words to yourself. Suddenly, you realize the connection between what you are reading and the problem you are trying to solve. The solution appears clearly.

You place the object in your pocket and begin walking down the path. Satisfied that your problem has been solved, you can return home. Your gait is now lively and you whistle a happy tune.

Open your eyes, stretch, and look around the room. You feel deeply refreshed and relieved to have solved this problem. Answer the following questions to help you achieve more clarity about the resolution.

EXERCISE

Evaluate Your Imagery

Are your images clear?

_____

_____

_____

What impresses you the most about the setting?

_____

_____

_____

Can you return to the setting and add further imagery to this basic scene?

_____

_____

_____

What object did you retrieve from the water?

_____

_____

_____

Do an amplification to unravel the underlying meaning.

What words are written on the object?

_____

_____

_____

How do these words help with the resolution of your problem?

_____

_____

_____

Use Internal Brainstorming to Examine the Options

Generally, brainstorming engages the productive energies of several people who pool the creative flow of their ideas. However, you are the only person required to attend the *internal brainstorming* session. You will go deep within by altering your consciousness to retrieve wonderful new possibilities that you never would have entertained from your usual beta level. Remember, this is a variation of IPS by suggesting a specific way to elicit the imagery.

Recall that in the alpha level you are tapping the subconscious flow. Internal brainstorming enables you to list many advantages and disadvantages that will help you answer your question or arrive at a solution. This list is very different from the one you would develop while sitting at your desk, where you would simply list the logical pros and cons. The intuitive mind is helping you by discovering many new possibilities.

Here is the internal brainstorming formulation.

1. Clearly and concisely formulate the *problem* in the form of a question.

2. Become focused using any of the *centering* tools.

3. To become more *receptive*, sit in a chair with your eyes closed. If possible, listen to instrumental music; it will help lead you to the alpha level. Before you begin your breathing and relaxation practice, take inventory, paying particular attention to any tense areas in your body. Mentally become aware of any intruding thoughts and banish them from consciousness. Make a gentle plea to relax any distracting emotions raging through your heart. Court the sensation of inner peace and stillness before you begin to silence any nagging feelings of spiritual discontent.

4. Stimulate the flow of *imagery* as you create a chalkboard with your inner mind. Write the word PRO on top and list all the positive ways to solve your particular problem. Run through these ideas again and see if any stand out or become surrounded with a glowing neon light. Command these ideas to stay in your mind while you proceed to the next step. They won't disappear from consciousness even though you erase these ideas and write the word CON at the top of the chalkboard. Once again, list all the factors or adverse conditions that interfere with a positive solution. Do any negative influences stand out? Make a special request for your consciousness to record these ideas so you can attend to them later.

   If you are concerned about forgetting the important pro and con ideas, take the time to record them. Return to the alpha level by taking several deep breaths and commanding yourself to "relax."

5. Ask your intuitive mind to present any *additional imagery* that will help you find a novel solution to your question.

6. Proceed to *interpret this imagery* by using amplification or any of the other interpretive techniques you have been practicing.

7. If necessary, you can return to your *inner mind's chalkboard*. Ask the best idea(s) to stand out in a neon light. You can amplify or make further associations to these ideas.

8. A *resting period* can be used, if needed, to let the resolution incubate.

9. What *confirming signals* have you received that the solution is correct? Recall the discussion of immediate confirming signals in the last chapter and note if you simply feel good about making the correct response? Are bodily sensations providing confirmation? Are you receiving validation from others? From your environment? Do you feel satisfied by clearly knowing that you have the correct answer?

An Example of Internal Brainstorming: Coping with Stress

Background: Tex is a sales engineer working for an international corporation. His territory encompasses approximately one-third of the country. Currently there are two other sales engineers in his department. One of these engineers has accepted a different position within the company, so Tex has been asked to cover both areas until a qualified person can be found to replace him. This has created an increase in the amount of the stress both at work and home. The added hours at work and additional travel have been totally consuming. Tex decides to engage in an internal brainstorming exercise to find out how to cope with the stress caused by this excessive overtime. Here is his process.

1. *Problem*: He asks himself, "How will I survive this grueling schedule until a suitable person is hired and trained?"

2. *Centering*: Tex repeats the focusing phrase "I will relax" several times.

3. *Receptivity*: To heighten his receptivity, Tex sits in a chair and closes his eyes. He plays an instrumental cassette tape to help him reach the alpha level. He takes inventory of himself and then practices his breathing and relaxation exercises. Tex pays particular attention to any tense areas during the relaxation. Mentally, he watches the intruding thoughts come into his mind and willfully banishes them from consciousness. Distracting influences also come when he thinks of his "new love." So he gently sends a message to his heart to settle down. Some parts of his body continue to ache, and he reminds them they will soon be relaxed and at rest.

4. *Imagery*: He creates a chalkboard with the inner intuitive mind. The word PRO is written on top. Tex proceeds to list all the positive ways he can solve his particular problem. He runs through these ideas again to see if any stand out or are surrounded by a glowing neon light. He takes a few minutes to jot down some notes. Then he erases these ideas and writes the word CON at the top of the mental chalkboard. Once again, he lists all the factors or adverse conditions that interfere with a positive resolution. This list shows that the PROs outweigh the CONs, even though his current fatigue overshadows any other input. This list shows:

Pro	*Con*
Enjoy the travel	Long hours
I have worked my way up	Too much traveling
Benefits are good	No personal time
Graduate school is paid for	Feel tired and weighty
Developed good friendships	

5. *Additional Imagery*: When he asks for an image that will lead to a novel solution, he elicits a nail. The associations to the amplification are

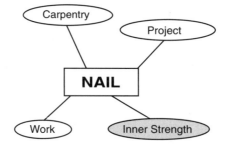

6. *Interpretation*: The association that stands out is "inner strength." Seeing the nail, he feels inwardly and outwardly strong. He just knows he will triumph.

7. *Return to the Chalkboard*: Feeling receptive to any additional imagery, Tex hears his intuitive voice screaming, "hang tough." He wants to generate additional ideas, which he lists on his inner mind blackboard. He asks to have his best idea(s) stand out in a neon light.

Among the following possibilities, one is outstanding.

- ◆ Learn to sleep less.
- ◆ Take a stress reduction course.
- ◆ Hire someone out of my own pocket to help out.
- ◆ Practice yoga breathing for refreshment.
- ◆ *Learn to relax by taking frequent 5-minute getaways.*

8. *Resting period*: Not needed.

9. *Confirmation*: He knows his solution to take frequent breaks is right! He feels that this is the correct action to take. His body also provides feedback with a positive feeling vibrating throughout his chest. Tex knows his temporary stress will pass if he takes small breaks more frequently.

EXERCISE

Your Turn to Practice Internal Brainstorming

Now, imagine that you are Geri and want to use Internal brainstorming to solve a problem. Geri, a manager in the Management Information Systems Division of a local insurance company, is responsible for computer security. She has two security administrators on her staff. Her problem is getting management to understand how the work load has increased and that the use of additional help is needed to automate the administration process. If you were Geri, how would you proceed to solve this dilemma using the following internal brainstorming steps?

Answer these questions:

1. How will you clearly formulate the problem or question?

   _____

   _____

2. How will you become centered?

   _____

   _____

3. What receptivity techniques will you use?

   _____

   _____

4. What imagery do you elicit from creating the inner mind blackboard?

Pro   *Con*

_____   _____

_____   _____

_____   _____

_____   _____

_____   _____

5. What additional imagery is presented?

_____

_____

6. How do you interpret this imagery?

_____

_____

7. Do you need to return to your inner mind blackboard? Ask to have the best idea(s) illuminated. When necessary, amplify.

_____

_____

8. How will you let the problem rest or incubate?

_____

_____

9. What confirmation do you receive immediately or later that your solution is correct? Do you suddenly know the right choice, solution or approach? Learn to hear what part of your body gives you intuitive feedback that you have made the right choice.

_____

_____

10. How is your intuition being integrated with your logic to help you arrive at the final determination?

_____

_____

11. Does your logical mind pose additional questions? If so, repeat steps 4–7 until you can go on.

_____

_____

Use the Metaphor Technique to Stimulate Associations

I am most grateful to Frances Vaughan for presenting the *metaphor technique* in her book, *Awakening Intuition*.[1] My adaptation is offered here for your use as part of the IPS process.

This is a wonderful tool for penetrating through character. Have you ever looked at someone and said, "I wonder what makes him (or her) tick?" Perhaps you have to make a hiring decision, and although the person's credentials are impeccable, you still feel that something is not quite right. Penetrating through an individual's character with the metaphor technique may help you confirm your decision.

Can you identify with this situation? You have been assigned to work on a committee with someone who is basically incompatible with you. On the surface, the person is pleasant and hard working, but your rumbling stomach tells you that something is not right with this working partnership. The metaphor technique can be used to help you understand this intangible feeling of discontent.

Directions: This exercise can be done with your eyes open or closed. What person do you want to focus on? Bring this person into your awareness as you become centered and quiet. Close your eyes and be aware of your breathing; notice any physical sensations that are present for you at this moment. Be aware of any feelings that you may be having; notice the thoughts that are going through your mind. Be aware of how it feels to be you at this moment, and what your energy field feels like. That is, if you were to visualize an energy field surrounding your body, what would it be like? Give yourself a few minutes of silence to be fully aware of your experience.

In this receptive mode, once again allow this person to come into your awareness. Can you get a clear picture of this person in your inner mind? Do not try to make anything happen. Simply notice what images come to mind. If nothing comes to mind, that is all right. Do not try to interpret or judge your images as they appear. Simply notice them and let them be.

If this person were an animal, what type of animal would he or she be?

Simply be quiet and receptive to any images that may emerge spontaneously as you continue to focus your attention on this person. Entertain any feelings you have about the images, but do not interpret them.

Bring your awareness back to the room. If the symbol is not clear, use the amplification and word association techniques to understand the underlying meaning of the images presented.

For example, when John sees Jill as a lion, he is surprised and can't relate to this symbol. He starts amplifying by retrieving the following associations: long hair, beast, brooks no interference, queenly, raging. Suddenly he realizes the lion is "born free." John interprets this to mean that Jill has a strong need for freedom, which accounts for her feeling cramped when working in a group of people. As the queen of the jungle she wants to be center stage and not have anyone else in the spotlight. The amplification of the lion shows

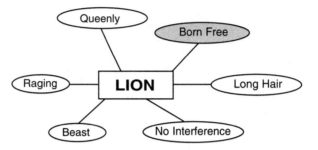

Do you know someone who reminds you of a lion? Do an amplification to determine how this symbol represents that person.

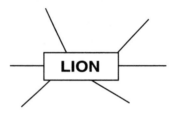

EXERCISE

Practicing the Metaphor Technique

Practice this technique by selecting someone you know well and someone you don't know as well. Use the amplification technique afterward to clarify why a particular symbol or association is presented. Record your experiences below. I used the animal as a metaphor, but you can use any of the following metaphors as well. Try creating some of your own categories. The metaphors are

- ◆ book title
- ◆ piece of furniture
- ◆ character from a book
- ◆ song title
- ◆ flower
- ◆ color
- ◆ book title
- ◆ automobile

- ◆ well known person
- ◆ musical instrument
- ◆ weather description (cloudy, sunshine, etc.)
- ◆ other _____

_____

_____

_____

_____

_____

In the next part, you will dip into the intuitive tool chest so you can start your practice program and actually apply IPS to your "problems."

Part Three

USING YOUR INTUITIVE TOOL BOX FOR SUCCESS

Change is intensely affecting all our lives. People in settings as varied as the boardroom, marketplace, political arena, counseling office, social club, or family dinner table are increasingly aware that wide-sweeping changes are taking place in their lives. The added intuitive edge can help you cope with the rapidly advancing technological and structural changes that are strongly impacting every facet of their lives.

Changes abound everywhere, and your head starts swimming as you wonder how to keep up with the fast pace. When you want to build something, you dig into your tool box and go to work. Analogously, that is just what you do to build and strengthen your intuition so you can activate your visions and dreams for success. But, what are your tools? How will you do that? If you have come this far, you know that the key for survival in the twenty-first century is expanding your inner awareness so you can access the intuitive mind. Intuition is the new tool that will put you on the cutting edge of innovation, regardless of your profession.

Completing the exercises in this book has helped you develop your intuitive muscle. Now, accept the challenge of strengthening this muscle. That means "working out" through practice with the various "intuitive tools" provided throughout this unit.

Practice makes perfect! Through practice you receive immediate feedback as the accuracy of your efforts is revealed. To appreciate all the facets and benefits of practice, familiarize yourself with the *intuitive practice acronym* that follows. Pay attention to this acronym to underscore the importance of intuitive practice:

INTUITIVE PRACTICE ACRONYM

P	peace	create inner stillness
R	relaxation	gain inner receptivity
A	affirmation	reinforce your desires
C	creativity	innovate or make new
T	timetable	use discipline for positive results
I	imagery	communicate from the inner mind
C	commitment	develop and use your intuition
E	exercise	get physical exercise for proper functioning
M	meditation	become still and know
A	authenticity	to thine own self be true
K	keep a journal	keep a record to reinforce consistent practice
E	enjoy dreaming	use the intuitive messages from your dreams
S	stress reduction	release and reduce stress
P	play games	make learning fun and lighten up for sharper receptivity
E	emotional release	liberate your feelings
R	risk	confidently act on hunches
F	faith	know you have intuitive ability
E	enjoyment	know that practice time is pleasurable
C	comradeship	have friends share the joy of discovery
T	trust	know your intuitive abilities are reliable

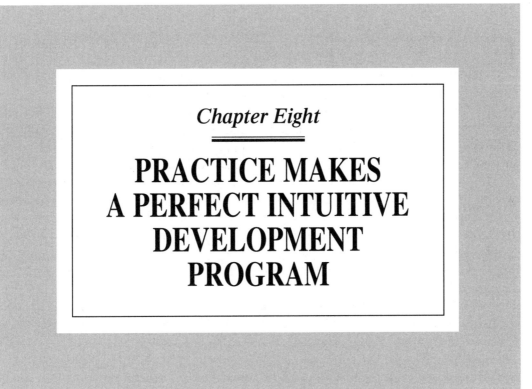

Chapter Eight

PRACTICE MAKES A PERFECT INTUITIVE DEVELOPMENT PROGRAM

Keeping a journal will enable you to discover which constellation of factors correspond with successful intuitions and which are associated with faulty ones. By keeping the journal diligently, you should become more aware of the signals when your intuitive voice is leading you in the right direction.

PHILIP GOLDBERG
The Intuitive Edge

ELEMENTS OF A SUCCESSFUL INTUITIVE DEVELOPMENT PROGRAM

Do you recall any teacher saying, "You will do it again and again until you get it right!" Practice does make perfect. There is very little to say. You simply must do it!

As part of his research into the use of intuition in decision making, Dr. Weston Agor surveyed the top 10% of the high intuitive scorers from his earlier studies and summarized the results in his book, *The Logic Of Intuitive Decision Making*.[1] The people he interviewed included the president of General Motors, a former governor of Michigan, board members of Chrysler Corporation, Burroughs Corporation, and Ford Foundation, and various high-level public officials. Through his interviews, he discovered that these industrial and governmental giants used *regular practice routines* to consistently develop their intuitive abilities. Their agendas included activities such as guided imagery, journal keeping, and meditation. In this chapter I will underscore what practices you should adopt to strengthen your intuitive functioning.

The prerequisites for establishing your successful program are:

- ◆ The belief that you can strengthen your intuition.
- ◆ Commitment to daily practice.
- ◆ Maintaining a quiet and private practice setting.

Start with a Time Log

All practice begins by entering a record of your activities in a time log. As with anything you are trying to learn or become proficient at, it is important that you be consistent in your practice or exercises. It is vital to establish a routine to build your intuitive skills and develop your intuitive muscle.

This sample time log shows the activities you must practice each day so you can be receptive to the messages sent by the intuitive mind. Notice the variety of activities. They are not necessarily attended to in one practice session but are interspersed throughout the day. I may take my quiet time in the morning, get physical activity at noon, and incorporate my IPS practice after work at 5 P.M. Practicing all these activities will help restore balance so you can become more attuned to the messages sent by your intuitive mind anywhere and at any time.

Here is a sample of my time log.

TIME LOG

ACTIVITY	JUNE 4	JUNE 5	JUNE 6	JUNE 7
IPS Skills				
Centering	Focusing	Affirmation	No	Affirmations
Breathing	Yes	Yes	No	Yes
Relaxation	Yes	No	No	Yes
Imagery	Yes	No	No	Yes
Physical Activity	50 min	40 min	No	5 min
Play Time	No	Yes	Yes	No
Journaling	Yes	Yes	No	Yes
Dream Recording	Yes	Yes	No	Yes
Meditation-Quiet	20 min	10 min	No	12 min

Remember, this log is for you! No one is testing, checking up on you, or giving you a report card for good practice. This record reinforces the seriousness of your intention to strengthen your intuitive ability through consistent practice.

Some of the areas that you will be noting in your time log, such as the IPS components, have been extensively reviewed in Chapters Three through Five. I will touch on them briefly and emphasize how you can strengthen these skills during practice. I will also write sparingly about activities you may already do, like physical exercise and play time. You will find out how to keep a journal and then learn about meditation, or quiet time, and dreams in the next two chapters.

A Practice Site

Activities, such as practicing the IPS components, keeping a journal, meditating, and recording your dreams will require a special setting. Select a practice site where you can be quiet and private for at least 15 to 20 minutes a day. When appropriate, consider shifting to a natural setting such as a park, lake, beach, or wooded site.

My ideal setting is

_____

Other settings I prefer are

_____

_____

_____

_____

Be alert to the many opportunities for spontaneous practice. For example, before going in for your staff meeting, play a game by estimating how many people will be there. When will the meeting end? This is using any opportunity to practice activating your intuitive muscle.

Informal practice sites come about unexpectedly. For example, have you ever felt irritated standing on line at the bank, post office, or grocery store? Use that time to meditate and/or play any game you want to test and strengthen your intuition. You can certainly "intuit" how long you will be standing on line.

Another way to evaluate your progress is to test and retest. Periodically take the "Intuitive Quotient Checklist" on pages 15–16 or discover other ways to evaluate your progress. In a few pages I will be encouraging you to play "intuitive games" that will give you feedback about how your intuitive muscle is working.

EXERCISE

Informal Practice

Where and how have you been practicing informally?

_____

_____

_____

_____

_____

Group practice with coworkers or friends is mutually reinforcing and can supplement rather than replace your daily practice. Joining others for practice activities increases your commitment and provides additional stimulation. Group input when interpreting imagery can be particularly useful. Ideally, a group of five or six people could meet once or twice a week to discuss and interpret their imagery.

All the elements that you need for your personal intuitive development training program are recorded in the time log. Let's go to each entry to find out how to implement this element or activity in a practice session. The description will help you understand its value in developing and strengthening your intuition. Each activity is an important reminder of what you need to develop the power of your intuition.

IMPLEMENTING YOUR INTUITIVE DEVELOPMENT PROGRAM

Practice Your IPS Skills for Mastery

Here we will incorporate everything you have learned about the IPS formula. The secret is to discover what centering or receptivity techniques work best for you and use them. Whenever you feel tense, for example, you have a breathing or relaxation tool that can unlock that tension and free up your intuitive mind. I will briefly review the IPS skills you can practice. They are centering, receptivity, and imagery.

CENTERING. To recall how using an affirmation will help you consistently access your intuition, review pages 40–42. For example, repeatedly stating that your "intuitive signals grow clearer every day" transmits this message to the intelligence embedded in every cell of your body. Discover what affirmations work to motivate you to practice and consistently receive clear messages from the intuitive mind.

Focusing techniques can be the lifeline thrown to you when you feel confused or stressed. Refocusing your perception helps drain away the stress and restore equilibrium. Review pages 42–43 to discover what focusing words or phrases work for you when you need to relax. Sometimes a focusing object will alter your perception so you can go from chaos to clarity. Recall these objects on pages 44–45 to remind you of the joy of discovery. I still love finding new objects, and keep a record of the plants and flowers that help me ease into the alpha level. I still continue to notice paintings and points of focus like the woodwork in my office, that are also effective. This is the joy of discovery and every new object or phrase can be noted in your time log and then described more extensively, if you wish to, in your journal.

Please review pages 46–48 to remind you that music as an important tool for centering, can usher you to that still place within. As you practice your IPS skills, discover what kind of soothing instrumental music can lull you into the receptive alpha level. Have your favorite audiocassettes handy for quiet periods, or any other time you want to take a mental break. Consider keeping a cassette recorder in your office.

The academic dean of a well-known college shared with me that his favorite cassette tape for taking a retreat is *Deep Breakfast* by Ray Lynch. You can find this tape in any record store. Whenever he has to resolve a challenging problem, he closes the door and plays this tape on his cassette. After hearing the first few bars, he is transported to a fantasy retreat so he can consider the variety of options needed to solve any dilemma.

RECEPTIVITY. Use these exercises to guide you into the alpha level so you can hear the intuitive mind speak. As you become familiar with all of the breathing and relaxation techniques, you will identify which are most suitable for your use. When practicing, notice how you block out any outer or inner noise that disrupts intuitive communication.

Review the following breathing techniques on pages 54–58: "total" breath, "reenergizing" breath, "ha!" breath, and the "hang-sah" breath. Again, which feels most comfortable? Validate my statement, for example, that doing the "total" breath in the morning will have a positive impact on your day. Or experiment with using the "ha!" breath to relieve stress.

Relaxation can be used to lull you into the alpha level as well as to eliminate excess anxiety and tension. Review these relaxation techniques on pages 59–65. They are the "autogenic" technique, the "extended autogenic relaxer" technique, the "stretching and breathing" technique, the "tense and release" technique, the "progressive relaxation" technique, and the "countdown" technique.

Stress reduction methods help you respond to your stress alarm by reducing anxiety. These receptivity techniques will help you function more effectively. You can also incorporate the physical postures found in yoga exercises. Some of these exercises can be used in place of your morning coffee break for a quick "pick-me-up."

IMAGERY. By now you are aware that the language of intuition is not words but the pictures, symbols, and images sent by the intuitive mind. Do your senses respond faintly to the imagery? Give yourself a workout again and revisit the exercises in Chapter Five from pages 67–100

With consistent practice you will be able to elicit strong and clear imagery. Then, you will become more aware of the richness of your intuitive communication as you "smell" a fragrant blossom that represents your upcoming sweet smelling success. Or clearly "see" the red or green flash of a stoplight to tell you whether the upcoming promotion is a stop or a go.

Give your senses a workout until you become aware of how your dominant sense helps you access the intuitive mind. *See* a beautiful sunset or be *touched* by a meaningful movie. You can *taste* good food or *feel* the gentleness of the wind and the warmth of the sun. You can *smell* the fragrances of flowers and high mountain pines. You can *hear* the bird's song and the sound of beautiful music.

Harmonize Your Mental, Emotional, and Spiritual Needs with Exercise

Physical exercise can also be introduced into daily practice and recorded in your time log. A healthy, stress-free body is also necessary to enhance intuitive receptivity. Ideally, daily participation in some form of physical exercise will help your body harmonize your mental, emotional, and spiritual needs. Immersion in physical activity ignited the intuitive spark for many of the top leaders of business and industry that I interviewed.

Bill Gonzalez, CEO of Butterworth Hospital, enjoys running and started this practice when he realized how sedentary his life had become. After a few years, he noticed that his special thoughts were saved up for his run, which is often his only uninterrupted quiet time. He frequently extends his run if he isn't finished thinking. Gonzalez's formula for creative success during these excursions is to run alone in a secluded area where he doesn't have to worry about cars and can just let the ideas drift in his head.

It may sound paradoxical that engaging in physical activity spurs the intuitive mind, but during this time all the verbal activity from the "logical" mind becomes faint. Two other "running" tales show how physical activity energizes the intuitive mind. Barry Bechtel, vice president of human resources at the Rapistan DeMag Corporation, starts running at five in the morning and is always amazed by the ideas that come into his mind during these jaunts. A nagging problem at work will come into his awareness when Bechtel is running along the dark street. Though he doesn't start his run by consciously thinking of a problem, he is no longer amazed when a unique solution pops into his mind during his run.

James Schiltz is the plant manager of Lomac. When he runs, he also prays, thinks, or meditates on his problems. One time, he went out for a 15-minute run to ponder a problem he was having linking two financial schedules together. During the run, the idea for creating the correct balance sheet "came from out of nowhere." By now you must realize that this seemingly "nowhere region" is full of subconscious activity; the intuitive mind is processing a variety of possible solutions. During the involvement in physical activity, the correct resolution manifests itself in the person's mind as the "great Ah'ha!" Receiving these insightful flashes is one of the many rewards of engaging in physical activity.

Take Time Out to Play and Rejuvenate

Another heading for play time could be "keep it light and lively." Four activities fall under this heading.

First, you can spend time in an enjoyable activity to retreat from the stressful world of words. Fun activity is like an incubation period as you take "time out" from analytical matters. During this time, weighty concerns of the logical mind are released so the intuitive mind can spring into action.

Second, as part of your play time activity, you can invent all kinds of games to strengthen your intuitive muscle. For example, ask your coworkers to guess who will arrive first at the weekly staff meeting, or who will say the first words. Then, your intuitive mind can respond by sending you a suitable picture, symbol, or image. Use games for consistent practice to help sharpen your intuitive receptivity.

Here are some other games you can play to strengthen your intuitive muscle. If you have a new client coming or you are meeting someone new, visualize what this person looks like before the actual meeting takes place. Imagine his physical features as well as the clothing he will be wearing. Notice if he is carrying anything. The variety of games is endless! You can guess or intuit what your mate will be preparing for dinner, the final score of a game before it is even played, when it will stop or start raining, or even how many people will come to a meeting.

The games we invent can streamline office procedures. Make it a game to discover what needs to be eliminated or added to help you work more productively. You can use a "game" to heal interpersonal problems. If you are having a misunderstanding with someone, step into their shoes to "intuitively know" how to approach them. Take some of the ache out of the situation by making this a "game" and imagine "you are them." How would you view this situation "inside out"?

The last "game" I want to suggest is related to planning priorities. Use your calendar, appointment book, or day planner to add another dimension to your planning. Review your daily events or tasks and intuit which ones will be the "hot topics" of the day. Which will you get the phone calls on and who will do the calling? Which ones will you spend the most time on?

You can devise many games. You can devise a game for work. For example, Laurie's job is to forecast discounting levels for the sales division. She matches her intuitive forecast with the forecast published by the financial division. Her game is to see whether her intuition or the financial model is closer to the actual figure. Devise a game in a "social setting." For example, you could go to a concert or theater and guess what your seat number will be without looking at the ticket. You can devise a "personal game." For example, as you are sending out invitations to a party, guess how many people will actually come. Just remember, it is not irreverent or silly to play these games. This is a fun way of practicing.

Third, you can treasure introspective time in a natural setting. Gaze at the starry sky, look at cloud formations, watch the ocean waves, or even listen to the whisper of the breeze. These introspective times are necessary to balance and realign your energies so the intuitive mind can emerge.

Last, daydreams and fleeting reveries contain priceless nuggets of intuitive wisdom. Engaging in daydreaming is not sheer folly. Paying more attention to the pictures, symbols, and images sent by the intuitive mind has its own reward as you access the wisdom emanating from the intuitive mind.

Here is my last admonishment about play time. Remember, all work and no play will make you a dull boy or girl. That is why light and lively activities are needed to balance your work and heavy personal concerns. The ultimate benefit is openness for intuitive receptivity.

Activate Your Intuitive Mind with an "Idea Book"

A journal or idea book is invaluable for recording your hunches and intuitive flashes. Consistent journaling brings many benefits and rewards. Recording your own experiences will sensitize you to the many times and ways your intuitive mind speaks to you. You will also discover that many people use and share the joy of intuitive discovery as you become more aware of intuitive examples and other references in the media.

This record can also help you confirm the accuracy of your "hunches." Watch them improve as you practice your intuitive skills. Set into motion the positive cycle of using your intuition, confirming the accuracy of these hunches, and then using intuition again.

Have you ever said, "I knew that was going to happen but didn't listen to my inner voice?" I'm sure you have made statements like this many times. By recording "gut feelings" in your journal, you will become attuned to even the faint whispers of your intuitive mind. In Chapter Six, you read about using a journal to record the signals and cues that validate your intuitive impressions. I suggest you do this and also make entries in your journal as you make discoveries about your dominant sense. Also, you can become more aware of how the various levels of intuition discussed in Chapter One are sending information to you.

A reporter once asked me to estimate my "intuitive batting average." It was easy to do since I had kept a journal of all my hunches, gut feelings, and so on. Another benefit from keeping this record is discovering that the intuitive mind constantly presents information. This steady stream of input is often drowned out in our busy sea of daily activities. Being attuned constantly to intuitive input will help you arrive at any decision, solution, or creative innovation quite effortlessly.

Keeping a journal is a relatively easy procedure. You can use any notebook to record your hunches or gut feelings. This journal should be private and used primarily to validate your intuitive impressions. Divide the journal so you can keep a sequential record of daily events in the first part. Make sure you leave room under each entry to note when and how the "hunch" is validated. As you collect your intuitive flashes, note how they come: on the job, relating to others, with family, scoping current events, and so on. You might want to include the results of games and premonitions and collect examples of intuition in the media that appear as cartoons, quotes, and stories about other people. Keep the following sections in your journal. I will explain what is included in each section by giving examples.

- ◆ Time log—This can be a part of your journal or kept separately.
- ◆ Your intuitive entries.
- ◆ Intuitive stories from others.
- ◆ Collectibles such as cartoons and quotes.
- ◆ Media stories about how others use intuition.
- ◆ Validate your hunches.

TIME LOG. Refresh your memory about the time log sections by referring back to page 146.

YOUR INTUITIVE ENTRIES. This section is most important. It includes the flashes and intuitive experiences you have had. Some of your entries might be rather trivial, while others are quite weighty and evidential. All share the common function of showing you that your intuitive signals are definitely working. The other sections reflect your growing awareness of intuition and the way this skill is included in your daily activities.

Jerry is a salesman. Here is a sample of the intuitive entries from Jerry's journal:

Thursday, June 9. On the way to work I was speeding and suddenly had a very mild feeling there was a police car somewhere. I slowed down without thinking about it and a squad car appeared immediately.

Friday, June 10. On my way home from work, I was in the outside lane and decided to pass a slower car in the inside lane. Something stopped me from changing lanes and immediately out of nowhere a car shot past me in the suicide lane.

Saturday, June 11. My father had surgery this morning. I felt relaxed and had no bad feelings about it. It turned out fine.

Monday, June 13. I met with someone about a business opportunity. My "gut feeling" says it's a ripoff and I don't trust him. I'll know in three weeks whether my gut feeling is correct.

Wednesday, June 15. I had planned to catch up with my paperwork at the office so I wanted to dress informally. But suddenly I had a flash about putting on a good suit. Soon after I got to work, our president came into my office and asked me to take his place at an important outside meeting. The other attendees were senior executives, so I was glad I trusted my intuition.

PEOPLE'S INTUITIONS. To help you become more aware of the broad workings of your intuitive mind, listen to other people and collect their intuitive tales. Remember that the intuitive examples that you collect can run the gamut from the profane to the mundane. At times the intuitive light bulb shines brightly to inspire revolutionary and useful new ideas. Recall, for example, how intuitive information led to ingenious inventions like the Xerox copier and Post-it™ Note. But not all intuition is that bright; sometimes the intuitive light pales and provides seemingly insignificant information. Honor these thoughts, too; they demonstrate that your intuitive antenna is alive and working.

Remember, it doesn't matter whether these intuitive tidbits are profound or trivial. What does matter is that you start becoming aware of the variety of intuitive experiences happening to you. The following exercise will help you retrieve and then record your intuitive proddings.

Intuition-in-Action

How many examples of "intuition-in-action" can you list?

_____

_____

_____

_____

_____

_____

_____

CARTOONS AND QUOTES. This is a fun section in your journal and can become filled sooner than you think. Here are, for example, some of the quotes I have collected over the years.

Intuition often turns dreams into demonstrable facts.

BUCKMINSTER FULLER

We create (sell) dreams.

WALT DISNEY

Hold fast to dreams, for if dreams die, life is a broken winged bird that cannot fly.

ANONYMOUS

The really valuable thing is intuition

ALBERT EINSTEIN

Never tell people how to do things. Tell them what to do and they will surprise you with their ingenuity.

GENERAL PATTON

Intelligence highly awakened is intuition which is the only true guide in life.

KRISHNAMURTI

EXERCISE

Start Your Quote Collection

Start recording your collectible quotes on this page.

_____

_____

_____

_____

_____

MEDIA STORIES. You can look through the sports section to find countless examples of athletes "knowing" just what to do during a game. During the 1993 National Basketball Association championship games, John Paxson of the Chicago Bulls was asked about his winning shot in the last game of the playoffs. He said his gut instinct told him that shot was going in, and when Michael Jordan was asked about it he said he "just knew" it was going in as well. In 1990, Vinnie Johnson came through with the winning shot for the Detroit Pistons to win the NBA title over the Portland Trail Blazers. Vinnie was having a very poor showing in that game. His playing time had been just 9 minutes, he had missed all three of his shots, and his leg was a little sore from a first-half collision. Teammate Bill Laimbeer pumped him up at half time by saying that the team was going to need him in the second half and that he was going to hit the winning shot. Laimbeer "just knew" that Vinnie was the man for that shot, which happened with less than 1 second remaining in the game.

Martina Navratilova, well known women's tennis champ, has honored her Dad's intuitive muscle for years. She recalled the year he predicted that she would lose the French Open and win Wimbledon—he was right. He's been accurately predicting the double faults in most of her matches, as well.

VALIDATE YOUR HUNCHES IN THE JOURNAL. A word or two about validation. The examples you have just read about come from many people who knew what the intuitive voice sounded like. For others, acknowledging this voice and honoring its suggestions are the next step of the journey and the reason to keep this journal. As part of your journal entries, note when you feel comfortable listening to your own inner voice and are rewarded by the correctness of your actions. Sometimes, when the intuitive voice tries to tell you that something is wrong, it comes as a nagging feeling. For example, Larry Adams, CEO of Harrow Industries, manufacturers of home building products, described how that nagging feeling harassed him as he was in the process of making some important management changes. Though he had articulated the changes to others in the company, he could not get comfortable with them. He continued to feel uncomfortable, and by acknowledging that nagging feeling that would not go away, he knew something was wrong and had to be changed. When he modified the decision, that bothersome feeling left and he felt confident the changes he was making were correct.

Another example of the nagging anxious inner tug happened when Jim Stark, one of my former students, came to share his intuitive discoveries with the class. The group giving the oral presentation ran overtime, which delayed Jim's presentation. When his time came, he insisted that he had to leave immediately so he could participate in a wedding. Although I was surprised that he had to leave an hour early, I certainly had to honor his agitated feeling and need to return home immediately. Days later, Jim described his sudden departure by explaining, "It was my understanding that the wedding I was to be a part of on Saturday afternoon was to begin at 3:00 P.M. In reality, it was to begin at 2:00 P.M. and the person who had given me the wrong time was sending out all kinds of 'mental messages.' The extreme discomfort was intuitively telling me that I had to leave when I did, and I was certainly glad I listened to my inner voice."

Do you get the picture? Can you "see" what I am saying? "Hear" it! Get the "feel" of the words. All these activities in your journal are intended to stimulate your intuitive processes. The following exercise will lead you into making a commitment for keeping a journal.

EXERCISE

Journal Keeping

Make a commitment to keep a journal by noting the following:

I will secure a notebook for my journal by this date:

_____

_____

I will start recording my hunches, and so on, on:

_____

_____

_____

_____

The sections in my journal will feature:

_____

_____

_____

_____

_____

Some recent occurrences that I would like to record in my journal are

_____

_____

_____

Journaling with the Subdominant Hand

Before closing this section on keeping a journal I want to introduce you to a unique journaling method that is being used by many to enhance their intuitive awareness.

This is a relatively new breakthrough emphasizing the power of your "other hand" to access the right side of the brain. If you are "right handed," your "other" hand is your left hand. Lucia Capacchione in her groundbreaking book, *The Power of Your Other Hand*,[2] gives extensive exercises designed to tap the inner wisdom of the right brain.

Basically, the dominant hand writes the question to which the "other hand" responds. For example, suppose you want to have a confrontation with a superior. This authority figure would be represented by the dominant hand. Your true feelings about what you really want to reveal will come through the "other" or "subdominant" hand. It is by writing with this "other hand" that new insights and feelings about the other person will emerge.

You can also dialogue with objects, such as products you want to sell. For example:

DH (dominant hand): How do you want to be presented?

OH (other hand): Turn me on my side and rotate several versions of me so I will be shown from all sides.

DH: Is there a special way to sell you?

OH: Put a recording next to me and imagine I am talking.

DH: Do you need a campaign for a special time of year?

OH: I am always special and can be recognized each day.

This may seem awkward, playful, and even nonsensical to you. But this is what experimentation is about. You are discovering the "right way to go" from within.

EXERCISE

Other Hand Experimentation

What issue or person would you like more insight about? Let your dominant hand speak by representing the person or issue. As you use your subdominant hand to respond, you will be eliciting wisdom about the situation.

_____

_____

_____

_____

To complete the time log, you need to record your dreams and meditation experiences. The remaining elements in this unit are dreamwork and meditation, which will be discussed in the next two chapters. Here is a brief description of what you can expect.

Honor the Wisdom in Your Dreams

Dreams are to be honored and taken seriously since this is one way the intuitive inner mind communicates with the outer aware self. The way to record your dreams and unravel the underlying meaning implicit in the dream symbolism will be presented in Chapter 9.

Meditate to Become Centered and Revitalized

Meditation, quiet time, or periods of stillness are vital to help you become more centered and revitalized before you face any responsibilities at work or in other settings. How to take a few moments of quiet time to revitalize yourself, clear your mind, and allow yourself to focus on your business or personal affairs more easily will be discussed more extensively in Chapter 10.

EXERCISE

Discovering Other Elements for Your Practice Program

Is your practice program complete? If yes, just do it. If not, what would you like to include in your practice program that is not listed here? Write it down.

_____

_____

_____

_____

_____

Which factors are easy to implement?

_____

_____

_____

_____

_____

Which are difficult to incorporate into your day or work routine? Why?

_____

_____

_____

_____

In the next chapter you will learn how to activate your intuition through dreamwork.

Chapter Nine

DECIPHERING THE WISDOM OF YOUR DREAMS

The dream is an invaluable commentator and illuminator of life. Listen to the wisdom of the dream.

CARL JUNG

THE RELATIONSHIP BETWEEN INTUITION AND DREAMS

The intuitive mind "invents" while you dream. Thomas Edison used to keep a pencil and paper on his bedstand and would write down ideas that came to him while he was sleeping. Mendeleev saw the periodic table of elements roll out for him in a dream. Physicist Niels Bohr visualized atomic structure when dreaming about the sun and planets. Nobel Prize winner Otto Loewi discovered proof of the chemical mediation of nerve impulses in a dream.

You can now go into your intuitive kit and extract dreamwork as another tool for activating your intuition. The information in this chapter will show you how to honor the wisdom of the dream! There are three goals in this chapter: First, to discover how to recall your dreams. Second, to learn how to interpret your dreams intuitively. Third, to learn more about dreams "that come true," which are called the precognitive dreams.

For many people, the intuitive gateway is opened through their dreams. That is why it is inconceivable to talk about intuition and not mention dreamwork. A dream can be compared to an inner intuitive advisor that comes during the quiet of the night, while you are taking a nap, or even while you daydream. When faced with a problem, have you ever said, "I have to sleep on it!" For example, if you have to choose between two compelling candidates for a managerial position, the dream advisor might show you shaking the hand of the "right candidate."

Many people struggle to understand the meaning of a dream. Your intuition can be used to clarify the meaning of your dreams. When your intuitive mind merges with the dreaming mind, it is easier to capture the elusive "Ah'ha!" about any puzzling facet of the dream. One night, for example, I dreamed I was watching someone being held up at gunpoint. Though I awoke surprised, my intuitive mind quickly signaled that an anticipated contract was being "held up."

Intuitive resolutions can come through dreams. Over the years, I have noticed how people significantly strengthen their intuitive abilities after they become involved in dreamwork.

Your intuition can use a dream to provide a preview of upcoming events. After hearing from an old friend in the dream, I received a letter from "an old friend" I hadn't heard from in some time. Intuitive dreams that go forward in time to prepare you for upcoming events are called precognitive dreams. A dream showing you in a car with failing brakes may be warning you to get the car fixed.

My favorite example of a well-known discovery resulting from a dream is the story of Elias Howe and the sewing machine. Howe was working hard for weeks on his new invention, trying to resolve one last detail. He couldn't figure out how to thread the needle and still have the top attached to the machine. After working long and hard one night, he fell into an exhausted sleep. In his dream, a cannibal captured him and told him he had to perfect the sewing machine within 24 hours or be eaten. As the cannibals marched around, he noticed that the spear held by the cannibal chief had a hole in the point. Suddenly awake, he had the long-sought-after solution. He knew that putting the hole in the sewing machine needle at the bottom near the point, instead of at the top, was the right answer.

Some Fascinating Facts and Figures About Dreams

You might be interested in these facts and figures about dreams before we go on to explore the role of intuition and dreams. Sigmund Freud said that "dreams are the royal road to the unconscious" (for which we are using the word subconscious). Your dreaming mind, or subconscious, registers all the sights and sounds you encounter during your waking hours. Some of these impressions you may be aware of while most are recorded in the subconscious without your awareness. The intuitive mind has access to all this information stored in your subconscious and communicates with your conscious mind by sending a message through the dream.

- Dreams are useful in learning more about the dreamer's feelings, thoughts, behaviors, motives, and values.

- Most remembered dreams occur during a phase of sleep called rapid eye movement (REM) sleep, which occurs about every 90 minutes, lasting 10 minutes just after the onset of sleep and lasting about 45 minutes in the last period just before awakening.

- Most dreams are in color, although people may not be aware of it.

- Nightmares can be caused by stress, traumatic experiences, emotional difficulties, drugs or medication, or illness.

- We dream approximately 20% of the time we spend in sleep.

- We dream for a variety of reasons.

- A guidance dream may give you an insight into a puzzling relationship.

- Problem-solving dreams can often show you perfectly clear solutions to seemingly unsolvable problems you struggle with when you are awake.

- With self-help and self-knowledge dreams, you can become your own teacher, counselor, or guide to make any learning experience easier.

- A healing dream can prompt you to get what your system needs nutritionally.

I encourage you to explore more about this area and retrieve information about the vast experimentation and points of view within this "field of dreams."[1] The more you delve, the more you will discover fascinating dream facts. This chapter is not intended to take the place of a dream course but is to "whet your appetite" for dreams.

THE LANGUAGE OF DREAMS

Dreams Can Be Literal (Manifest) or Symbolic (Latent)

As you become involved with dream interpretation, you will become adept at interpreting the messages sent by the dreaming mind. A dream symbol or image can be viewed in two different ways. First, the symbol can be literal, or manifest. With these symbols, what you see is what you get; so if you dream of having a baby, don't be surprised to find out that a new family member is on the way.

The second way that dreams can be interpreted is to unravel the meaning of the latent or underlying symbol. The dreaming mind can sort through endless possibilities before finally choosing a relevant symbol to represent people or events in your life. For example, a dream of having a baby could symbolically represent "a new project on the way" or even giving birth to "a new you." If you are surprised to dream about a particular person, you may have to decipher what this person symbolizes or represents. If you dream of Jack, does he symbolically stand for another person named Jack, or someone that looks like Jack, or even an individual that shares the same profession as Jack? Uncoding these symbols is the detective part of dreamwork.

Dreams Can Come Unrequested or upon Request

Without requesting specific input, you can let a dream come spontaneously and unsolicited. With this unguided approach, your dream content may or may not relate to a specific problem. That does not imply the dream content will not be meaningful; just that it may not address a particular problem on your mind. To court a spontaneous dream, simply be receptive to receive a dream about anything.

Many people actively program a dream to resolve a nagging problem, get insight into another person's action, or discover creative inspiration. If you want your dreaming mind to show you how to bridge the gap with your new assistant, you pose the question, "How can my new assistant and I improve our communication?" Dr. Gayle Delaney, a California psychologist, calls this process "dream incubation." I recommend reading her books, *Living Your Dreams* and *Breakthrough Dreaming*,[2] to deepen your understanding of dream incubation or programming.

Basically, you formulate a question before going to sleep to summon an answer or clarification from your dreaming mind. Here is an example of dream incubation. Are you wondering about forming a closer relationship with someone at work? Program your dreaming mind to give you a response to this situation by writing the following question in your dream journal: Will I spend time outside of work with my new workmate?

Decision-making questions can also be used for programming. If you are asking about the feasibility of starting a new career at this point in your life, you might ask, "Should I make a career change?"

SIX STEPS FOR SUCCESSFUL DREAM RECALL

With practice, you can recall your dreams. You will find tapes listed on page 291 that will help you master the basics of dreaming and take you into the sleep state. Successful dream recall entails the following six steps.

1. *Engage in daytime activities that facilitate dream recall.* Several times throughout the day, give yourself the suggestion "I will remember my dreams" and then, at bedtime, go to sleep anticipating a dream that will give you insight. If you choose to program a dream, it is essential to pose a question for a dream response. For example, if you are concerned about a career change, you want to focus on this situation intermittently throughout the day. Suggest to your dreaming mind several times throughout the day that you will remember your dream about making a career change.

2. *Set up your dream journal.* This can be a notebook or spiral memo book that is easy to carry. Have a pen, which can be used while you are lying down or sitting up. And last, see if you can obtain a small penlight that can be attached to your journal. I suggest placing the journal, pen, and penlight on a nightstand next to your bed. Keeping these materials close at hand reflects a serious commitment to record your dreams.

3. *Prepare your dream area.* This will help encourage dream recall so you can avoid distractions. For example, a blaring alarm clock in the morning can be jarring whereas a clock radio playing gentle instrumental music can be soothing. Be certain that you are comfortable in your sleep environment. If you have difficulty sleeping because the room is too cold or too warm, this will preoccupy you and distract the dreaming mind.

4. *Develop presleep rituals.* Slow down the outer activities as you approach bedtime. Try to avoid stimulants such as alcohol, coffee, or tea with caffeine. You might meditate, listen to relaxing music, or take a soothing hot bath before getting into bed. Once in bed, take your dream journal out and write the date in the left-hand margin. To ensure complete clarity, date it the night and morning it was dreamed. If I put down May 25/26, this would mean the night of the 25th and morning of the 26th during the month of May.

If you are programming a dream, you want to record the day residue, incubation discussion, and incubation phrase in your dream notebook.

Day Residue: Write a brief paragraph under the heading "Day Residue." In a few sentences, describe your day's activities. You might also note any emotional or physical reactions left over from the day that might influence your dreams. For example, are you feeling joy or sadness? Have you felt alert, tired, drained, or weary during the past day? Are you unusually hot, cold, or sweaty? These "day notes" can also be written for a spontaneous dream if you choose.

Incubation Discussion: Record a discussion that will center on the question you want to resolve. Probe by asking

- What could have caused this situation?

- Are there alternative ways to resolve this dilemma?

- What is the most challenging outcome?

- What could be the most desirous result?

- How would my life change as a result of this resolution?

Incubation or Programming Phrase: Then write your incubation or programming phrase, which is a one line question that will help you answer this predicament. This may be simply put by asking, "Is a career move appropriate for me at this time of my life?" When drifting off to sleep, focus on that programming phrase and give yourself the suggestion several times that your dream will show you the right perspective about making a career move.

For both the spontaneous and programmed dream, do the following as you go to sleep:

- Tell your dreaming mind before you fall asleep, I will sleep soundly, awaken feeling refreshed, and remember my dreams.

- Turn off the light and make sure you are comfortable in bed. You can listen to soothing music as you do any of the breathing and relaxation exercises to help you enter the alpha level or listen to a tape that will put you into the sleep state.

5. *Take care on awakening (to collect and hold on to your dream)*. Be gentle upon awakening and don't move or even open your eyes until you are ready to record. This is a delicate time, so lie as still as possible while you are recalling the dream. Changing positions or quick movements will quickly chase away the dream memory.

Focus completely on retrieving any dream image. If you are having difficulty remembering the dream, lie still until you can "pull up a thread" to help you retrieve the complete dream. For example, one morning I seemed to wait endlessly for a clue. Suddenly, I remembered seeing a "stop sign." With that thread, I easily reconstructed the rest of the dream.

Start with the last scene and work backward until you are led to the previous scene. You might want to rehearse these dream details several times until the dream is clearly embedded in your memory. I must emphasize that it is vital to lie still while any fleeting thoughts, feelings, and images surface.

6. *Record the dream in your journal*. Now you are ready to record the dream in your journal. Sometimes the hardest thing is to get up and record these dream memories. At the very least, force yourself to make notes. Even if you awaken in the middle of the night or early morning, record any notes that will help you recall the dream later. If you awaken during the middle of the night and don't feel coherent enough to write in your journal, have a pad handy to record any recollections.

Each dream can be recorded on a separate page. Honor any fragment, flash, emotion, or one-liner. Every bit of information is important. Eventually, your dreams will become longer and more detailed. Make certain you are including the setting, the characters appearing in the dream with whom you may be familiar or unfamiliar, and any other significant symbols.

After making your entry, give the dream a title. You might want to note any emotional feelings you have as a result of the dream. If anything stands out graphically, draw those figures in your journal.

Leave some space so you can relate the dream information to your waking experience. You will make bridges between the symbolic images presented and the reality of your life. As you continue to make entries in your dream book, the symbolic meanings of the symbols will become clarified.

Here are some sample entries, including the dream titles.

Feb. 4/5   The Deer Hunter

I am deer hunting on my property. Brother had a four-point buck go right next to him but didn't shoot. Buck turned into a doe. When I awaken, I realize that I need to spend more "quality" time with my brother and his family.

Feb. 8/9   Mowing the Lake House Lawn

My wife and I have been looking at buying some lake property. Last night I dreamed of mowing the lawn of a lake house with my riding mower. The prior night I had been talking with my father about what a good decision it was to trade my large Ford tractor for the new smaller lawn tractor. Although I didn't want to part with my old Ford, it was the right thing to do.

Interpretation: I believe this dream confirmed that our continued search for the "right" lake house is the right thing to do. I also believe that the dream indicated that the right place will come along, just as the right tractor did. The details of the lake house in the dream are sketchy at best, but I'll bet it is similar to the place we end up with.

EXERCISE

Encourage Spontaneous Dream Recall

Following the spontaneous dream recall steps, record your dream in this space.

_____

_____

_____

_____

_____

_____

Engage in Dream Programming

Program a dream by following the directions for recording the day residue, incubation discussion, and incubation phrase in this space.

_____

_____

_____

_____

INTUITIVE DREAM INTERPRETATION

Since you are the producer and creator of your dreams, you must play a key role in the interpretation. Perhaps the strongest advice I can give is, don't run to see what a dream book has to say about your dream symbols. Your dreaming mind has sent information that is custom designed for you. So, you will be the best interpreter of your dreams!

The benefit of recording your dreams is developing an understanding of your unique symbols. The meaning of symbols will be revealed to you as patterns begin to emerge. I know many people who have overlooked the vital warning messages sent through their dreams because their head is tucked away in a dream book searching for answers that do not apply. Whenever I am asked to offer interpretive help, I preface my words by saying, "If this were my dream, this is what the symbol would mean to me."

Many of the following steps are used in traditional dream practice. I have added the intuitive touch to help you retrieve insights effortlessly.

Seven Steps Toward Understanding the Dream Message

1. *Give the dream a title.* Use up to eight words for a title that describes the dream theme.

2. *Extract the theme.* In a sentence, tell who is doing what to or with whom.

3. *Underline the major symbols or concepts presented in the dream.*

4. *Determine the emotional content of the dream.* How do you feel? This will be an important clue.

5. *Draw any part of the dream to capture your feelings and recollections.* This step is optional but often gives clarity in trying to decipher the symbol.

6. *Use amplification and/or word association to analyze the most important symbols.*

7. *Integrate the logical and intuitive minds.* When you finish, ask: "How does the intuitive resolution relate to my initial question?" The logical mind's task is to integrate the intuitive information and do a reality check on the feasibility of incorporating this intuitive input. After analyzing the dream content, you want the logical mind to tell you how to

implement the interpreted information. For example, if your dream shows you losing a front tooth, your intuitive mind is symbolically highlighting your concern with public speaking. The logical mind then discovers that you have an upcoming speaking engagement and prompts you to develop more confidence in your speaking skills.

Periodically review your dream interpretations to see if any new insights have emerged. Leave room in your journal after the dream entry to record your interpretation and make additional entries.

Practice Dream Interpretation

Record and then interpret a dream. Do this for both a spontaneous dream and a programmed dream.

Spontaneous Dream:

_____

_____

_____

_____

_____

Programmed Dream:

_____

_____

_____

_____

_____

New insights will continually emerge. Now I will show how I intuitively analyzed a dream. Try to make your intuitive interpretation before looking at mine. *Go with your first impressions*, which are intuitive and definitely correct for you.

SAMPLE DREAM ANALYSIS. This dream was presented by a student in class. Initially, she had no idea about the true or underlying meaning of the dream symbolism. Step into the dreamer's shoes and see if you can get any clues about the dream's meaning. After reading the dream, make an analysis by applying the dream analysis steps found on page 165. Then you can write down your interpretation in the space provided.

Dream: I dreamed that I woke up in the middle of the night. I awakened my husband and we went down the stairs. The bedroom was ours, but the downstairs was the house I grew up in. As we looked over the banister into the living room below, we saw that someone had robbed us—the room was a wreck. Everything of value was taken. As I looked, I saw the silverware chest empty. I thought, "Wouldn't it have been easier to carry the silver in the chest?" Then I said, "Why didn't the dogs bark?" Both dogs were sleeping. We didn't hear anything, and they didn't either. My husband didn't say a word in the dream.

EXERCISE

Make an Intuitive Dream Interpretation

What does this dream intuitively suggest? Write your interpretation in this space, including any associations from amplification and word association. Then you can compare your analysis to mine on the next page. Use this space for your amplification or word association.

My interpretation is:

_____

_____

_____

_____

_____

EXERCISE

Marcia Emery's Interpretation of This Dream

1. *Title*: Something of Value Is Gone

2. *Theme*: A couple has been robbed of their valuables.

3. *Major symbols (underlined)*: I woke up in the <u>middle of the night</u>. I awakened my <u>husband</u> and we went down the <u>stairs</u>. The <u>bedroom</u> was ours, but the <u>downstairs</u> was the <u>house I grew up in</u>. As we looked over the banister into the living room below, we saw that someone had <u>robbed us</u>—the <u>room was a wreck</u>. <u>Everything of value was taken</u>. As I looked, I saw the <u>silverware chest empty</u>. I thought, "Wouldn't it have been easier to carry the silver in the chest?" Then I said, "Why didn't the <u>dogs bark</u>?" Both <u>dogs were sleeping</u>. We <u>didn't hear anything</u>, and they didn't either. My <u>husband didn't say a word</u> in the dream.

4. *Emotional content*: The woman was puzzled but not concerned about anything being stolen.

5. *Drawing*: Not necessary.

6. *Amplification*: The symbol that jumped out for amplification was the empty silverware chest. This is how I guided the student in the amplification. Remember, this is her dream, and eliciting her associations was paramount.

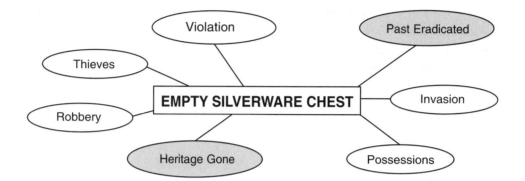

How did your amplification compare with this? Make any notes here.

_____

_____

_____

_____

7. *Integrating the logical and intuitive minds*: The strongest association reached through the amplification process was "past eradicated." I asked the woman if she owned a silver chest and she said no. This type of chest often represents a dowry or a family possession passed on to heirs. Her husband said nothing in the dream, indicating that all responsibility for words or action depended on her. The intuitive dream interpretation substantiated that she was wrestling with letting go of past family ties.

Can you see the intuitive connection between empty chest and letting go of past ties? The logical mind stepped in to substantiate when I questioned the dreamer. When I initially asked the woman if she had any idea what the dream was telling her, she said no, she was quite puzzled. I, too, had no immediate connection upon hearing her tell the dream. How could I, then, be in a position to help her interpret her dream?

As we worked with the dream her mouth suddenly dropped open as she realized the importance of the intuitive connection. She talked about the difficulty she was having with her dysfunctional mother and had been thinking of severing all communication. The dream with the symbol showing "heritage gone" made her evaluate the finality of this decision.

The people with whom you share the dream become intuitively attuned to the dream content and can help with the interpretation. For example, the symbol in need of amplification intuitively is presented to me by "coming forward" or being highlighted in some way. This process is duplicated if another symbol from the same dream is in need of amplification. It is very important to remember that when I offer this information to the dreamer, I also use the disclaimer I mentioned previously, "If this were my dream, this is what it would mean to me."

Last but not least, don't forget that you are the best interpreter of your dreams.

Interpret Your Dreams

Return to the spontaneous and programmed dreams you recorded on page 164. Use the seven steps on page 165 to intuitively decipher the message from each of these dreams.

Use your journal if you need additional space.

_____

_____

_____

_____

How did the inside information revealed through this analysis help you clarify your problem or original question?

_____

_____

_____

_____

Make a commitment to read at least one of the dream books suggested in the reference section by listing the name of that book in this space.

_____

_____

Make a pledge to record all forthcoming dreams in a section of your Journal. Or you may want to record all dreams in a separate "Dream Notebook."

Interpreting the Symbol

I encourage you to keep a record of your dream symbols. As you become immersed in dream interpretation, you will see that a symbol can be interpreted in various ways. For example, dreaming of flying is common.

Sigmund Freud felt that flying symbolized sexual intercourse.

In contrast, Carl Jung felt that flying dreams represented upcoming and profound life changes.

T. C. Brink, a California psychologist, correlated flying dreams with an increase in self-confidence, sense of freedom, and creativeness.

Several contemporary psychotherapists have reported that patients who were beginning to rise above their present circumstances by taking more control of their lives frequently reported flying dreams.[3]

EXERCISE

Your Turn to Explore Flying

What does flying mean to you? Make as many associations as possible.

_____

_____

Elicit flying associations from other people. Can you see the variety of associations attached to one concept?

EXERCISE

How to Share Your Dreams with Others

Dreamwork becomes more meaningful when shared with someone else. Here is how you can share your dreams.

1. You can program a dream for someone you know who is in difficulty by asking for clarity about their situation. You may not understand the symbolism you elicit, but it can be clarified when you share the dream content with the troubled person.

2. You can tell someone your dream and see what perspective is provided. Someone else may "hear" or "see" connections that elude you.

3. You can organize a dream group that will meet once a week to discuss and analyze dreams.

4. You can join the Association for the Study of Dreams (ASD) to find out about a dream group in your geographical locale. You might also enjoy attending their annual conferences, where dream experts, educators, and laypeople interested in this area join for a week of exciting dream exploration. Please see the reference section for further details.

DREAMS THAT COME TRUE ARE CALLED PRECOGNITIVE

Precognition is that facet of parapsychology, or psi, that highlights the ability to know about future events with a high degree of accuracy. Having a dream that eventually comes true attests to the mind's expanded capability to reach forward in time and preview an upcoming event.

Considerable experimentation with precognition has occurred in connection with dreams. These future-oriented dreams have the function of preparing the dreamer for upcoming events. Warnings coming through dreams have prevailed for centuries. President Lincoln had a dream in which he rose and walked into the East Room. "Who is dead in the white room?" he asked. "The president," came the answer. "He was killed by an assassin." Robert Louis Stevenson wrote the classic thriller *Dr. Jekyll and Mr. Hyde* after seeing the story in a nightmare. Writer Graham Greene saw a great shipwreck in a dream the night before the ocean liner *Titanic* sank.

Pioneering precognitive dream studies were conducted at the Maimonides Hospital, in Brooklyn, New York, in the 1960s. The results of this work is summarized in the book *Dream Telepathy* by Ullman, Krippner, and Vaughan.[4] In these studies, Malcolm Bessent, the prime precognitive dream subject, was able to foresee randomly created events of the next day more than 87.5% of the time. Alan Vaughan, one of the original researchers, points out that a variety of people with and without apparent intuitive ability participated in the Maimonides studies over the years. Out of 148 attempts by participants to envision the future through dreams, 111 or (75%) were successful in activating their intuitive ability in dreams.[5]

For the past seven years I have been studying various facets of the precognitive dream.[6] According to many participants in these studies, precognitive dreams that eventually come true are an unforgettable experience. The vividly clear dream content seems to grab the dreamer by the shoulders, give a good shake, and demand to be remembered. Days later, reality replaces reverie as an experience literally fulfills the drama originally presented in the dream. This phenomenon is a clear example of the intuitive mind speaking through the dream state to project a future reality.

The following examples of precognitive dreams will, I hope, excite you to collect your own.

◆ Kathy dreamed "The butler entered the room and presented the woman with a gift. He said, this is from your husband because he wants to see you happy. He placed in her hands a small painted porcelain Easter egg. She thought it was a lovely gift, but it wasn't Easter and she was confused." On Easter, Kathy was overjoyed to find out that she was pregnant and finally having a child after eight years of marriage.

◆ Peter has a friend who is a mechanic for the U.S. Postal Service in Chicago. They had a jeep that had broken down, and despite extensive testing, nobody could figure out why it wouldn't run. The boss decided not to let anybody work on this jeep because too much time had already been wasted in repair efforts. Then Peter's friend had a dream about the jeep in which a solution appeared. The next morning, he went over to the jeep and interchanged two wires that had been reversed, quickly correcting the situation.

◆ I, Marcia Emery, asked my dreaming mind to help me locate a "long lost friend." I was trying to find Mike Malone, a well-known choreographer whom I hadn't seen for many years. Although he had recently resided in Washington, D.C., I felt he had moved and had no idea as to his whereabouts. Finally, a dream provided the answer.

I dreamed I was talking to Debbie Allen, star of the television program "Fame" and renowned choreographer. I asked her how she liked living in California. I told her I was trying to find Mike. Debbie said, "That's easy, he's living on the West Side of New York."

As Detective Emery, I was eager to follow up this lead the next day and called the information operator in New York City, who gave me a number for a Mike Malone living on the West Side. Mike answered the phone and immediately recognized my voice. He said, "How did you find me? I just moved here yesterday!"

Please note that these dreams bring both good and bad messages. But, if you honor the sneak preview presented in your dreams, you will be prepared for life's most significant events. For example, a promotion can be anticipated, a problem solved, or a new friendship previewed. Precognitive dreams can come spontaneously or through programming.

Through the years, many people in my dream research group were able to identify their precognitive dreams from a signal or cue in the dream. As a part of the programming they asked, "Can you send me a signal so I will know that this dream represents an occurrence that can go forward in time?" Some of the symbols sent were a white dove, an eagle, a white light, a deer, a cat, and a piece of cake. One of the most interesting symbols came to Nanci, who saw the actress Jane Seymour. We were all amused by the "punny" nature of her dreaming mind—by presenting someone who wanted her to SEE MORE!

You can learn to program a precognitive dream by saying, I need advice and guidance from my dreaming mind. I need a dream that will answer my question (insert your question in here). My dreaming mind will show me a simple picture I can understand. Send me a symbol showing that the dream is precognitive. I will awaken with the dream picture fresh in my mind. I will remember the dream easily and record it in my notebook. The meaning of the dream will become clear to me.[7]

EXERCISE

Practice Programming a Precognitive Dream

Write your programming question and the dream that is sent in response.

_____

_____

_____

_____

Where Do You Think This Advance Information Comes From?

The late Edgar Cayce once said, "Nothing of significance happens in our lives unless we first preview it in a dream."[8] Where does this input about the future come from? I will briefly offer a perspective about how your subconscious presents information about the future.

Often, higher spiritual states are accessed through dreams. A dream can occur in *chairos* time, that is, sacred time or the eternal now. During sleep, the dreamer is carried to a sacred dimension, where a transfer of wisdom and energy occur. The subconscious steps into this sacred time to bring wisdom, energy, clarification, and insight from sacred time into *chronos*, or chronological, time.

EXERCISE

Evaluating Precognitive Input

Remember, your mind is like a parachute and functions only when open. How open are you to accepting the validity of precognitive experiences?

_____

_____

Now on to the next chapter to learn about meditation, another way to activate your intuition.

Chapter Ten

ACCESS YOUR INTUITIVE MIND THROUGH MEDITATION

Anyone who has practiced meditation knows how difficult it can be to quiet our "mind talk" in order to connect with our deeper, wise, intuitive mind....We can tell the difference between the limiting, habitual mind talk, and the voice of our inner guidance.

SHAKTI GAWAIN
Reflections in the Light

WHAT IS MEDITATION?

In this chapter, you'll learn to use meditation, the remaining tool needed to activate your intuition. There are various associations to this word. Meditation is *not* what you think! And meditation is not *what* you think. With meditation, you become still and enter the alpha level so you can access your intuitive mind. In contrast, your logical mind is responding when you "think."

In her book *Awakening Intuition*,[1] transpersonal psychologist Frances Vaughan emphasizes that meditation facilitates intuitive attunement. During your meditation time, you will notice how the logical mind slips into the background while the intuitive mind emerges.

If you are uncomfortable with the term "meditation," you might prefer to substitute the words "introspection," "stillness," or "quiet time." Some people use their quiet time for prayer. It doesn't matter what word(s) you use to describe meditation; it is important to know that this is a time of stillness.

As you enter the receptive alpha level, you can do any of the following:

- Retrieve a solution to a vexing problem.
- Help with decision making.
- Relax and become more energized.
- Discover a creative or innovative touch.
- Send positive thoughts and healing energies to someone in need.
- Discover a profound universal truth.
- Gather spiritual support.

Meditation becomes an unbroken focus on the object of concentration. When you block out everything but the focal point commanding your attention, you are meditating. The commuter riding the train to work and reading the paper is, in a sense, meditating because all surrounding talk and activity are shut off. The same for the jogger or athlete practicing a sport. In fact, many top-level managers and CEOs have told me that focusing on problems while jogging helps them arrive at wonderfully innovative solutions. Some people even meditate while mowing their lawn or vacuuming the house.

A senior corporate management development consultant for McDermott Inc. in New Orleans, specialists in marine construction services and power generation systems and equipment, talked about getting his intuitive high every morning from 6:45 A.M. to 7:00 A.M. when he meditated. The information that came to him during that time has been incorporated into his two books. He also ran every day and considered that a meditative state. As he ran, he received the intuitive flashes, which he wrote down when he got home. A part of the stress management training he provided was teaching others how to meditate. He continued to receive feedback years after this training was provided from participants who told him, "I've been using the meditation and feel so much better."

You have been practicing a facet of meditation by becoming centered and using your receptivity techniques to go into the alpha level. Meditation can be passive or unguided as you let any image spontaneously come into your awareness. The phrase "unguided meditation" best describes this process of spontaneous receptivity to whatever imagery emerges. In contrast, when you are actively directed with guided imagery to go "sit down by the lake," you are actively or deliberately retrieving these images. All the "fantasy" trips you have encountered so far in this book have been guided imagery. You might review the following: guided imagery trip on pages 71–73, the guided journey to the beach on page 80, the alpha to omega technique on page 89, the nature walk you took on pages 93–95, the trip to the "house of intuition" on pages 97–100, the candle color exercise on pages 114–115, and the guided fantasy journey you took on pages 132–133.

At times, your meditation can be a combination of the guided and unguided. You may be actively guided to walk through the forest and discover a house and then, without being guided, you can move through the house to explore the inside.

There is no ritual or special formula for meditation. This is your time to become centered and still. Engaging in daily meditation sessions will not only strengthen your intuitive abilities, but it will also put you in a very balanced and centered mode to effectively handle all your responsibilities and challenges.

HOW TO PRACTICE MEDITATION

Make a commitment for daily practice. The best time to meditate is when you first awaken in the morning, after you have washed but before you eat. At that point, you are less assaulted with the demands of the coming day and evening. If this is not possible, choose the next best time for you. Most important, be consistent by meditating at the same time each day.

Select an appropriate setting. Find a relatively quiet room or space where you can feel comfortable. A distraught body will send tense messages and disturb the meditation. A quiet setting is important to minimize outside noise and interference. Disconnect the phone so you won't be abruptly interrupted by the ring. Be astute in deciding what area of your living quarters is most appropriate for meditation.

This is not the time for sleep. Affirm before starting, "I will stay awake and be alert to any messages from my intuitive mind."

This is not the time to rejoice. You may experience joy or laughter during the meditation but don't deliberately create these feelings.

MEDITATION EXERCISES

Use any of the imagery scripts in this book as an example of how to create a guided imagery meditation to suit your own needs. As suggested previously, you can ask a friend to read this to you or record the meditation on an audio cassette tape.

Here are four meditation exercises. In the first two, the guided imagery is intended to lead you into the stillness so you can problem solve, create, become refreshed, or allow the intuitive thoughts to flow. These meditations were created by Jim Emery and are listed in the resource section. In the third exercise, the guided imagery is provided so you can receive assistance from a problem-solving helper. The final meditation exercise is designed for relaxation.

Have a pad of paper and a pen available to write down any symbols, words, or pictures that might come into your mind after each guided meditation.

MEDITATION 1: USING GUIDED IMAGERY—THE CAMPFIRE. **Directions:** Sit up straight in your chair with your feet flat on the floor, arms uncrossed, hands in your lap. Take seven "hang-sah" breaths to put yourself into the alpha level of consciousness. Begin: "hang-sah," "hang-sah," "hang-sah," "hang-sah," "hang-sah," "hang-sah," "hang-sah."

Send this message from your mind to your body. "Every cell in my body feels relaxed and comfortable. Every cell in my body feels relaxed and comfortable. Every cell in my body is relaxed and comfortable."

Imagine that you are in a campground where you have already pitched your tent and are ready to build a campfire in the fire pit in front of your campsite. The fire pit is circular with about a 2-foot diameter and the outer edge is lined with a dozen rocks to contain the ashes of the fire. You have your sleeping bag folded in half with the upper part resting on a large log on the ground so you can lean back comfortably to enjoy your campfire. As you light the dry twigs and dead pine needles in the center of the fire pit, the flames jump skyward with a snapping and crackling sound. The pitch from the pine branches causes billows of dark smoke to rise into the air. Sometimes the smoke seems to take on the form of a human figure dancing in the light of the fire. Quickly the larger pieces of wood begin to burn and the fire is soon burning brightly. You close your eyes and feel the warmth of the fire on your face as it takes the chill out of the evening air. When you open your eyes, you begin to watch the flames as they lick at each new branch that is pushed to the center of the fire pit. Occasionally, you throw on a few dry pine needles to watch their sparks rise high above the fire, dancing up into the darkness of the night sky until the cool night air extinguishes their glow. It's a clear, starry night and the moon is nearly full. As you look up at the sky, you can see pictures that seem to be formed by the stars. It's like the game you played as a child where you connected the dots to discover what the picture was. Your mind continues to play this game as it mentally connects the patterns that you find in the stars. Look at that group over there to the right. They form a perfect kite when the imaginary lines connect them together. What else can you see? Look at the moon. Can you see the face that's there? As you sit and watch the sky, you begin to think about the vastness of space that is out there. A chilling feeling of isolation runs up your spine as you feel how empty and lonely it could be if you were in space all by yourself, but you are still fascinated by the idea of infinity. The eternity of time is another thought that comes into your mind. You look back now at the fire pit, where the flames have been replaced with bright orange, yellow, and red coals. As you stare into the coals, you again begin to think about space and time, infinity, and eternity. Many other thoughts come into your mind at this time. You reflect on them for a couple minutes and then, as your head nods forward, you notice that the coals are nearly out. You spread them with a stick and pour a little water on the few live ones remaining. Then, you carry your sleeping bag into the tent, climb into it, and lay back, putting your mind and body to rest.

Take three counts to return your awareness to this setting and feel the energy coming back into your hands and feet. Open your eyes, stand up, and stretch, feeling refreshed and reenergized.

EXERCISE

How Did You Experience the Campfire?

Write down your experiences from this meditation. Then draw a picture of the most memorable scene in this meditation experience in the space provided.

_____

_____

_____

_____

Draw the picture in this space:

MEDITATION 2: USING GUIDED IMAGERY—AT THE OCEAN. Directions: Sit up straight in your chair with your feet flat on the floor, arms uncrossed, hands in your lap. Take seven "hang-sah" breaths to put yourself into the alpha level of consciousness. Begin: "hang-sah," "hang-sah," "hang-sah," "hang-sah," "hang-sah," "hang-sah," "hang-sah."

Send this message from your mind to your body. "Every cell in my body feels relaxed and comfortable. Every cell in my body feels relaxed and comfortable. Every cell in my body is relaxed and comfortable."

Picture yourself hiking down a mountain trail through huge pine trees. You have just spent the night camping on the mountain. As you climb down the trail, you get an occasional glimpse of the ocean through the trees. The forest has been quiet this morning, and the pine needles in the sand beneath your feet cushion the trail to make your descent an easy one. You become aware of a noise ahead of you that sounds like rushing water. As you quicken your pace the sound becomes louder and you can now see a small waterfall just 30 feet to the left of the trail. The sandy trail becomes rocky again as you approach the small stream that crosses the trail ahead. When you get to the stream, you begin to follow its edge upstream to get a closer look at the waterfall. As you look up you can see that the water is cascading over a gigantic rock, 20 to 25 feet in height. A pool has formed at the place where the water lands and you can see some fish swimming in the shadow of the big rock. From the pool a stream carries the water on its journey toward the ocean below, and you easily jump across to the other side of the stream where you are standing. You follow the stream back to the trail and continue down the path. The trees are thinning out now and the ground beneath your feet is becoming more sandy with fewer and fewer pine needles. The ocean is easily seen as you come out of the trees onto a sandy knoll. After taking your shoes and socks off and stuffing them into your pack, you run down the sandy hill with large leaping steps. The sand feels good on the soles of your feet. When you reach the bottom of the hill, you stop to feel the texture of the sand with your toes. Your rapid breathing from running causes you to take a deep inhale breath. As you do, you can smell the salty air from the ocean breeze. The smell is so strong that you can almost taste the salt. Your whole body feels invigorated with a fresh, new, alive feeling. Quickly walking across the sand, you approach the water that is gently lapping at the shore. There is only a slight breeze, and the roll of the waves is soothing to both the eyes and ears as you step into the wet sand, letting the waves lick at your feet. As you stand in the water and look down at the many stones and broken shells, a perfectly formed shell washes in near your feet. It is a shell with a spiraling turban shape. You carry the shell back to the dry sand, take off your pack, and sit down near a large piece of driftwood. As you study the shell closely, you are aware of the wonders of art that mother nature produces. The cry of a sea gull cuts through the air, and you look up to see several circling the beach in search of lunch. Leaning back against the driftwood, you close your eyes and listen to the sound of the ocean. A wonderful feeling of peace and tranquility washes over you as you rest from your journey down the mountain.

EXERCISE

Describe Your Beach Experience

Write down your experiences from this meditation. Then draw a picture of the most memorable scene in this meditation experience in the space provided.

_____

_____

_____

_____

_____

Draw a picture showing your beach experience in this space.

MEDITATION 3: FIND YOUR INTUITIVE PROBLEM-SOLVING HELPER. The exercises throughout this book have been designed to help you problem solve by accessing your intuition. As part of this process, you can even ask for help from your intuitive problem-solving helper. Assistance in the form of a person, object, or other type of being can be created to help you solve problems.

The following guided meditation will help you call upon your own personal helper in order to get a new perspective on nagging problems.

First, take a moment to list any bothersome problem(s).

Is there one major problem upsetting you?

Do several unrelated issues have to be resolved?

Formulate what is bothering you in a brief question.

Problem(s):

_____

_____

_____

Directions: Sit up straight in your chair with your feet flat on the floor, arms uncrossed, hands in your lap. Take seven "hang-sah" breaths to put yourself into the alpha level of consciousness. Begin: "hang-sah," "hang-sah," "hang-sah," "hang-sah," "hang-sah," "hang-sah," "hang-sah."

Send this message from your mind to your body. "Every cell in my body feels relaxed and comfortable. Every cell in my body feels relaxed and comfortable. Every cell in my body is relaxed and comfortable."

Close your eyes and imagine you are walking along a beach, you gaze at the blue-green ocean. Feeling elated, you walk along the edge and let your toes touch the water. You momentarily forget all your worries and cares. The salt air and wind caress your face, bringing back fond memories of beach fun. You walk toward the jetty, and go out to the end of the pier and sit down. You know the time is right for intuitive problem solving.

After posing your question(s), look up and see your helper. What direction is your helper coming from? Is someone standing in back of you or seated by your side? Is someone coming toward you in a boat? Has a friendly sea gull landed near you? Help has arrived! Greet your helper and give thanks for the intuitive assistance you will receive for your problems. You might want to find out such details as your helper's name, whether they have served you before, and how you can establish future contact.

Briefly state the problem and listen for the reply from your helper. Perhaps the answer is phrased in yes or no terms. You may be presented with a special word, phrase, sentence or symbol. Express gratitude for the assistance and make plans to contact your helper again in the near future. You know you have the correct answer. Happily, you get up and walk back to the beach and prepare to return home in order to put the solution into action. Return your awareness to the room feeling deeply refreshed and relaxed.

EXERCISE

Describe Your Experience with Your Problem-Solving Helper

Describe your helper.

_____

_____

_____

_____

Note any problem-solving advice you received.

_____

_____

_____

MEDITATION 4: ELICITING RELAXATION IMAGERY. This guided meditation is intended to help you achieve a relaxed state. The imagery that is elicited through the guided meditation directions will help you relax each part of your body.

Preparation: To ease into a receptive alpha level, take seven "hang-sah" breaths followed by the autogenic relaxer.

Directions: Close your eyes and imagine walking down to the lake, taking in the beautiful view as you go. The trees wear their finest greenery, and the nearby flowers bloom radiantly. Although the water looks inviting, you choose not to go for a swim. Instead, you walk to the big tree at the edge of the lake, sit down comfortably, and lean against the tree. You remove your shoes in a hurry so you can put your feet in the water. Your toes and heels touch the water as you sit back relaxing. As you inhale, you feel the cool water caressing your feet and ankles. Your feet are relaxed and comfortable from this light massage.

On an inhale breath, imagine the sensation of water coming inside your skin, moving up around your heels, and then running up around the ankles as all muscles and tendons are relaxed. On an exhale, imagine the water flowing down and out the bottom of your feet. On the next inhale, imagine the water flowing under the skin again as it moves up into the calves of your legs, massaging the muscles and soothing them. On the exhale, imagine the water flowing down through the ankles and out through the bottom of your feet. As you inhale again, imagine the water moving up through your ankles and the calves of your legs up into your knees and upper legs. When you exhale, the water flows down to your feet, drawing all the tension out of your legs. When you inhale again, you imagine the water moving quickly up the legs into the midsection of your body as it swirls around the kidneys, bladder, and spleen, cleansing those organs. As you exhale, the water flows down your legs and out through the bottom of your feet. You now feel a wonderful relaxing feeling in the lower half of your body. You continue drawing the water through your feet on the next inhale, moving it quickly up the legs, through the waist, and up into the chest and back. It soothes and caresses the muscles around your heart and in your upper back. As you exhale the water works its way down your spine and through your lower back and takes all the tension with it, moving down the legs and out through the bottom of your feet again. You are becoming more relaxed and so very comfortable. This time you inhale and draw the water up through your body until it reaches your shoulders. Your shoulders become more relaxed as the water massages this area. The tension is drawn out of this area as the water flows down each of your arms, over your elbows, past your wrists and out each finger tip. As your hands and arms tingle, you know that tension is easing out. When you take your next inhale, imagine the water moving quickly up your legs, through your waist, up your spine, into your neck and head. The water washes all the tension away from your forehead, face, and neck. You exhale with a sigh of relief as the water continues traveling all the way down to your feet and out into the stream of water in front of you. You can now appreciate what a totally relaxed body is like as you savor this comfortable, tranquil feeling throughout your being. You continue to sit by the lake, feeling relaxed from the top of your head to the tip of your toes. After a few minutes have passed, you get up to return home, knowing you can always return to this relaxing image whenever the need arises.

Now open your eyes, stretch, and return your awareness to the room, feeling deeply refreshed and relaxed.

EXERCISE

Become Aware of Your Relaxation Imagery

What imagery helped you relax?

_____

_____

_____

_____

What would you like to add to this relaxation script?

_____

_____

_____

_____

Keep noting your progress eliciting clear and concise imagery.

_____

_____

_____

_____

COMMIT TO MEDITATION

Write down

The time of day you will meditate. _____

The place where you will meditate. _____

The amount of time you will spend meditating. _____

Do you prefer active, or guided, meditation? Record your reactions to guided meditation.

_____

_____

Do you prefer passive meditation, where you can sit quietly and let the images spontaneously emerge?

_____

_____

Record any comments about your practice that includes a combination of the active and passive.

_____

_____

_____

_____

_____

Now you can go into your intuitive tool box at any time to retrieve whatever you need to solve a problem that seems insoluble. You can achieve that special understanding of a coworker, family member, or friend. You will also discover creative approaches to old problems. Do you have any problems or issues you want to resolve? I'm sure you do. And I'm also certain that many of your problems will be described in Part Four, which shows how IPS helps resolve work problems and/or in Part Five, where IPS is applied to a spectrum of personal problems.

Part Four

INTUITION: THE ESSENTIAL BUSINESS TOOL

When you allow your intuitive skills to supply missing data, risk taking can be minimized and you will make decisions with greater confidence. In Part Four, you will see how intuition can be used effortlessly to access an elusive solution to a problem and "supply the missing data" in the business environment. The value of using intuition in business is expressed by Richard Antonini, president and CEO of the Foremost Insurance Company. He believes that intuition is a key component of management. You can make a decision with facts alone, he observes, but there are always holes that only intuition can fill. He recalls telling some of his employees who tend to be somewhat analytical that "the world is not just two and two is four. There is a lot more to decision making and management than they can put in a calculator." This added dimension is intuition.

There are many people who admittedly "fill in the blanks" in their work environment. Charles McCallum is an attorney and partner of a very large and reputable firm. During our interview, he mentioned that a lot of decisions have to be made on insufficient facts because the timing of many decisions doesn't allow for sufficient fact gathering. When a client begins to sketch out a problem, McCallum's intuitive mind is already filling in the blanks by showing him the rest of the problem and the solution. Then, when time permits, he goes back to fill in the supporting logic and give a convincing set of reasons so the client can accept the conclusions.

We are all decision makers and have to respond in many situations when the facts are incomplete. What do you do? Armed with the intuitive problem-solving process, you can respond more quickly and effectively in any situation. Notice how Drew turns the following disabling situation into one where he feels fully empowered and effective.

There was a time when Drew felt disgruntled because his customers used the threat of competition to get him to lower his prices. Recently, a customer adamantly demanded that he lower his prices or the firm would take its business elsewhere. Drew wanted to stand firm but was in a quandary as to whether this was the right thing to do. He used the intuitive problem solving to find out if he should refuse to lower his prices for this angry customer. He became centered and receptive using the intuitive problem-solving (IPS) techniques, and an image of an anchor appeared. After sorting through several associations to the anchor, he had the intuitive insight he was being shown to "hold fast" and not lower his prices. He also sensed that anchors represented hope, telling him to hold fast, not to despair, and he would not lose the business. After Drew told the customer he could not lower his prices, the customer replied, "I will give you the order anyway since I am very happy with your quality and service."

As you read through these cases, the ease with which solutions are retrieved may seem questionable. I always find it amusing how solutions have come about to problems that have eluded the team members for many months. I am constantly amazed to see how my students, firmly ensconced in their rational analyses at work, learn to use IPS and discover shortcuts to long procedures as well as to retrieve innovative solutions.

As you work your way through this book, you will see that you, too, can retrieve unique solutions in record time. One day a student related how he applied IPS to a business problem that needed attention. He used IPS and was amazed that he retrieved a solution in 15 minutes. Feeling quite skeptical about this new intuitive procedure, he took the usual "analytical" steps to find the solution. Guess what! Using his usual logical procedure took him a little over four hours to arrive at the same solution that IPS produced. He found an added bonus. When he looked back at his original notes, several options were suggested through the amplification procedure that he had never considered.

Other things may puzzle you as you read through these cases. You might wonder how people actually "see" pages of a calendar turning, or even watch a "stoplight" turn different colors. You might feel that you could never see or sense any of this imagery. If you want to implement the IPS in your decision-making activities, then you have to commit yourself to some of the practice activities described in Chapter Eight. Then, in a short time, you too will be able to "see" or become more aware of how your dominant sense "feeds" you the intuitive information. This does take practice. And just as any athlete or virtuoso who practices consistently to excel, you too have to work at learning how to become centered and receptive so you can effortlessly retrieve the imagery.

Many of the people who have used the IPS process in the cases you are about to read were quite skeptical. Yet they persisted and found the needed solution. I can tell you from my experience and theirs that it "does work." But, more important, as you discover the solution to elusive problems, you will be validating the usefulness of intuitive problem solving.

In Chapter Eleven, we are going to go inside the organization to look at problems that can affect the worker and the organization as a whole. Then, in Chapter Twelve, we will see how interpersonal dynamics generate problems that can also be resolved by intuitive problem solving. In Chapter Thirteen, we will also highlight specific jobs such as sales, marketing, and advertising. And in Chapter Fourteen, we show how IPS has empowered others to confront the issue of changing jobs at some time in their career by making quick, cogent, and responsible choices.

Many people have contributed to the examples or cases presented throughout this book. Students, seminar participants, and clients have applied IPS to these various situations at work and in their personal lives. Each has shared the need to find a solution to a pressing problem. These cases are intended to serve as a guide when you find yourself in a similar situation. Review the index and find a problem or two that truly engages you so you can see how the IPS process has been applied to arrive at a solution. Then you can start at the beginning and review each case more systematically.

Since reading one case after another can be overwhelming and tedious, I suggest the following:

- ◆ Read two or three cases at a time.

- ◆ Pause longer to study any case that is "closer to home."

- ◆ Be comfortable with both the third and first person accounts presented interchangeably.

- ◆ Complete the exercises interspersed among the cases. These are intended to help you clarify your use of IPS in any situation.

APPLYING INTUITION TO SUCCEED IN THE WORKPLACE

Intuitive managers have special skills that are likely to become more valuable in tomorrow's rapidly changing environment. They are likely to be the people who dream up the new products of tomorrow. They are the people who have a feel for what the consumer wants and how much he or she is willing to pay for it.

WESTON AGOR
Professor of Public Administration
University of Texas, El Paso

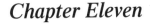

INTUITION AND LOGIC: A POTENT MIX TO EXCEL

What are the three most critical work-related decisions you have had to make recently? How long did it take to make these decisions? What was your investment in time and money? Did these decisions affect your relations with other people? In this chapter you will learn how to use the intuitive problem-solving (IPS) formula to successfully solve business-related problems and retrieve ingenious solutions, regardless of the dilemma.

The issues that are addressed are

- ◆ Using intuitive problem solving to resolve work issues.

- ◆ Using intuitive problem solving to focus on organizational concerns.

- ◆ Using intuitive problem solving to implement intuitive strategies within an organization.

The Chinese word for crisis is *weiji*, which combines two characters that separately mean danger and opportunity. You can use IPS to discover what opportunity is presented by any calamitous situation. Can you recall the last time you had to make a quick decision without having the facts available to you? How did you act? Were you paralyzed by indecision? Acting quickly can be risky, especially if the data are incomplete. By retrieving the needed intuitive input you will be engaging in risk taking, which is the key for placing yourself on the cutting edge of anything you do.

Before you begin this chapter, review Chapter Five, which has shown you how to elicit intuitive imagery. Suppose you raise the question, "How can I make some positive change on my new job assignment?" In reply, your intuitive mind sends you a simple image of a bed spring. Now you actually *spring into action* by making several associations to this image. The word spring may remind you of the following: support, bounce, coil, flowers, season, and flexible. Wow! By altering your perception, you realize that flexibility is the key. With this understanding, you will minimize any resistance by gaining the confidence and support of others as you take advantage of the opportunity this change offers you when you release your fear.

The image of a spring has come spontaneously and is readily retrieved and interpreted by your intuitive mind. Suppose you don't retrieve any imagery to the question you posed, "How can I make a positive change on the new job assignment?" You might actively elicit or create the imagery by imagining the offices of people at different levels within the company. Then, notice which office your intuitive mind highlights, showing you whom to approach to make this change.

Remember, the logical and intuitive mind work together as part of a "whole brain" in problem solving. As a result, the intuitive mind goes forward to preview the long-range effects and access unknown factors while the logical mind reviews the feasibility of applying these resolutions.

You were introduced to the intuitive problem-solving formula in Chapter Two. Now, you can see the ongoing working interchange between the intuitive and logical mind in this process. We are now going to look at several real-life situations and see how individuals have used IPS successfully.

USING INTUITIVE PROBLEM SOLVING
TO RESOLVE WORK-RELATED PROBLEMS

The first set of examples underscores how issues in the work environment can be resolved when they arise. Highlighted are

- Requesting a raise.
- Promotions and upward mobility.
- Shouldering unexpected responsibility.
- Learning a new skill.

Requesting a Raise

In the following case, extensive probing between the intuitive and logical minds is required before a solution is presented.

CASE: WHEN AND HOW. **Background:** Larry is being overwhelmed by the rising costs of raising his two children. He feels he must request a raise. This is how Larry applies IPS to his dilemma.

Problems: Should I ask my boss for an increase now? How should I make this request?

Centering: I sit on my favorite deck chair at the beach and listen to the waves. Focusing on the grains in the sand, I begin turning my attention within. I stare into the water and become still and tranquil.

Receptivity: I can feel every muscle in my body relax as I slowly close my eyes. I take three deep "total" breaths and let them out with a sigh. Then I am ready to receive the images into my mind to find an answer to my problem.

Imagery: I ask myself some questions, hoping the imagery will lead to a clear solution.

- Would it be worth my time and trouble to ask my boss for an increase now? I imagine that there are objects that look like shells in front of me. When I lift them, they either say "yes" or "no" underneath. I pose the question just asked and see myself reaching for the shell on the left. Underneath, the word "no" is illuminated. I am disappointed but continue questioning.

- Why should I not ask for a raise? I clear my mind of all thoughts and ask "why?" Immediately a picture of a judge's gavel enters my mind. The symbol fails to make sense to me. Does it have something to do with being judged or sentenced? I still don't know what this means but decide to ask my next query.

- When shall I ask for a salary increase? In the relaxed state, I look at a calendar on a wall. The pages began flying off the calendar month by month, beginning with January. The pages stop at the month of September. I try to put the images together to make sense, yet I am still confused.

- If I don't request a raise now, should I ask for a larger increase when the opportunity arises? I see a faint light in the corner of a dark room and, as it comes closer, it looks like a twinkling star.

Interpretation: I try making sense of these various images, which seem rather unorganized and irrelevant. I have a "no," a gavel, the month of September, and a twinkling star. After posing the main question again, these images begin to make sense. My intuitive mind tells me it is not the time to ask for a raise. It looks as if September might be better. I take the gavel to mean that if I ask for a raise, it will be vetoed, as if by a judge who is angered. This makes sense since my company is cutting costs and is rather meager with increases. I realize that my annual review is in September, and I will probably receive an increase at that point. The star seems to reflect that I will get recognition for my abilities at that time, like a "shining star."

Activating the Solution: With the picture of the judge's gavel strongly etched in mind, I decide not to ask for a raise at this time. I'm particularly glad that I have decided to wait when I find out that my company has a standard practice of hiring and promoting people that everyone has to follow. My informant says it would be futile to ask for an increase now, so I plan to present my position at the next annual review.

Promotions and Upward Mobility

Promotions and upward mobility are both serious concerns in the work environment and arise when an employee wants to assume more responsibility. Cases 1 and 2 address the desire for a promotion. Then Cases 3 and 4 show that the person aspiring to upward mobility is having difficulty convincing a superior that the next step up the corporate ladder can be taken. Case 4 also examines the extent to which the fear culprit influences the imagery interpretation.

CASE 1: ANTICIPATING A PROMOTION

Problem: Will I be promoted in the next year?

Centering: I look at a favorite picture and play soothing music.

Receptivity: Then I take a few deep "total" breaths and "progressively" relax my body.

Imagery: A dark cloud comes up spontaneously.

Interpretation: Using the amplification technique, I received the following associations.

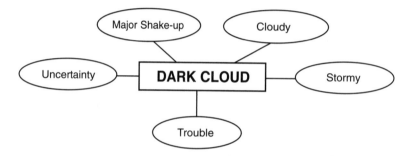

I can't get a real feeling for which association is right. So I ask another question:

♦ When might I get more information? I see a Christmas tree and once again use amplification to the Christmas tree image, which shows the following:

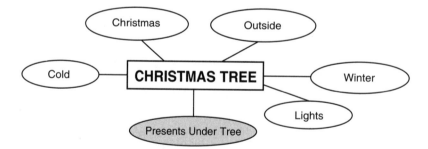

Further Interpretation: The "presents under the tree" association feels right and shows me that I will be offered something this winter, even though according to the first amplification, some rough times might come before then.

CASE 2: HOW TO TURN A "NO" TO A PROMOTION INTO "YES." **Background:** Niall is a manufacturing engineer with a large office furniture and equipment manufacturer. He is currently responsible for reorganizing the Filing Division into a smaller, more efficient manufacturing unit. His immediate supervisor has nominated him for a promotion, but the plant manager, his supervisor's boss, has denied this request.

Niall relates his strategy:

Problem: How can I get my plant manager to give me a promotion?

Centering: I sit down at my desk and look at the picture on the wall, which has a peaceful pastoral scene. I repeat "peace, be still" until all the stress is released from my body.

Receptivity: I close my eyes and do the "tense and release" technique.

Imagery: My mind leads me to an oasis in a desert. I begin looking into the peaceful, still pool of water. After looking at the water, I see a bull at the other end of the pool. It is one angry animal that is snorting and sneering.

Interpretation: Using amplification, the association to this bull reveals

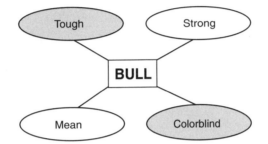

I realize that this means my plant manager is a tough, demanding person to work for. Also, the bull is colorblind and cannot see very well. That brings to mind that maybe the plant manager is not seeing something in me! The following question arises:

◆ What can I bring to my plant manager's attention to make him reconsider his evaluation of me?

Resting Period: I go out running. The image of a calculator appears to me while I am in the alpha level.

Further Interpretation: The calculator means that I need to produce numbers.

Activating the Solution: The plant manager is a real numbers man. If he sees me produce these numbers, that may prompt him to reconsider my promotion.

EXERCISE

Discovering Your Promotion Possibilities

Get relaxed and create imagery specifically designed to help you answer these questions. For example,

Do you see an open or closed doorway?

Is this doorway far away or close to you (telling you if this will happen short term or long term)?

What is the environment on the other side of the door? (Is it friendly or hostile?)

Is the smell of the environment one that is familiar or foreign to you?

What other imagery would you add?

CASE 3: GAINING RECOGNITION. **Background:** Bill, as the following case shows, is most unhappy because he wants to have more input in shaping company policy. Bill relates, "The most difficult part is that I have the responsibility for developing and executing the marketing plan within the organization, but I'm not being recognized for my efforts. The problem I have is based on my career expectations. While I have done very well with my company, I may need to move to another organization to keep my career moving forward. I am concerned that my boss and the rest of the officers of the company will promote others and overlook me. I want my superiors to understand that I am doing my job and am responsible for many of the positive things happening in the company. I am not sure if they are fully aware of my contribution and will grant a promotion based on my efforts."

Problem: Can Bill rise in the organization and be recognized for his efforts?

Centering: To become centered, Bill repeats the focusing phrase "peace, be still" several times, then takes a picture of a mountain cabin from his desk drawer. Bill retreats from the world into this cabin to find incredible peace. As he continues to look at the picture, he becomes more receptive.

Receptivity: To become more relaxed, he imagines himself walking down ten steps to the door of his "cabin in the woods." Entering cautiously, he sits down in his intuitive problem-solving chair. Feeling relaxed, he knows he will receive the imagery sent by the intuitive mind.

Imagery: Bill elicits imagery to these questions:

◆ Do promotional opportunities exist? Bill sits quietly and asks to be shown a key if a promotion will be given to him. He sees a large golden key. This is a good sign and encourages Bill to probe further with his questions.

◆ What position will I occupy? Bill sees nameplates on the office doors of his superiors. He goes down the line to see if the key opens any of these doors. When the fourth door opens, Bill walks in and even sees his name on the desk. Peering into the future, he watches himself confidently sitting behind the desk preparing an office memo. On the door he sees a nameplate that says "First Vice President."

◆ When will this change in mobility occur? He looks up at a graph and sees that the five-month mark is significant. In seeing this, he knows that he has to be patient for awhile.

◆ He then asks, "How will I cope over the next five months?" When he raises this question, an image of a large golden star is presented.

Interpretation: Bill is puzzled by this symbol and uses amplification to reveal the following associations:

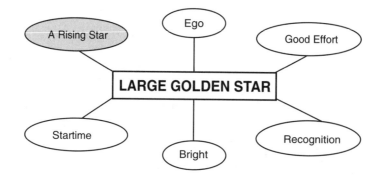

Further Interpretation: Bill is given strong intuitive feedback that he is definitely a rising star in the company. He realizes he needs to be more patient and knows from the imagery he receives that he is being recognized and appreciated.

Activating the Solution: Bill avidly applies his energies to the in-house concerns rather than focusing his energies on attaining a new position elsewhere.

***CASE 4: LOOKING FOR RESPONSIBILITY BUT NOT GETTING IT.* Background:** Rose wants to convince her director that she is ready to take over managerial responsibilities for the department. She feels that her hard-to-reach boss is autocratic. Rose knows that she is capable of handling more responsibilities. Recently, she was passed over for a promotion when two positions were available. Consequently, she feels depressed and rejected. Rose wants some insight into how things will eventually work. Specifically, she wants to be promoted to the position of a department manager and given more responsibility.

Problem: Will a promotion with added responsibilities be offered?

Centering: Rose sits down in her office with the door closed and focuses on the leaves of a plant.

Receptivity: She begins by taking several "total" breaths and progressively relaxes the various parts of her body, starting with her feet and ending with her head. Finally, Rose feels very relaxed.

Imagery: Rose asks a number of questions to find out more about her promotion.

- "Where do I stand now?" She waits until an image is presented and sees herself in dark clothing that resembles mourning garb. This vision shows her sitting in a bleak room with drawn shades. After seeing this picture, Rose thinks that being passed up means she will be reduced to the most meager of circumstances. She realizes, however, that her intense need for a promotion has probably induced this depressing picture. Rose wants to explore further to see if the fear culprit has influenced her imagery.

- Has fear influenced my imagery? This is easily tested by her imagining two light bulbs. One has fear response written on it and the other is labeled intuitive response. When she asks what this imagery represents, the fear light bulb lights up.

The next query is

- Is a promotion in sight? To gain some insight into this possibility, Rose imagines that she is a temperature scale. She tells her intuitive mind to have the mercury rise if a promotion is in sight. If not, let the mercury stay stationary or even go down if a demotion is pending. The mercury rises when she focuses on the thermometer image.

- Is the promotion in my present company? Rose wonders if the elevation reflects her status at her present job. She actively creates imagery to see if the door of her company is open or closed. The door is open.

Interpretation: She is satisfied when the door opens but feels incomplete, wondering how she will bide her time until a promotion is finally offered.

Further Interpretation: Rose wants to elicit a symbol that would show what she should be doing in the coming months. In response, her intuitive mind sends an image of a computer as a strong reminder to her that she needs to write a paper for the local management society.

Activating the Solution: Her creative energies will be used productively while waiting for the coveted promotion.

Check Your Upward Mobility Quotient (UMQ)

Do you envision yourself as a rising star about to be discovered? Or have you been passed over for promotion? What imagery can you create to help you answer the following?

Question: What opportunities for upward mobility exist for you at work?

Imagery: Create the image of a thermometer. Does the thermometer rise or fall?

Question: When will significant changes in your job status manifest themselves at work?

Imagery: Create a bar chart. What month has the highest bar? This will show when you will be making a vital move within or out of the company.

Question: Is a promotion slated for the present work setting?

Imagery: Visualize a door. Is it open or closed?

Question: What UMQ rating would you receive on a test?

Imagery: See a number appear. What is the number?

Shouldering Unexpected Responsibility

People often have to assume unexpected responsibility. Do you remember reading about Darwin Clark, General Motor's European vice president in sales, services, and parts, in Chapter Two? His broad shoulders suddenly received a very heavy weight when he was asked to preside over an important conference. After he recovered from the shock of being asked to do that, he realized his intuitive mind would guide him through the situation. The following cases are presented to show how intuitive input quickly reveals how a new responsibility should be handled.

CASE 1: ASSUMING UNEXPECTED RESPONSIBILITY. **Background:** Craig has to take over the meeting agenda for an operations session in place of his boss who has been suddenly called away. Although he is told to "wing his presentation," he is still uncomfortable. He wants to draw everyone together with a strong topic for discussion.

Craig adopts the following strategy:

Problem: What would be a strong topic that would draw everyone together?

Centering: Becoming still is quite a challenge since we have office cubicles where you can be interrupted at any time. Also, the sound of the computer always comes into my consciousness. I look up at the pattern on the ceiling and visualize myself standing in the middle of this geometric design.

Receptivity: Then I use the "hang-sah" breath. I repeat "peace" several times and ask my question.

Imagery: The images of a calendar and Jamie, head of the Claims Department, appear. I become quiet to get a clearer image of a calendar, which shows the months of May and June.

Interpretation: Using the amplification method I discover

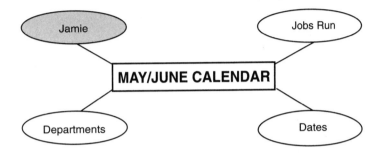

I don't get the connection until I do a word association and link Jamie and the calendar together.

Jamie→calendar→her calendar→production schedule and how it works

Intuition leads me to decide to run a meeting on the production schedule and to get Jamie to assist.

Activating the Solution: The session is excellent. We all learn a lot and Jamie prepares an excellent handout. I also learn that my mind has a cache of creative answers I can tap if only I take the time to be still and listen.

CASE 2: STEPPING INTO NEW SHOES. **Background:** Scott was recently called into a meeting because his boss was about to assign him a new job responsibility. His boss stated, "Scott, you have excellent sales skills. We would like you to work in the field with some of our newer sales representatives to help them get up to speed. I'm sure this will be beneficial to them and you as well, considering that you are studying management in the Masters program." Scott is delighted by the challenges at first, but then becomes concerned about how he will relate to his peers. He wonders how they will react to him in a management position. Since this new assignment is scheduled to begin the following week, he has little time to prepare.

Problem: How should Scott handle the new responsibility with his peers?

Centering: Scott stares at the Ansel Adams painting of a running stream in the woods.

Receptivity: He uses the "hang-sah" breath to relax and focus.

Imagery: Going into the alpha level, he sees two distinct images. One is a handshake and the other is a star.

Interpretation: The handshake suggests that Scott just "be friends," not like a boss, but as an equal with the newer reps. This means he should treat the sales representatives in the same manner he always has, which is as friends. Scott is concerned about appearing to them as a manager or superior, which would probably make them feel uncomfortable. Scott feels that the star is showing him that he is a rising star in the organization. This new assignment is the preparation for his eventual duties as a future sales manager.

Activating the Solution: The advice from his intuitive mind is right on target. By being a friendly advice-giver to the representatives, Scott finds everyone is much more productive than if Scott had done a "power play." By building a comfortable atmosphere, the reps are more open to ideas and constructive criticism from Scott.

EXERCISE

How Big Are Your Shoulders?

Do you suddenly have to "shoulder" responsibility? What will you do? What type of imagery can you create to show you how to handle this weighty responsibility? As a starter, can you imagine your shoulders and see how they will hold up under the weight of the new activity?

_____

_____

Are you smiling or frowning after you assume your new responsibility?

_____

_____

Learning a New Skill

New procedures and innovations are constantly presented in the workplace. Can the proverbial old dogs be receptive to learning new tricks? Often, a supervisor is charged with the weighty task of motivating employees to learn new skills. Here is how Karen (in Case 1) and Kevin (in Case 2) used the intuitive mind to show them how to cope with learning a new skill.

CASE 1: TEACHING YOURSELF A NEW SKILL. **Background:** Karen works in the Cost Accounting Department and is involved in learning a new skill. In this situation, the impetus to learn the new skill and forge through all the difficulties of digesting this new process rests strictly on her shoulders. She is learning how to be a programmer with a "user-friendly" computer language. In the four months she has had this position, Karen is delighted about the opportunity to learn a new skill. Her challenge comes in digesting this difficult program. Karen was the expert in her previous position and knew all the nuances of the job. Now she feels humble by having to learn from scratch again. Karen wonders if she will be up to this challenge. Her boss and coworkers seem to have unlimited faith in her despite the low opinion she is currently maintaining of herself while learning this new computer system.

Problem: Can her mind master this new technique?

Centering: Karen shifts focus to the intuitive mind by staring at the leaves of the plant on her desk. The beautiful symmetry in the greenery of this natural geometric design helps her become more centered.

Receptivity: She does several repetitions of the "reenergizing" breath. Feeling relaxed, she is now able to receive the intuitive imagery.

Imagery: Karen elicits imagery to these questions:

◆ Is she capable of learning new information? To assess her learning potential in this new situation, Karen imagines that she is a glass or pitcher. She closes her eyes and watches the new information pouring into the vessel. She wants to see how the new information comes in and is retained in the vessel. She looks carefully to see if leaks and cracks are present from a strain on the vessel. The imagery she elicits shows that the liquid pouring into the pitcher is easily retained.

◆ When will the learning process become less stressful? To assess the current difficulty and see when the present stress will be alleviated, Karen creates a bar graph. She wants to see when she will easily cope with learning this new information. Her graph showed the days, weeks, and months ahead. The imagery elicited highlights the two-week mark. Knowing this indicates an easier time ahead helps her go forward.

◆ Can the information be assimilated more easily? Though the image of the pitcher shows that she is retaining the new material, Karen still feels uncomfortable. She asks for a symbol showing how she feels about mastering this new information. She sees a large cookie jar that is bursting at the seams.

Interpretation: The associations to her stuffed cookie jar are shown in the following amplification. When this image is presented, Karen realizes she is too full to retain any more.

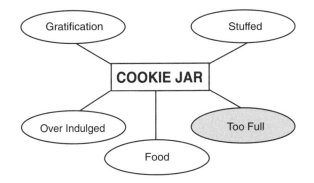

Then Karen asks to be shown what is at the end of the road after the new computer techniques are mastered. She sees herself smiling as a golden glow emanates from her whole body.

Activating the Solution: This intuitive input encourages Karen to press on regardless. However, she does ask her employers for a brief respite so she can practice what she is learning and not have to cram new material into her tired mind. She then knows she will be feeling less stressed in two weeks and will once again resume learning the new skill.

CASE 2: HELPING OTHERS SHARPEN THEIR SKILLS. **Background:** Kevin is the director of engineering for a manufacturing company that produces metal stampings and assemblies for the automotive consumer electronics industries. He supervises a staff of six people.

In addressing the situation, Kevin proceeds as follows:

Problem: How do I develop the computer skills of all my employees without causing them to miss considerable time from work?

Centering: I go into my office, shut the door, and stare at the blank piece of graph paper on my desk.

Imagery: I freely let my associations flow to this "computer problem."

Interpretation: As the amplification diagram shows, I have three people in my department who have advanced computer skills (experts) and three people with minimal computer skills (nonexperts). I want everyone to know the "Timeline" program for project timing charts and also basic Lotus spreadsheets. I know "Timeline" has a tutorial program, so I add this to my diagram. I next think about how to teach basic Lotus 1-2-3. I then think of Mel, the engineer with the most computer expertise. This is what my amplification looks like.

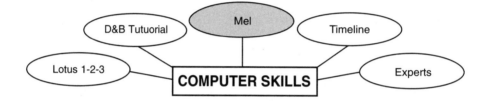

I interpret my amplification to mean that Mel will have a large role in helping me accomplish my goal.

Activating the Solution: I bring Mel into my office and share my amplification with him. He suggests purchasing a Dun & Bradstreet tutorial on Lotus 1-2-3 that he has seen. Then Mel volunteers to lead the program! Mel has had two tutorial sessions with all members of the engineering department. At this time, we are not all computer experts, but we are all learning more and more with each session.

EXERCISE

How Do You Feel About Learning Something New?

Ask your intuitive mind to show you a face that is either smiling or frowning. This will provide feedback about whether you are happy or sad about what you are learning.

_____

_____

Are you too filled with information at this time? To check if you are saturated with information, elicit imagery in the form of a body. How is the shape presented? Is it lean, average sized, or bloated? What is this telling you about how much data you have consumed?

_____

_____

_____

_____

How well will you learn this new technique? Ask for an image showing you using this new technique in your workplace. In addition, create imagery showing you getting congratulations and glowing reports from your coworkers. To solidify this image, you can create an affirmation that will attest to your competency. You might say, "I am feeling more confident learning this new phase of my job."

_____

_____

_____

_____

Create your own affirmation:

_____

_____

_____

_____

USING INTUITIVE PROBLEM-SOLVING TO FOCUS ON ORGANIZATIONAL CONCERNS

In this section, we'll see how the IPS system can add to your on-the-job effectiveness and productivity.

Getting Ideas Across

CASE 1: HOLDING EFFECTIVE MEETINGS. **Background:** Brenda wants to make meetings creative, stimulating, and participative. She proceeds as follows:

Problem: How do I run an effective meeting?

Centering: I close my eyes and repeat the word "relax" several times. I imagine myself lounging on the beach by a lake. The sun feels hot but that is offset by a cool breeze. The waves pound against the shoreline and slowly retreat back into the lake. Sea gulls are flying overhead and diving for fresh fish.

Receptivity: I take three "reenergizing" breaths and begin feeling more relaxed. Then I "tense and release" my muscles.

Imagery: I elicit a red rectangle.

Interpretation: Amplifying, I see that the rectangle could be a table, a sheet of cement, or a hard object.

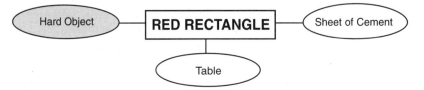

I realize that to be effective in a meeting, I need to take a hard stance. The red of the rectangle tells me that I need to be strong to take a firm line. Additional questions are the following:

◆ Is the meeting held at a good time? I close my eyes and see the sun rising, which reinforces my belief that the meeting should be in the morning before the workday starts, when people are fresh.

◆ What day shall I hold a meeting? I preview banners going by with the days of the week featured. Suddenly, a banner saying Wednesday is elevated.

◆ Will I facilitate a good meeting? I see a number of people sitting together and holding up a sign that has a "+" in the middle. This is positive feedback coming from all the people sitting together.

Further Interpretation: To encourage more ideas, I decide to do a mind map on the effective meeting theme. Just letting my ideas freely flow reveals the following themes. On these "tracks" I have elicited inner feedback concerning the agenda preparation, positive atmosphere, keeping the meeting short, group participation, and ending on a positive note. This map provides a clear scheme of what I need for an effective meeting.

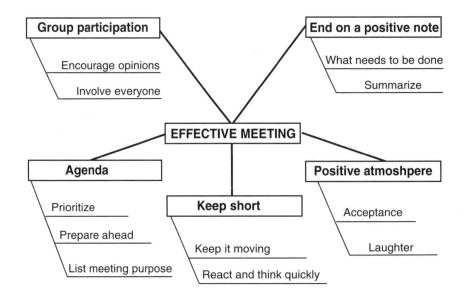

CASE 2: GIVING FEEDBACK TO THE BOSS. **Background:** Bruce plans to meet with his boss John, the executive director of a social service agency. They are scheduled to talk about Bruce's current and future role in the organization, as well as his contributions and performance. Bruce and his boss have worked together for over nine years and know each other well. Although they have often disagreed about issues, Bruce has always tried to be honest and direct with John, which has sometimes caused tension in their relationship. Bruce is wondering whether he should give John some honest feedback about his autocratic and controlling style of management. Although John talks about participative management and empowerment, Bruce feels that John does not always practice this. Several people have left the organization, in large part due to John's authoritarian style. Bruce is motivated to share these comments with John, who invites feedback from others to find out more about the staff's perceptions. Bruce wonders, though, if this evaluation meeting is the right time to present this feedback about John's leadership style in their staff meetings.

Problem: Bruce asks, "Should I give John feedback in our private meeting about his style and how it affects others?"

Centering and Receptivity: Bruce listens to a guided imagery tape and easily projects himself to the trail in the woods.

Imagery: Bruce imagines himself walking along the trail and begins asking, "Should I give John feedback on his management style during the upcoming meeting?" Bruce walks along the trail until he comes to the rock where he sits down to rest. He repeats the question, and almost immediately a very bright, almost blinding, light comes down from the sky. All he can see are the rays of light coming down, much like the sun rays shining through a hole in the clouds. He is surprised at how bright the light is, especially since his eyes are closed.

Interpretation: The words "illumination" and "enlightenment" come to mind right away. Bruce feels that John will be enlightened by the feedback and that he will "see the light." Because the light comes down so fast and is so bright, Bruce is certain his intuition is speaking to him. He is also impressed by how quickly the words "illumination" and "enlightenment" came to him. He realizes he is being given the right solution and decides to give John the feedback.

Resting Period: His logical mind does not agree with this solution, so he lets the problem rest awhile and looks for further imagery or confirmation. Bruce feels that it is quite risky to give John the feedback, even though he will be "getting it off his chest."

Further Interpretation: Bruce tests the answer while out on a long run. Something in him keeps saying, "just do it!" He still has four more days before the meeting. Each time he poses the question, he gets a positive feeling and a sense that it is the right thing to do.

Activating the Solution: When Bruce confronts his boss during his evaluation meeting, the boss receives the feedback quite well. In the next week, John lets his staff air their views more than usual.

Motivating Employees to Work as a Team

CASE 1: MOTIVATING A GROUP TO REMAIN UNIFIED.

Problem: What form of motivation do I implement to motivate a large group to remain unified and focused?

Centering: I repeatedly say the word "motivation" and also focus on a picture of a peaceful setting to become centered.

Receptivity: I use the "reenergizing" breath to control my breathing and the "tense and release" method for relaxation. The instrumental music in the background helps me relax so I can easily enter the alpha level.

Imagery: I start out by imagining a group of people sitting around a campfire and hope this setting will stimulate ideas for a solution. The only image that keeps appearing in the fire is the shape of a triangle or the triangular outline of the dancing fire.

Interpretation: Upon seeing the triangle symbol, I decide to do some clustering to see what this might mean.

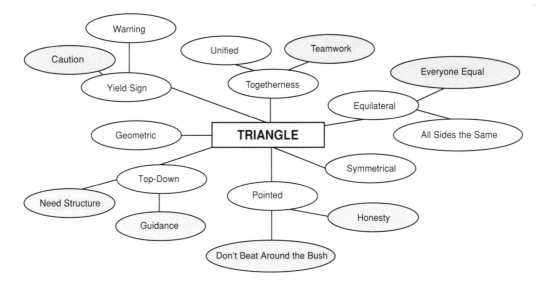

The clustering brings out some interesting facts. I realize that ground rules for teamwork are missing in the group. We have assumed up front that everyone knows what is expected and we have never created a structure outlining responsibilities. While everyone needs the comfort of being honest and equal, this is not happening. The entire teamwork concept has never been laid out. The "yield sign" warns me to be cautious about trying to change the group too quickly.

Activating the Solution: I realize that the basic ingredients for a successful team are missing. We have been together for a long time but have assumed we all know how to act on a team. I suggest that we go back and set up the ground rules, which everyone accepts favorably. We will be introducing some training in this area, and I anticipate positive benefits in our future.

CASE 2: WORKING WITH AN OUTSIDE TEAM. **Background:** Jane owns an advertising agency. Her main love is creating ideas and promotional programs rather than managing a business. She has to make a vital and quick decision about her staff aligning with another company for a national campaign. There are advantages and disadvantages for making this temporary merger. Jane wants the final decision to be in the best interest of her employees and to sustain their motivation for productivity.

Problem: Shall my company temporarily merge with another company in the upcoming campaign?

Centering: To arrive at an immediate decision, Jane decides to take herself for an imaginary walk in the woods. She stands at the base of a mountain and notices how the fresh snow glitters like diamonds. The sky is clear with only occasional wisps of clouds. Jane walks into the woods, which is beautiful. The snow is clinging to the branches of the trees. There is a large variety of trees, including red pine, white pine, oak, and maple. In walking through the woods, she hears the chirping of birds and sees small sparrows flying about. She even notices a red tailed hawk. Continuing, she sees deer tracks and wonders where the deer are. Coming to an empty deer blind, Jane sits down to elicit an intuitive resolution for the merger problem.

Receptivity: In this perfect spot, Jane focuses on nature and then takes three "total" breaths and does a "progressive" relaxation.

Imagery: Jane sees herself at a staff meeting with members from both companies. She is listening and taking parts of ideas from one person and combining them with pieces from someone else. She creates a beautiful tapestry with these various views. She wants to find a title for this finished product, which she knows reflects the merger decision. There are two distinct groups of ideas with their indigenous patterns in the tapestry. She intuitively labels the piece "merging views" and clearly knows the merger will be effective.

Activating the Solution: The label of merging views gives Jane clear intuitive input. She is satisfied and confident that she is making the right decision by deciding to join forces with the other company. By aligning with another company, Jane now realizes that her workers will be motivated to perform.

EXERCISE

Make an Important Managerial Decision

Take yourself to the woods using Jane's images from her "fantasy retreat" to create a special receptivity environment. As the CEO, manager, or unit leader, you have to make an important managerial decision. You want the managers and department heads to cooperate so you can work regularly together for the good of the entire organization.

What imagery can you elicit to create a united vision?

_____

_____

Are any of the pictures unclear? Use the amplification technique to unravel any of your symbolism.

IMPLEMENTING INTUITIVE STRATEGIES
IN THE ORGANIZATION

I have always been impressed with this story about the successful exploits of business magnate Conrad Hilton as he climbed the ladder to success by listening to his intuitive mind. The following excerpt is an example of Hilton's intuitive mind at work.

"No businessman likes sealed bids," Conrad Hilton remarked, yet he too managed to deal with them. During World War II, Hilton decided that if he couldn't own Chicago's Stevens Hotel, which had been taken over by the Air Force, then he'd like to own the Stevens Corporation. The company's other assets might prove profitable, and he'd have a line on the hotel if the government released it. The Stevens Corporation trustees called for sealed bids.

"My first bid, hastily made, was $165,000." Hilton recalls. "Then, somehow, that didn't feel right to me. Another figure, $180,000, kept coming to mind. It satisfied me. It seemed fair. It felt right. I changed my bid to the larger figure on that hunch. When they were opened, the closest bid to mine was $179,800. I got the Stevens Corporation by a narrow margin of $200. Eventually the assets returned me $2 million."

Many businesspeople have talked about the need "to intuitively peer into the envelope" when sealed bids are involved. Leon Hess of Hess-Getty Oil also admits that his hunches frequently give him a clear picture of what the other sealed bids will be and have helped him make profitable bids.

Have you ever made a decision without relying on facts and figures for support? Too often, intuitive insights are ignored because these intangible ideas don't have a logical base. The examples in this last section show how to use intuition to

- Achieve a quick and innovative solution.

- Sell a new approach to others.

CASE 1: ACHIEVING A QUICK AND INNOVATIVE SOLUTION. **Background:** Kim finds herself in a dilemma over a "pricing problem" that has had her stumped for several weeks. All the pricing methods and procedures are so different that she is unable to develop a record layout and supporting file structure to handle all the variations.

Kim states her problem as follows:

Problem: "How do I handle the pricing problem for the manufacturing project I am designing for a client?"

Centering: She begins by affirming that her intuitive mind has the answer and will help her find the right solution.

Receptivity: Kim does the "total" breath and used the "tense and release" relaxation technique.

Imagery: The image that she elicits is that of a baby bottle.

Interpretation: Using the amplification method, she began associating to the baby bottle and thinks of things like

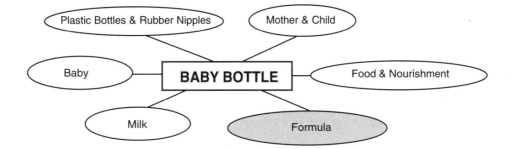

Formula is the symbol that seems to fit her pricing problem. She has not thought of using the pricing formulas to drive the file structure. The record layouts can be the same format; only the pricing formulas will be different. Formulas, the arithmetic kind, not the baby food variety, can be used to handle all the different pricing relationships. The records can all be the same format, while the formulas could be used to handle the variability.

Activating the Solution: This is best described in Kim's words as she comments, "I can't express how important this formula discovery is. I have spent so much time trying to figure this problem out. I only wish I had used the intuitive problem-solving process earlier. I have laid out the necessary structure for the project, and our data base administrator has approved the layout. He even questioned me on how I was able to come up with such a creative idea!"

CASE 2: SELLING A NEW APPROACH TO OTHERS. **Background:** Barry is a senior project planner in charge of distribution planning for new products. He feels that success in the introduction of new products hinges on many factors which cannot be calculated. He laments that most of the management team is numbers oriented, relying on the "data." Although distribution planning by way of gut feelings is replacing much of his previous use of analysis, Barry's area of concern is how to sell his intuitive decisions and influence others to break with their reliance on pure data in decision making.

He states his problems as

Problems: "How do I communicate a plan I know is correct without having factual support?" and "How do I encourage others to use their intuition along with logic in their decision making?"

Centering: Barry looks at the pattern in his carpeted office.

Receptivity: Then he begins to relax by taking three deep breaths to a count of six when inhaling and exhaling. To become more relaxed, he imagines himself at the top of a flight of stairs walking down ten steps. As he takes each step, he feels more and more relaxed.

Imagery: Barry wonders how to encourage his associates to be more open-minded to intuitive decision-making practices. He creates imagery in which he is attending a lecture on "Implementing Intuitive Management Strategies in Your Company." He hears suggestions given and notices that others are impressed.

Interpretation: He starts thinking of how national leaders and innovators have let intuitive thinking influence their decisions and major inventions. He realizes that everything in the room was once started as an intuitive light bulb in the inventor's mind. He looks down at the self-adhesive memo pad and recalls that this idea was initially generated at the 3M company.

Activating the Solution: Armed with several examples of innovation within and outside his company, he had viable cases of "intuition in action" to share with others.

EXERCISE

Organizational Feedback

Intuitively, discover more about your company by comparing it to a person. What do you learn by describing the age, function, and any other developmental features?

_____

_____

_____

_____

EXERCISE

Implementing Intuitive Thinking

How can you intuitively keep one step ahead of your boss or supervisor to know what he or she is thinking? How can you implement creative thinking to develop programs for the company's benefit and anticipate future needs?

_____

_____

_____

EXERCISE

Anticipating Future Needs

As a product manager, you are in communication with suppliers, production facilities, and customers. Many times when you are setting up new products, you have to anticipate future problems. How can you learn to substantiate your gut feelings? Would keeping a record of your intuitive hits and misses in a journal help?

_____

_____

_____

_____

You have discovered that it is easier to explain your "gut feeling" to your boss or customer if you can provide fairly concrete reasons. How do you step back and view the whole situation so you can give a tenable explanation to support your intuitive input?

_____

_____

_____

_____

EXERCISE

Your Business Problems

Did these situations remind you of any pressing concerns in your work environment? Use this space to formulate any problems of your own so you can continue to use IPS for retrieving intuitive resolutions.

_____

_____

_____

_____

You are now ready to go to Chapter Twelve. There, you will find out how IPS can be used to clear up misunderstandings with other people, get a deeper look into an individual's character, and discover how to approach others with equanimity.

Chapter Twelve

USING INTUITION TO IMPROVE ON-THE-JOB RELATIONSHIPS

Cease trying to work everything out with your minds. It will get you nowhere. Live by intuition and inspiration and let your whole life be a Revelation.

EILEEN CADDY
Footprints on the Path

When all cogs function properly, the wheel readily turns and goes forward. The cogs in this situation are the full cast of characters in the work environment. This includes the "directors" at the top and the "people they direct" or support staff. Productivity is ensured when satisfied people at all levels work efficiently.

Troublesome interpersonal relationships often halt progress. The cases presented in this chapter show how IPS input is used to gain an understanding of someone's personality, heal past wounds, and correct faulty perceptions so productive operations can be resumed.

In this chapter the interpersonal relations in need of improvement stem from

- Difficulties with superiors.
- Dissatisfaction with support staff.
- Strained relationships among coworkers.
- Need to adjust to a new environment.
- Requirement for cooperation to achieve greater productivity.
- Customer and/or client problems.
- Human Resource problems.

DIFFICULTIES WITH SUPERIORS

Approaching a boss or superior can be an awesome task. Yet choosing the right approach is the gateway to success. The dilemma in Case 1 is resolved by raising a number of specific questions in the IPS process. In Case 2, a basic image produces enough clarity about a situation to solve the problem. In each example, what seems intimidating becomes probable and possible after an intuitive insight is gleaned and acted upon.

CASE 1: BECOMING COMFORTABLE WITH A "NEW" BOSS

Problem: How can Linda become more comfortable with her new boss?

Centering: Linda darkens her living room blinds to shut out the bright light except for a stream of sunlight shining through. Focusing on that stream, she repeats the word "peace" several times.

Receptivity: Sitting on her living room couch, Linda slowly takes some deep breaths and wiggles her toes. She becomes calm and relaxed.

Imagery: She poses the following questions to get clarity about her problem.

- Do I unconsciously fear my boss or feel inferior in some way? The first image presented is a picture of a serene beach. She decides that neither feelings of fear or inferiority apply to their relationship.

- If my boss were an animal or object, what would he be? The image of a clown dancing and holding a ruler appears in her mind. Using amplification, many related associations surface.

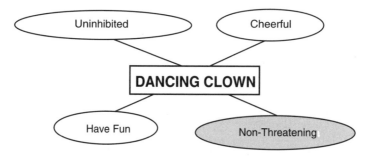

The underlying meaning is still elusive so Linda continues to probe.

- Is the uneasiness I feel in our relationship controllable by me? If so, how? She imagined two signs next to each other. One reads "Parking" and the other, "No parking."

  The "Parking" sign sways back and forth when this question is posed. She then asks "Why?" and the image of a long list of paper appears.

- Does this list mean I have too many tasks or projects? Since no image comes to mind, solving this problem is becoming difficult. She thinks about the original problem again and tries to associate to the clown and list. The only other picture that emerges shows a dimly lit light bulb.

Interpretation: Putting together the various images becomes revealing. The clown represents a nonthreatening boss that Linda doesn't fear or feel intimidated by in any way.

This reminds her that the boss is actually likable and much fun. The clown holding a ruler represents the authoritative power the boss holds over Linda. The picture of the list is initially confusing until she realizes this reflects demands or goals she places on herself. The light bulb still makes no sense.

When she ignores the clown image and thinks of the list and bulb, she begins to make more connections. She feels the list represents objectives or tasks on her mind. She wonders if she needs to share these tasks with her boss. In reflection, she really wants the opportunity to sit down and get to know him better and discuss her personal and work objectives.

Suddenly, the imagery begins to make perfect sense to Linda. Sharing her goals will not only help her boss know her job expectations but will invite feedback from him. She feels this will add comfort and increased understanding to the relationship.

Activating the Solution: Linda schedules a lunch meeting with her boss to discuss her work goals and expectations.

CASE 2: COMMUNICATING WITH A BOSS

Problem: Why am I having difficulty communicating with my boss?

Centering: Sitting in my room, I hear the rain falling down. It reminds me of an environmental sound cassette tape. I watch the oscillating fan.

Receptivity: I begin my breathing and concentrate on the noise of the fan and smell of the rain.

Imagery: I imagine a closed door and retrieve the following associations to my amplification.

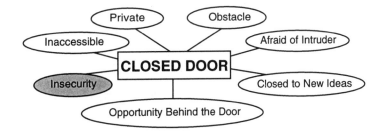

The word insecurity is associated with the closed door. To understand this association and achieve further clarity, I pose the following questions:

♦ Does this insecurity belong to me or my boss? I try to see a traffic light. Red represents my boss and green is me. I see the red light flashing and know the insecurity is his.

♦ Is there something I can do to help my boss feel more secure in our relationship? I see a deck of cards. The card I turn over says "yes."

♦ What can I do? I see the image of a teddy bear.

Interpretation: Amplifying to this symbol reveals the following:

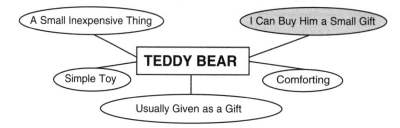

My boss is avoiding me because he is insecure. He is afraid of me for some reason and probably views me as a threat to his position. I have to make the first move to help him feel secure, which can be giving him a small gift to help ease the tension.

Activating the Solution: I will buy him a cup of coffee and reassure him that I am on his team and am not after his job. Next week, I will have to insist that we take time out and sit down together.

DISSATISFACTION WITH SUPPORT STAFF

Case 1 addresses serious infractions that could have engendered more resentment and caused further deterioration of the relationship between a supervisor and employees if the insight provided by IPS hadn't been considered. In Cases 2 and 3, the challenge of improving communication so parties can be clearly understood is aided through the intuitive input.

CASE 1: DISCIPLINING AN EMPLOYEE. **Background**: Paul manages several supervisors who handle the daily interactions with the production workers. One of these supervisors asks Paul's opinion about disciplining an employee. The reason for the potential disciplinary action is that the individual had called in to say he will miss work, but not in the timely fashion expected by the supervisor. He doesn't call in until noon. To make the situation even more difficult, the employee in question is just an average worker, not a standout, but not a troublemaker either.

If they do not discipline this individual, the entire work team might look at this action as a sign of favoritism or weakness on the part of the supervisor. Also, the employee in question might then continue with this unacceptable behavior. If they do discipline the person, the favoritism and weakness issues will not materialize. The employee will know he needs to adhere to and respect the company's policy.

Paul asks the following question:

Problem: How should we discipline?

Centering: I begin to ask this question as I lie in bed in the evening prior to falling asleep. To become centered, I listen to the Deuter *Cicada* audiocassette tape. The pattern on the ceiling wall is great to focus upon.

Receptivity: I take several deep breaths and then "tense and release" my muscles to relax more.

Imagery: The thought of soccer comes to mind after I pose the discipline question.

Interpretation: As I began to associate to the word "soccer," another cluster appears to the word coaching.

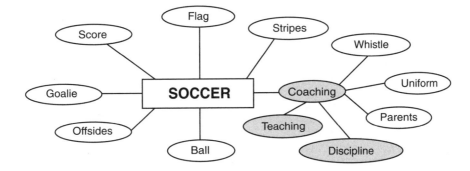

I ask, "Should we discipline?" and think about a stoplight with the red light on. This sets me back because I really want to go to sleep. Then I turn to teaching, the other term that is prominent, and ask, "Should we teach rather than discipline?" Now I feel an urge to get up and write the IPS steps down. I think about teaching, which is working with the individual to find out what is wrong. The teacher should take the time to help correct the problem before it goes too far. The result might be discipline, as everyone knows a teacher must be able to control the environment so everyone benefits and learns.

As I think about teaching, the image of a chalkboard becomes clear, so I know teaching or, in this case, one-on-one discussion of the problem and our expectations, is in order.

Activating the Solution: I recommend that the supervisor take the time to talk to the individual to find out what is wrong. I also encourage him to invite our human resource representative to attend the meeting. Consequently, they discover that this person is having a serious marital problem and is contemplating divorce. The fight the night before the absence lasted most of the night. The employee is gently reminded that he needs to manage his personal problems effectively so they don't end up costing him his job. To that end, the human resource representative also sets up a counseling appointment for the employee and his wife.

CASE 2: HANDLING MISPLACED ANGER. Background: A working relationship became embittered when Sue, the secretary, lost out on a promotion, which resulted in animosity being directed at Linda, her boss. Other incidents also resulted in strained communication. Examining the problem logically, Linda decides that the issue is not whether Sue treated her fairly but if she treated Sue fairly. Also, it does not matter if Sue likes her as long as the job is performed adequately.

Linda formulates the following three questions:

Problems: "Is Sue getting her job done?" "What would make Sue happier in her job? How can I better supervise Sue?"

Centering: To attain inner stillness, Linda goes for a walk during lunch hour and finds a park bench on a bridge overlooking the river. Listening to the water, she repeats the phrase, "Let it flow."

Receptivity: Linda starts breathing deeply. With closed eyes, her body relaxes, starting with the feet and ending with her head. Linda pictures herself strolling along the lake shore trail. As the sun warms her body, the smell of the fresh water mixed with pine trees fills her senses. She walks down a set of steps in the trail leaving her cares and responsibilities behind.

Imagery: Linda repeats the three questions to retrieve imagery to resolve her dilemma.

- ◆ Is Sue's job getting done? An image appears showing the side view of an open eye looking forward.

- ◆ What would make Sue happy? After quite a while, a butterfly appears.

- ◆ How can I better supervise Sue? A collie appears.

Interpretation: Using amplification for the eye reveals the following associations:

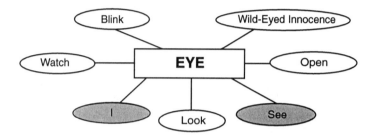

The obvious solution is that Linda should see if Sue is getting her work done. This simple solution makes sense, since Linda has avoided all contact with Sue for the past three weeks and cannot realistically know whether Sue's work is getting done unless someone complains. The eye looking forward reminds Linda to look forward and not let the past taint her present review of Sue's performance.

The amplification to the butterfly brings to mind

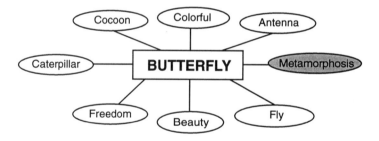

The association with metamorphosis really "rings a bell" since this is characterized by a marked change in appearance, character, condition, or function. Since Sue has been doing the same type of work for over 17 years, Linda feels that Sue might be craving a "marked change" or metamorphosis.

Amplification to the collie leads to

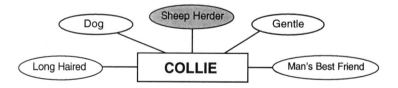

The sheep herder provides the strong "Ah'ha!" since Linda feels collies are gentle but firm in their responsibility to herd the sheep. They beckon them on with a bark, run playfully with the leaders, and circle around to nip at the heels of the sheep lagging behind. She realizes that she needs to gently but firmly remind Sue that she, not Sue, is the boss.

Activating the Solution: She continued thinking of how the sheep herder never stops the progress of the herd but rounds up the slow sheep and encourages them to keep up with the pack. Linda realizes that she doesn't want to inhibit Sue's productivity by interfering with Sue's way of doing things, but she feels a greater commitment to notice when things fall behind so she can "nip at Sue's heels." Finally, after retrieving this IPS solution, Linda comments, "The communication problem with Sue has been weighing on my mind for a long time, and for the first time in months I feel at peace with the situation."

EXERCISE

How to Heal Disagreements

Have you had a disagreement or misunderstanding with someone in your work environment in the past six months? Close your eyes and picture this person facing you.

Are they smiling or frowning?

_____

Record any other impressions you are getting about how they are thinking or feeling.

_____

_____

Notice their hands. How are they placed? For example, are they reaching out to you, or are they held behind the back?

_____

_____

Activate your image of this person by imagining they are walking toward you and then whispering something in your ear. You are hearing the words or message they would like you to say to heal this disagreement. Can you write down what they are saying?

_____

_____

_____

_____

CASE 3: ACHIEVING HARMONY ON A NEW ASSIGNMENT. **Background**: Kelly is a senior quality engineer at General Motors. As a group leader in supplier development and certification, her responsibilities include leading and developing five quality engineers. She is also responsible for the purchased parts quality on the heating ventilation and air conditioning systems on three car lines. Her new department assignment is acting as a quality coach to seven buyers. A coworker, Matt, has been given a similar assignment to coach six different buyers. She knows it is important that they are consistent in their coaching method and approach. She has worked with him before and knows he is someone who prefers working alone. His ideas are good but he doesn't volunteer them very readily.

Kelly poses the following problem and tells us how IPS provided the guidelines to interacting with Matt.

Problem: How do I work effectively with Matt in our new assignment?

Centering: I come home from work, turn on the ceiling fan, and concentrate on it spinning slowly around and around.

Receptivity: As I am doing this, I practice the "hang-sah" breath and do the "tense and relax" technique.

Imagery: I close my eyes and ask about working effectively with Matt in our new assignment. The image that presents itself is a fiery red ball.

Interpretation: I use amplification to interpret what this means. The words that came to mind are "hot," "brilliant sunrise," "comet," "explosion," "simmering," and "bright idea." The words that stand out are "hot" and "brilliant sunrise." The word hot means to me that our new assignment is a hot one and that we don't have any time to waste getting started. Brilliant sunrise means that this assignment is a new beginning for both of us to improve our working relationship.

Activating the Solution: The imagery tells me that I need to get started on my new assignment right away; procrastinating is the last thing to do. This assignment will give us a new opportunity to put our skills and creative minds together to implement the concept of the quality coach. Instead of dreading our teamwork, I will now see it more positively as a new beginning.

EXERCISE

How to Understand a Coworker

Imagine stepping into the shoes of a coworker you just had a misunderstanding with to see how that person feels about the discomfort from this situation. Answer these questions as if you were the other person.

How do you "feel" emotionally about this dispute?

_____

What do you "think" caused it?

_____

_____

What must you "do" to satisfactorily repair the situation?

_____

_____

_____

What intuitive input have you received by "stepping into this person's shoes" to answer the last three questions?

_____

_____

_____

_____

ADJUSTING TO A NEW ENVIRONMENT

Someone coming into a "new" work environment can feel bewildered and lost. Do you remember how you felt when you first started your job? Often, responsibilities arise that need to be clarified. That is why those first few weeks and even months on the job can be confusing and sometimes overwhelming. The following two cases show how to help someone new adapt in the work environment.

CASE 1: HELPING A NEW ASSISTANT ADJUST

Problem: Will the new rehabilitation assistant stay on the job?

Centering: Anita sits in her study, stares at a vase with geometric lines carved into it, and repeats the focusing phrase, "Be peaceful and you will know." Then, she lights a scented barberry candle and plays a Paul Horn tape.

Receptivity: She uses the "hang-sah" breath along with the "stretching and breathing" technique.

Imagery: When Anita poses the question, "Will the new rehab assistant stay on the job?" she asks her intuitive mind to show her a picture of this new assistant smiling if she is going to stay. She knows if the picture is glum, the assistant will be leaving soon. The picture shows the assistant laughing. From this, Anita knows that her assistant will be staying in the position. She then asks, "How can I best help her learn and perform successfully?" She is presented with the image of a dark green candle with a flickering orange flame.

Interpretation: Anita looks at the candle and uses amplification to make the following associations:

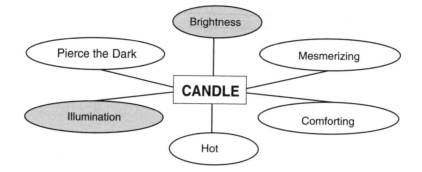

With this interpretation, Anita realizes her assistant is a bright person who does not require a lot of direction. She realizes that the training approach should concentrate on the job responsibilities to illuminate the necessary points. Then, she knows that the green candle color signifies a relationship that will bring prosperity. The orange flame suggests that the assistant's personality will be a balanced one, unlike the previous assistant's.

Activating the Solution: Anita resolves to be available and helpful but not overbearing. She knows the new assistant will absorb a lot from experiencing the basics on the job.

CASE 2: COMMUNICATING WITH A NEW MANAGER. Jenny is frustrated with her "new" manager. They communicate only when they absolutely must. The new manager frequently offends Jenny by giving directives without explanation. Jenny then proceeds to carry out the assignment in a state of confusion and resentment.

Jenny asks,

Problem: "How can I open communication with my manager?"

Centering: Jenny focuses on a pattern in the carpet under her feet to feel more receptive.

Relaxation: Then, she uses the "reenergizing" breath to relax and clear her mind.

Imagery: Using the metaphor technique, she thinks of her boss and elicits the image of a mouse.

Interpretation: The amplification to this metaphor reveals the following:

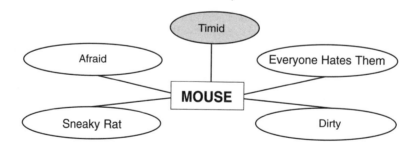

At first she thinks of her boss as a dirty, sneaky rat, but when the word timid comes up, things are put into a different perspective. Rather than appearing as sneaky or as attempting to hide something, Jenny realizes that her boss is afraid to talk to her. Jenny feels that whenever she approaches her boss, it is as if he can't wait to get rid of her.

Activating the Solution: Doing this exercise changes Jenny's entire attitude and behavior. Instead of going in with the attitude of "he'd better let me do this," Jenny approaches him and asks for his ideas and what he thinks. Jenny is amazed by the difference and admits that she attracted a lot of the initial negativity by the limiting attitude she held of her boss.

EXERCISE

Understanding How a New Employee Feels

Try to understand how a new person is adapting to your work environment by using the metaphor technique. See this new person as an "animal" and as a "piece of furniture." Do an amplification and word association for both metaphors. Intuitively, what information are you receiving from these metaphors to help you understand this new person?

Amplification:

Word Association:

Intuitive Interpretation:

_____

_____

_____

_____

GAINING COOPERATION FOR GREATER PRODUCTIVITY

There are times when a disagreement involves more than two participants, so the tension is felt among all the team members. Cases 1 and 2 show how to use IPS to find out how to achieve cohesiveness within the team.

CASE 1: MONITORING STAFF. **Background**: Dale, an assistant vice president and credit manager at a bank, has the following concern about her staff. She feels that three staff members, one clerical and two at the management level, are becoming nonproductive because of their excessive socializing in the office. This also affects other people within the very open work environment. Dale constantly reminds the "frivolous three" about these disruptive conversations. Although they are oblivious to their noisy impact on others, they have to be made aware initially that these distractions are adversely effecting productivity. The following question is posed to elicit intuitive input for resolving this dilemma.

Problem: How can excessive socializing in the workplace be handled?

Centering and Receptivity: Dale retreats to her favorite beach. Walking along, she felt the sand beneath her feet. When she sits down to watch the waves breaking on the shore, she becomes mesmerized and rapidly enters the alpha level of awareness.

Imagery: Dale imagines everyone at a cocktail party and watches as all the employees spontaneously form small groups. The three socializers are closely linked with each other.

Interpretation: From this observation, Dale is able to formulate break groups—small groups who will be taking breaks at the same time. She realizes that by allowing the three to take breaks together, she will alleviate their need to socialize on the job.

Activating the Solution: Later, Dale announces these break groups to the company. She adds 10 minutes to the usual break time as a special bonus to compensate for the fact that employees are unable to socialize on the job due to the open environment. Dale tactfully suggests that a longer break will help everyone get the talking out of their system so they can settle down to work.

CASE 2: RESOLVING TENSIONS AMONG THE MANAGEMENT TEAM. **Background**: John is second in command of a large metropolitan Urban League. The president of the League has recently taken a new position. When he left, he asked John along with two other officers to work as a management team. With the concurrence of the advisory board, he also appointed John interim president. Immediately, this arrangement created an inherent structural problem. The outgoing president empowered the management team to make decisions on all matters. Although John is given the responsibility for the agency, he doesn't have any authority. When several problems related to this structure come up the first week, John makes decisions he believes are within his authority. This upsets the other management team members. John uses IPS to come up with a solution.

Problem: How do we resolve the tensions in the team which this structure has created?

Centering: I sit out on the porch of the house we are building and listened to the natural sound of the crickets making music. I affirm that "my intuitive mind will show me to the right solution."

Receptivity: After taking five "hang-sah" breaths, I feel totally relaxed.

Imagery: When I present the problem for my intuitive mind to work on, I don't get a visual image but become aware of the sound from the spring peepers in the wetland down the road from our house. Spring peepers are small tree frogs that become active at dusk and dawn. Part of their mating process is hundreds of them filling the air with a peep-peep-peep chorus.

Interpretation: The imagery by way of the sounds first seems quite removed, and I wonder if I come up with it simply because it is dusk. I come up with the following associations to the spring peepers: a lot of noise from something so tiny, part of nature, they stop peeping when you get near them, and not a bad or obnoxious sound but a pleasant reminder of spring. The one that jumps out at me is that tree frogs get quiet when you get close to where they are. I interpret that to mean I should address the issue directly with the others, which will quiet the "noise" they are making.

Resting Period: I am not altogether comfortable with the imagery or my interpretation of it, so I decide to let it rest awhile. The next morning, I get up early to go running. As I ran down the driveway, I hear the peepers get quiet as I approach. That reminds me of the image, so I let my subconscious mind dwell on the question as I run. When I return, I feel more comfortable with the imagery and the interpretation.

Further Interpretation: While running, some of the different parts of the problem come to mind as well as ways to address them: put the issue on the agenda for our regular weekly staff meeting, note the various components of the issue, and invite discussion.

Activating the Solution: We have the staff meeting today and it goes well. We agree there is an inherent dilemma in the structure, and for the first time the others agree that if I am to be interim president, then some authority goes with the responsibility. We outline, at least in broad strokes, how that will work in the day-to-day operation of the agency.

EXERCISE

Creating a Positive Attitude

As a manager, you are concerned about creating a positive attitude among the employees which could increase worker morale. How would you visualize the necessary steps to make this change?

_____

_____

Does a schism exist between management and the employees? Note in your imagery what you can do to bridge this gap. Then use a bridge image to connect these two groups. Describe your "bridging the gap" imagery to resolve this problem.

_____

_____

_____

_____

EXTENDING A HELPING HAND
TO A CUSTOMER AND/OR CLIENT

The next two cases focus on the need to create a positive impression when approaching a client or customer. Often, one is focused only on their own situation and blinded to the circumstances of the person they are trying to approach. When reaching out to others, intuitive input can provide a wealth of information to reveal the needs of the other person in the situation.

CASE 1: REACHING OUT TO CLIENTS

Problem: What is the best way to approach the new sectors of my market area?

Centering: Betty first approaches this problem in her office. It is morning, so the building is quiet and peaceful. She keeps the lights off in the office and watches the morning sun filter through the blinds. She sits back in her chair and looks at the plant on the desk until she begins feeling receptive.

Receptivity: She becomes totally receptive by relaxing all her muscles using the "autogenic" technique.

Imagery: The following questions are posed to help her resolve the main problem.

- Should I approach each customer personally after researching them through various sources? In her mind, she sees two light bulbs. The one on the right is labeled "researched approach." The one on the left is labeled "casual approach," representing her just dropping by and introducing herself. The bulbs are both dark until the one on the left lights up. This suggests it would be more efficient to introduce herself briefly to customers. Betty is confused because the left light is blinking and she waits for the other light to do something. It remains darkened. Then she asks the following questions:

- How much time do I spend with each customer? Betty imagines a clock on the wall and watches the hands move. They keep moving and finally stop at 10:00. She takes this to mean that her initial meeting with customers should be a brief 10 minutes.

- How often do I need to meet with each customer on the average? She takes a deep breath and sees a blank chalkboard in her inner mind. Suddenly a bunch of numbers appear on the board ranging from 0 to 15. These don't make any sense, and when she tries to read a pattern into them, the board becomes blank and no other numbers appear.

Interpretation: Betty pieces these images together one by one. The light bulb lighting up and blinking might mean that it would be best for her to initially introduce herself to the new customers. Perhaps she should also do limited research on the larger clients who would be able to give her a larger volume of business. This sounds not only plausible but not quite as time consuming as this project first seemed. Ten minutes or so would give her enough time for the introduction and help her learn more about each customer. The numbers on the chalkboard don't make any sense, and Betty finally concludes that there is no set number of times or frequency that she should call on a customer. In the final analysis, it depends on their needs.

Activating the Solution: Betty is in the process of detailing which customers are in the new market and which businesses are working with a competitor. She plans to use this information to make informal business visits so she can introduce herself and discover their needs.

CASE 2: NEGOTIATING A PRICE

Problem: How can I approach my supplier regarding a price reduction?

Centering: I practice IPS at work in my office by focusing on the wall, which is covered by fabric. The material has lines in it which make you think it has depth.

Receptivity: While practicing the "total" breath, I get "still" and take another trip to the house of intuition.

Imagery: As I walk through the door, I instantly feel the peacefulness in this home. I sit in the chair next to the fireplace and feel very relaxed. Then, the cigar box on the end of the table catches my attention. Opening it, I find an assortment of coins.

Interpretation: When associating to the word "coins," I form a cluster to the word "nickel."

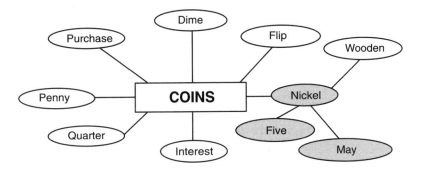

Rest Period: I let this imagery rest for a few days and consult my boss on how I should approach this supplier.

Further Interpretation: I recommend to my boss that we request a 5 cent piece price reduction in May of this year.

EXERCISE

Determining How to Successfully Approach Someone

Imagine you, too, have to approach someone. Close your eyes and imagine your hand reaching out to receive a closed envelope. You open the envelope to discover what you have to do to successfully approach this person. This message can come in words or pictures. Record what you find in the envelope. Use your favorite interpretation technique to find out what this means.

_____

_____

_____

_____

USING INTUITIVE PROBLEM-SOLVING
FOR ACCURATE HUMAN RESOURCE DECISIONS

Anyone concerned with the human relations activities of hiring and firing can affirm the invaluable role intuition plays in these processes. For example, you might be looking at a well-dressed person with a pleasant demeanor when your intuitive voice tells you that you "can't judge a book by its cover."

Throughout his professional career, Jim Adamson, now CEO of Burger King, has interviewed many people. He believes that although you've got the resume for evaluation purposes, what often ends up happening in an interview is based on chemistry between both people and what your gut tells you. He feels the intuitive mind, or gut reaction, during the hiring process is an important key to determining how the person is going to work. He also cautions that intuition must be accompanied by logically evaluating the individual's experience as well. He recalls interviewing some people who he thought would be fantastic, but the background checks showed that they were not right for the job. This underscores the need for the logical and intuitive minds to work together for effective hiring decisions.

Cases 1 and 2 show how IPS can be invaluable as a guide to hiring decisions and evaluating employees.

CASE 1: CHOOSING THE RIGHT PERSON FOR THE JOB. **Background**: Larry is a respiratory therapist in a hospital. He has just been given the go-ahead to hire two full-time individuals (or enough people to make up these positions). So far, he has interviewed six people and has to make a final decision in two weeks. Two of the applicants want the full-time positions and four want the part-time positions. These positions have never been offered in Larry's department, so he wants to make the right choice. The individuals must be of high quality, not only in their expertise but also in their grasp of the importance of customer service. Larry's is not an easy decision to make because each candidate is of extremely high character and has his or her own special abilities to offer.

> *Problem*: Who should I hire?
>
> *Centering*: I relax in my office by focusing on the leaves of a nearby plant.
>
> *Receptivity*: I take two "total" breaths followed by the "tense and release" technique.
>
> *Imagery*: I decide to use the stoplight approach of red, green, or yellow. Opening myself to suggestion, I start to imagine the essence of each of the six candidates and then concentrate on the stoplight. Nancy, who wants a full-time position, comes out yellow/green. She appears to be the perfect therapist, but I am concerned that she could easily become bored with my small facility and want the excitement of a big-city hospital. I believe the two colors mean I should hire her but be sure to give her enough of a challenge to make it worthwhile for her to stay. It might be beneficial to give her some free reign in designing some of her own job description.
>
> Esther, who wants full time, shows red. I'm not really sure why, since she is extremely capable. One of my nursing friends who has worked with her tells me she is a "know it all." Maybe I'm somewhat uneasy about this fact. I sure don't want someone who's questioning all my decisions.
>
> Two other candidates, Jana and Kerri, immediately come up green. They both want part-time positions and can create one full-time equivalent between the two of them.

Both these women lack confidence but are very bright. I feel they will blossom into valuable assets with a little coaching and experience.

Then, the last two possibilities both flash red on my stoplight. The woman is not sure at all if she wants to leave the institution she's at now, and she also wants a raise, which is hard to come by at the present time. The man wants a part-time position in addition to the full-time one he already has. This would prove to be rather inflexible as I need people who can cover each other at a moment's notice.

Interpretation: I have identified the three candidates who would be my choices for hiring, since they all received a green light.

Activating the Solution: I feel confident about extending the offers next week.

CASE 2: EVALUATING AN EMPLOYEE. Background: Kerry is a supervisor in the Supplier Quality Department of General Motors in Lansing, Michigan. In this capacity, she is responsible for completing employee appraisals.

When it is difficult to complete a particular employee's yearly appraisal, she asks her intuitive mind to show her what to do.

Problem: What closing comments shall I use to complete Dana's appraisal?

Centering: I go into my office and start shutting down my noisy logical mind by looking at the picture on the wall.

Receptivity: I listen to the breathing exercises on Jim Emery's tape. Through the exercises, I become more aware of inhaling through my nose and exhaling through my mouth. Slowly, I start to relax, my face tingles and I feel the tension release out of my back, shoulders, and neck. My mind starts to relax.

Imagery: The tape ends as I focus on the appraisal I need to complete. My mind is clear of all cluttered thoughts. I see myself writing down Dana's strengths in a concise and organized manner, and then move to the areas she needs to improve upon. Mentally, I start to list the skills Dana needs to work on to achieve his career goals. The list includes leadership, assertiveness, verbal and written communication, and taking the initiative to resolve problems.

Interpretation: In the area where Dana needs to improve his skills, the words leadership and assertiveness stand out to me. When I examine this further, I realize that he needs to improve his skills in these two areas in the upcoming year to significantly help himself toward his career goals. My job is to identify and let him know what areas he is weak in, and then provide ongoing coaching and development for him so that he can improve his skills.

Activating the Solution: Now that I know what areas to emphasize in Dana's appraisal, I will complete it. I feel good about the meaningful feedback I will be giving Dana and how I will close the appraisal.

You are now ready to go on to Chapter Thirteen where you will discover how IPS can be used in sales, marketing and advertising.

Chapter Thirteen

USING INTUITIVE PROBLEM-SOLVING TO MARKET, ADVERTISE, AND SELL

I am involved in marketing and sales management. The material in this book has sharpened my decision-making ability, and increased my effectiveness in sales by helping me to better understand my customers. Business is basically about people and the best way to understand people is by using the intuitive process.

BOB CROFT
Area Manager-Product and Sales,
Sakata Seed America, Inc.

INTUITION: A KEY INGREDIENT FOR MARKETING, ADVERTISING, AND SALES

Intuition can come as a *flash* or as a *flow of ideas*, each one sparking the next until you have an explosion of innovative thoughts and actions. Mr. Geoffrey Bloom, chief operating officer (COO) of Wolverine World Wide, the shoe manufacturer known internationally for its trademark Hush Puppy shoes, related a story about one of his main competitors in the highly volatile shoe industry.

As he tells it, Paul Fireman made the decision to purchase the rights to an unknown British trademark called Reebok and began manufacturing "aerobic shoes" under that name. He made this leap strictly on an *intuitive hunch*. At that time, there *was no* "aerobic exercise" boom. There were just small pockets of activity that could hardly foretell what was to come.

In addition, the "aerobic shoe" was being manufactured of garment leather, which was much softer than the traditional leather used in tennis shoes. It was questionable whether this leather was strong enough to keep the toes from popping through during intense exercise.

A finely tuned *intuitive sense* helped Mr. Fireman pick up on the whispered beginnings of a major trend. He went against the facts and logical information, which clearly indicated that the product and market were wrong and could lead him to risk financial ruin. He persisted with this hunch to the tune of $2.8 billion in sales in fewer than eight years.

As Mr. Bloom commented, "Any Harvard MBA would have seen that this decision was a terrible mistake and have gone on to something else. The risky decision made by Mr. Fireman is one of the most remarkable success stories in recent times. Basically, *it all began as a hunch*."

Many CEOs, business leaders, and upper-level managers have told me that intuition is a necessary part of almost any job in their company. For example, areas that require strategy undoubtedly benefit from intuitive input. There are many specific areas, such as design, customer understanding, customer partnership, hiring, and any human resource activity, that also benefit tremendously from intuitive input. The list can go on indefinitely as you add your experiences and those of your associates. Consider your own job. Irrespective of title or job description, I am sure you are now discovering how IPS can apply to your own work. The cases in this chapter will show how intuitive input has provided fresh ideas and new perspectives to market, advertise, or sell a product.

I'm calling upon Bob Smith, a hypothetical character with a fictitious company, the XYZ Gizmo Company, to show you how intuitive input can help you market, advertise, and sell. As the product marketing manager, Bob is in charge of the development and commercialization of a revolutionary new gizmo. Bob's boss, Mr. Whichway, is very demanding and unpredictable. Sometimes he is a logical clear thinker and, at other times, irrational, and intolerant of new ideas. Bob is responsible for recommendations on a number of issues and uses intuitive input along with logic to make many critical decisions. Bob's effective marketing, advertising, and sales plans are shown in the next three cases. You will see how his logical mind continually questions as the intuitive mind provides the necessary imagery for clarification.

CASE 1: MARKETING A PRODUCT. **Background**: Late one afternoon, Mr. Whichway barges into Bob's office, questions Bob's marketing plan, and demands more specific information regarding Bob's forecasts. As he drives home, Bob begins to wonder if his new gizmo will be a success in the marketplace and formulates a question to begin his IPS inquiry.

Problem: Will this product plan be successful?

Centering: Bob awakens early the next morning to go jogging. The exercise relaxes him, gets his blood flowing, and increases his oxygen intake. After his shower, Bob sits in his basement office and stares at a painting of a vase with flowers.

Receptivity: He practices the "total" breath until he feels deeply relaxed.

Imagery: Bob creates imagery to find the answers to the following questions:

- ◆ Will the demand for my product rise or fall in the next year? Bob imagines that he is in a car taking a trip. The car approaches a fork in the road, with one path leading up a mountainside and the other traveling down into a valley. Bob clearly sees his car starting to climb the mountain, which he interprets as growth in demand (i.e., a demand curve).

Bob then wants to discover:

◆ How high will the demand go? He uses the images of trees and rocks to indicate the degree of success. As his car travels above the tree line, he sees only large rocks and little vegetation, indicating a very high altitude. This suggests a very high demand for his product.

Finally, Bob wants to know

◆ When will the demand for my product peak? He imagines four quarters of a pie, representing the four quarters of his fiscal year. As he focuses his attention on each successive quarter, the third "pie slice" is highlighted.

Interpretation: The imagery shows a bright overall picture. Then, Bob uses word association to deepen his understanding.

mountain→hard work→stress and strain to achieve goals

path→treacherous→proceed with caution

large rocks→steep mountain→decline on other side is steep

Bob remembers that his car is the only car on the road, so he can expect little competition in the near term.

Activating the Solution: Bob concludes that the demand for his product will grow very rapidly, peaking in the third quarter of this year. With that short explosive growth phase, he will convince his boss to engage all available resources now to respond to this demand. He also recognizes that the fourth quarter of the year will not be as attractive, with demand dropping rapidly. Armed with this intuitive insight, he can prepare to counter that decrease with additional advertising and promotional funds to maintain demand at an acceptable level. Finally, Bob concludes that this market is very volatile and that for the sake of his personal track record, he should begin talking with others, including his boss, to prepare them for these radical shifts in market dynamics.

CASE 2: ADVERTISING A PRODUCT. **Background**: Having successfully presented this information to Mr. Whichway, Bob begins his promotional strategy. His boss wants a report as soon as Bob has updated his plans, to answer the following:

Problems: What types of advertising could promote his product? How should the advertising change over the life of the product?

Centering: Bob takes an extended lunch hour and goes down to his favorite fishing spot on a warm, sunny day. He spreads a thick blanket on the soft grass and sits down to relax. He stares at the grass and notices many different patterns among the strands.

Receptivity: Bob has his Walkman with him so he can play his favorite *Kitaro* tape. Listening to the music, he takes several "total" breaths to relax.

Imagery: Bob poses several questions to find out about his advertising campaign.

◆ Should I run ads on TV, on radio, or in national magazines? He actively develops three images to correspond with each of these advertising media: a light bulb for TV, a bell for radio, and a pen for magazines and journals. Shielding out all other sources of input, he repeats these images over and over in his head, until he simultaneously "sees" the light flash and "hears" the bell. With that input, Bob knows that he will concentrate his resources on TV and radio advertising to reach the appropriate audiences. Then Bob asks about the content of the campaign.

- ◆ Should the initial commercials promote awareness or stress product features? As he focuses on a cloud formation hovering in the afternoon sky, Bob imagines two flags. One has the patent registration symbol (brand awareness) and the other the outline of a gizmo on it (product features). Imagining the flags to be waving in the breeze, Bob notices that the flag with the patent symbol is more erect in the wind, while the gizmo flag hangs lifeless.

- ◆ Finally, Bob needs to understand what change in direction the program might need to take as market conditions develop. Once again focusing on the cloud formations, Bob sees two flags waving, but this time they are the gizmo flag and one that has a pen on it. He also notices that both flags appear to be stationed on the opposite side of the mountain.

Interpretation: Bob used amplification to clarify his symbols.

The flags indicate a clear identity or position, which is something every marketing manager wants for his product in the marketplace. The brisk wind holding the flags erect shows a lot of energy or activity in the marketplace. It could also be a precursor of the stormy times that lay ahead in the fourth quarter of next year, like winds before a summer storm. Bob also interprets the position of the gizmo and pen flags on the opposite side of the mountain to indicate appropriate strategies during the downturn in demand.

Activating the Solution: Rising from the blanket to return to his car, Bob summarizes what he has learned from this intuitive experience. With rapid growth in demand and little competition in the first three quarters of the year, he will concentrate his TV and radio spots on brand awareness. This will rapidly establish his gizmo in the recognized leadership position in the marketplace. With this identity firmly in place despite competitive responses, Bob will shift his advertising dollars to more technical copy in magazines and trade journals.

CASE 3: SELLING A PRODUCT. Background: Although impressed with Bob's creativity and insight, Mr. Whichway feels that Bob will need a stronger sales plan to maintain levels of demand and meet his volume quotas for the coming year. To get his marketing plan approved in time, Bob has to quickly demonstrate that his sales strategy is sound. He tells Mr. Whichway that he will have his recommendations the following morning.

Problem: What is an effective sales strategy?

Centering: Because of his short deadline, Bob decides to retreat to the XYZ Resource Center for a couple of hours. Finding an empty carrel in a secluded corner, he centers by repeatedly affirming, "I am creative, intelligent, insightful, and successful."

Receptivity: Bob needs to release some of the tension caused by Mr. Whichway's ongoing criticism of his efforts. He closes his eyes, takes several deep breaths, and "tenses and releases" his muscles. Bob wants to relax even more and imagines that he is at the top of a flight of stairs and starts walking down each step to become more relaxed.

Imagery: To complete his sales strategy, Bob uses imagery to discover more about the following issues:

◆ Should I recommend investing in additional sales resources to handle the product demand?

Bob lets his mind drift for a while and then suddenly an image of a bowl appears. As he studies the image more carefully, it changes into a stadium. As the stadium becomes sharper and more defined, Bob imagines himself floating above the stadium, which is filled to capacity. He then sees that his "lean and mean" team are outnumbered by the competition but still manage to win the contest taking place in the arena. Having resolved that the sales force will not need to be augmented, Bob attempts to answer the question

◆ Should the XYZ sales force concentrate its efforts toward the homemaker (the end user of the gizmo) or at the breadwinner (the economic buyer)?

Bob again returns to the stadium image. On one side of the stadium are the homemakers, representing the end users of the gizmo, waving banners and shouting the slogan, "More features!" On the other side are the breadwinners or economic buyers going through similar motions, shouting "Less costly!" Since Bob is unable to discern any appreciable differences in numbers or volume, this issue is left unresolved.

Interpretation: In reviewing the symbols that he has imagined, Bob's sales strategy and plan start to take shape. The bowl image relates directly to his product, since a gizmo and a bowl are often actually used together by the customer. Using word association, he notes that

bowl→fullness→vessel for containing sustenance

For Bob, this symbolizes prosperous and bountiful times ahead. As the bowl changes into the stadium, he realizes the competitive nature of his marketplace and decides that a "team" selling approach will raise morale, increase personal motivation, and undoubtedly maximize the productivity of the sales force. His floating over the stadium indicates that he needs to be involved in the day-to-day sales activities but also has to remove himself periodically to gain an overall strategic perspective on the sales process.

Further Interpretation: With regard to the "more features" versus "less costly" debate, Bob wonders where Mr. Whichway stands on that subject. He again returns to the stadium image, recalling the opposing factions and their cheering. He then visualizes Mr. Whichway walking down the middle of the field, apparently orchestrating both sides.

Activating the Solution: Bob reports back to Mr. Whichway the next morning and presents his revised sales plan. To achieve corporate goals in a highly competitive environment, Bob recommends a team-based approach in which each salesperson benefits from others' successes as well as their own. Bob will monitor this situation carefully, make adjustments when necessary, and deliver progress reports to Mr.Whichway on a quarterly basis. Bob also recommends that the sales plan employ a "push and pull" strategy. The sales program will "push" the features and performance to satisfy the home-maker demand, while it will "pull" the breadwinners by advertising the economy and durability of the product.

How Would You Market, Advertise, or Sell?

Anyone can do this exercise since your title, job, or formal work assignment is irrelevant. The focus is you and marketing, selling, or advertising your services. Use the IPS process to show you how to proceed with your "campaign" to sell yourself.

_____

_____

_____

_____

Take the challenge of marketing or promoting a work partner or friend. How will you proceed with this challenging assignment?

_____

_____

_____

_____

How to Use Intuitive Problem-Solving to Create Successful Sales and Advertising Campaigns

CASE 1: DESIGNING AN AD CAMPAIGN. **Background**: Brian is employed by a large company in the Colorants Division of a plastics applications business unit. He is the group section leader of the technical service laboratory. His responsibilities include support for sales, marketing, and production through applications testing of colorants in all plastics applications. He wants to develop an advertising campaign for a new replacement product line for heavy metal products and feels that trade magazine display ads and direct mail will be the best vehicles for the campaign. The challenge is developing a theme for this campaign that will be the common thread between the display ad and mailer. Searching for the theme, he poses the following question:

Problem: What will be the theme of my display ad and mailer?

Centering: My wife has taken the children to their piano lessons, which gives me a rare opportunity for "alone" time. I put an environmental tape called "Rain" on the stereo and listen to the gentle sounds of a summer rain shower.

Receptivity: Sitting comfortably on the couch with my eyes closed, I take several "hang-sah" breaths. Listening to the tape, I imagine the gentle rainfall washing away my tensions as I continue to take slow and deep breaths. I am relaxed and ask what the theme of the campaign should be.

Imagery: I picture Abraham Lincoln giving a speech and am not clear about the relevance of this image, but know I can decipher the meaning with an amplification.

Interpretation: I elicit the following associations to Abraham Lincoln: honesty, Emancipation Proclamation, Gettysburg Address, sixteenth president, stovepipe hat, tall, and homely. The word that strikes me is "honesty." I feel that ads should be honest, direct, straightforward, and to the point. The flash that comes to me about how to do this in the ad campaign comes when I ask the question, "Is the customer having problems matching color without heavy metals?" If so, we have the solution in our alternative products. This is the theme I decide to develop for the campaign.

Resting Period: I don't give this too much time to rest, but produce the artwork for the display ad and the mailer entitled, "Having trouble color matching without heavy metals?" I show my secretary the idea for the display ad and she is very impressed. It speaks right to the point and does it in an "Honest Abe" sort of way.

Activating the Solution: My boss likes the idea of this presentation for our company and decides that we will present it to corporate advertising for further development and implementation.

CASE 2: *FORMULATING A CAMPAIGN TO SELL A PRODUCT.* **Background**: The sales and marketing manager for the circulation department of a local newspaper has a challenging assignment. His work associates have begun a targeted promotional mailer to solicit subscriptions for weekend newspaper home delivery. He needs to determine whether the campaign will be successful and to make alternate plans if it is not.

Problem: Will the promotional campaign we are now using enlist subscribers for the weekend home delivery?

Centering: I settle into my lounge chair at home and look out the window at the trees. I can clearly see a pattern in the pine trees.

Receptivity: To relieve all tension, I do the "ha!" breath several times, followed by the "tense and release" exercise.

Imagery: Feeling very relaxed, I visualize catalogs sitting on a table in a busy hallway. As people walk by, I watch to see if they pick up a catalog. I see very few people picking up the catalogs and feel this indicates a doomed campaign.

Resting Period: Two weeks after this expensive campaign is kicked off, my imagery is confirmed, as we have generated only a few subscriptions.

Additional Interpretation: I return to the original imagery my intuitive mind sent and ask to see to what display the people in the hallway are looking at. I see a restaurant. The amplification shows

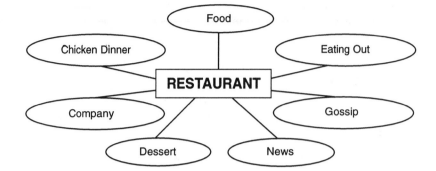

These associations don't make any significant connections, so I return to the restaurant in my thoughts. I decide to put myself at a table in the restaurant and see if I can pick up on anything. I order coffee. It seems this is a coffee house.

Eureka! This coffee is held in coffee mugs (not cups) with the restaurant's name on the mugs. I decide mugs with our name on them will go well with a campaign soliciting weekend subscriptions to the newspaper. Customers will receive a free mug with their subscription.

Activating the Solution: I wonder how many to order and the number 406 comes to mind. I order 500 mugs that afternoon. Two weeks into the campaign, the orders are at 403. Why did I order 500 mugs? I don't know what I am going to do with 90 extra mugs. Next time I will honor the input from my intuitive mind.

CASE 3: ACQUIRING NEW ACCOUNTS. **Background**: As the Midwest territory sales manager, Drew's income is significantly impacted by his ability to acquire new accounts. He has been struggling with new ideas and approaches to obtaining additional business with only moderate success. He needs fresh ideas for new markets or ways to increase his current accounts.

Problem: What should I do to increase my new account sales?

Centering: I try to address this problem when I am the most alert, which is early in the morning after a good night of sleep. I affirm that the intuitive solution will come to me easily.

Receptivity: I find out that it is easy for me to relax and enter the alpha level by using the "hang-sah" breath. I also imagine myself at the helm of a large sailboat, alone at night with only the slightest breeze and a clear sky.

Imagery: After a short interlude, an image of green and yellow balloons comes to mind.

Interpretation: I interpret the balloons to have several possible meanings. I feel that the balloons themselves could be significant of expansion, which would mean to look outside my current markets for new opportunities. I think that the choice of green and yellow is significant. Green stands for go, which means I should pursue this possible expansion. The yellow tells me to go cautiously and not try to expand too quickly.

Resting Period: I think about the imagery presented to this problem and decide to pursue this avenue by discussing the topic with my boss.

Activating the Solution: The outcome of this exercise is very interesting. I have just been given the "go-ahead" to expand into Iowa. However, I am told that I can't have

Minnesota as part of my territory yet. Wow! This fits right into the scenario that I received in this exercise.

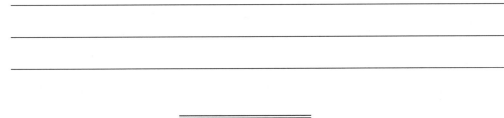

EXERCISE

Selling Successfully

Use your favorite centering and relaxation techniques. Picture the item you want to sell. The item can come from your work or home setting. Have a dialogue with this item to "find out" the best way to make the sale. Record the insights you receive in this space.

_____

_____

_____

_____

USING INTUITIVE PROBLEM-SOLVING
FOR INNOVATIVE SOLUTIONS

Intuitive problem solving is an ideal process for people in research who need to find new and innovative procedures. As Cases 1 and 2 show, IPS exploration can provide the missing piece in product development.

CASE 1: FINDING A QUICK DESIGN SOLUTION. **Background**: Sometimes, the intuitive flash can come easily. This is what happened to Kevin, who is the director of engineering for a manufacturing company that produces metal stampings and assemblies for the automotive consumer electronics industries. They came up with an innovative design for a new product, but the customer needed more strength from the lightweight material.

> *Problem*: How do we resolve the design problem and meet both demands?

> *Centering and Receptivity*: On the plane ride back from the customers, I close my eyes and relax. I let my mind wander to seek possible solutions to the problem.

> *Imagery*: I see a mountain range made up of several jagged peaks.

> *Interpretation*: The jagged peaks dart into the skyline. I relate the mountain range and its jagged peaks to our product and instantly know the answer to our design problem.

> *Activating the Solution*: We implement triangle-shaped embosses into the product to act as stiffening darts. The product is now out of the prototype stage and is in the validation stage.

CASE 2: INTRODUCING A NEW PRODUCT. **Background**: Brenda is an elected official serving as Clerk of the Cascade Charter Township, which is located southeast of Grand Rapids, Michigan. She will be using new voting equipment at the upcoming primary election. There needs to be a way to educate the voters so that they are not frustrated on election day with the change.

Problem: How should I introduce the Optech voting system to the voters?

Centering and Receptivity: To become prepared to answer this question, I listen to a meditation tape. I follow with the "hang-sah" breaths and the relaxation exercise. Doing this, I can feel the tension leaving my body, opening my mind to receive a message.

Imagery: I see a hand holding a pencil over a pad of paper.

Interpretation: Using amplification I do a cluster association that clarifies my problem:

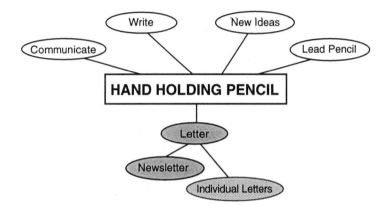

After I elicit the word "letter," I know that this is right, but I don't know what kind of letter to use. After further amplification of this word, I receive "newsletter" and "individual letters." I know that the newsletter is the correct forum for the education.

I am also drawn by the word lead as in pencil and realize that the voters need to be led through the steps of voting with the new equipment.

Activating the Solution: I will write an article for the township newsletter leading the voters through a step-by-step process for using the new voting machines.

All the cases that have been presented in the past three chapters have highlighted people in their work environment. In the next chapter, you will see how to use IPS to make a career change.

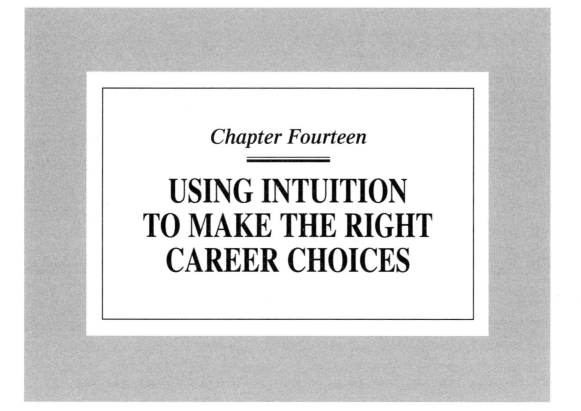

Chapter Fourteen

USING INTUITION TO MAKE THE RIGHT CAREER CHOICES

I didn't grow up on a lot of strategic planning and that sort of thing. Most of what I have done is based on intuitive gut reaction and how things feel at the moment. I've probably done most things that were important that way.

FRANK MERLOTTI
Retired CEO
Steelcase, Incorporated

One of the most agonizing decisions nearly everyone faces at one time or another has to do with some facet of career change. These work-related transitions come about in a variety of ways: the company you are working for decides to merge, downsizes, or goes out of business are obvious examples. Career transitions can also take place "in house" and frequently affect the upwardly mobile employee climbing the corporate ladder who savors various positions on the way to the top. Even the securely employed individual who seems relatively immune to any type of job upheaval dramatically confronts change when a rival company dangles the golden carrot to draw the "recruit" into a new job outside the present company.

Many people involved in career change activities focus on basic employment questions. These may relate to the type of work pursued, timing issues, or etiquette for approaching a potential employer about a job position.

Change need not be feared. On the contrary, forging ahead to innovate and create or participate in a new business can be exciting. Yet each of us responds differently to the challenge of a career change.

Carol Lopucki is the executive director of EXCEL, a training program for women business owners. Carol told me that she and her husband, a school administrator, react to "job change" in diametrically different ways. Carol, wholeheartedly embraces change. She is 40 years old and has made three major career changes. Her husband, in contrast, has worked within a school system in a more structured and predictable work environment. Now he too is in the throes of change, but he is not as comfortable as Carol, who flows with the ever-changing tide. He has learned much from watching Carol enthusiastically use her intuitive insights to flow right into each new situation. Carol describes her last career change as dramatic. She was intuitively prompted to make this move because of the kinship she felt with the energy level of the women who interviewed her and the joint visions they shared of wanting "to grow" something important. Intuitively, Carol knew it was the right time to make a move and to leave a career at which she had spent many years of her life.

In this chapter, you will see how IPS has been applied in a variety of situations, including decisions about:

- Making a career change.

- Company transitions: staying or relocating.

- Staying in the old, or going to something new.

- Moving to a new career.

- Venturing into a new business.

TO CHANGE OR NOT TO CHANGE JOBS: THAT IS THE QUESTION

The following two cases highlight some basic questions that are asked about making a career change. No matter how simple the questions may seem, this agonizing decision may take a long time to resolve as the logical and intuitive minds blend to piece together the various facts, figures, and images of the employment puzzle. That is why IPS is so useful in revealing the right choice or perspective in a relatively brief time.

The background of Case 1 is secondary. Of primary importance is noticing how the person focuses on a solution to his timely question about changing jobs.

CASE 1: TIMING A JOB CHANGE.

Problem: Should I change jobs now?

Centering: Everyone in my house is in bed as I sit in the cool basement, late at night, knowing I can get into a relaxed state without interruption. I say the focusing phrase "peace and quiet" several times.

Receptivity: The instrumental music on the stereo is an appropriate background for my doing the "total" breath and "tense and release" techniques.

Imagery: Using the internal brainstorming variation of IPS, I create a chalkboard in my inner mind and begin to list all the advantages of staying in my present position. I jot down those that light up and do the same thing for the disadvantages. This is the final list showing the pros and cons.

Pro	*Con*
Flexible work schedule	Organization is slow to change
Vested in pension plan	Lack of challenge
Good employees to work with	Low financial reward
Programs are successful	Limited ability to move up
Time provided for research and education	
Tuition reimbursement benefits	

After my options are presented, I quietly wait for an image to present itself. I see a boat on the water that is lazily drifting along on a sunshine-filled day. It seems very peaceful and calm.

Interpretation: When I used amplification around the image, I come up with the following: free time, family, no direction, moving, listless, floating along, leisure, and restful. Inwardly, I felt a very strong pull toward the "free time" and "family" options.

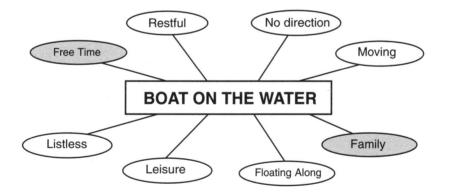

Activating the Solution: I'm better off honoring the IPS input and not making any changes at this time. I just finished my Master's Degree and two years of hard work implementing new programs at work. This has been a great sacrifice for my wife and children. The IPS resolution clearly helped me see that attention at this time should be directed to family needs.

Weighing the Advantages and Disadvantages of Changing Jobs

This is your turn to engage in internal brainstorming. Create a chalkboard in your inner mind and in the space below, list the advantages (pros) and disadvantages (cons) of making a job change at this time. Review the options on each side. Which light up or suggest that making a change is advisable, or even inadvisable, at this time?

Pro   *Con*

_____   _____

_____   _____

_____   _____

_____   _____

_____   _____

Indicate how going through this internal brainstorming has clarified your options about making a job change. What are your options now?

_____

_____

_____

_____

CASE 1: REASSESSING CAREER GOALS. **Background**: Bridget is temporarily out of a job and needs to reassess her career goals and consider other options.

Problems: Should she work full time or part time? Should she start a new career?

Centering: While listening to a Paul Horn tape, Bridget looks at the wood grains on the wall of her office.

Receptivity: Starting from her toes and moving to the scalp area, she thinks of relaxing each muscle and letting all the accumulated tensions flow out of her body. Breathing deeply and slowly, she tries to picture what is going on in her body.

Imagery: Then Bridget sees a crossroads. The many signs are each pointing in a different direction. Each sign represents a choice that is facing her. Before she chooses any path, she wants to think about what skills she has. She has recently learned communication and research skills. From past jobs, she has acquired problem-solving skills, supervisory skills, and the ability to delegate tasks. She has also learned to be more confident, assertive, and independent.

The first sign she looks at says: Choose between making a career change and staying in the same field. This leads Bridget to reflect that she has previously done accounting or tax work and has had several years of supervisory experience. She has always worked in a banking environment, except for a period in a law firm. A sudden flash presents the option of working in a manufacturing environment.

Another sign reads: Decide between part-time and full-time employment. Bridget feels that internal brainstorming can help her make this decision. The pros and cons that she sees in the theater of her intuitive mind that relate to full-time employment are

Advantages	*Disadvantages*
Life insurance	Longer working hours
Health insurance	Lack of personal time
Sick leave	
Profit-sharing or pension plan	
Vacation time	
Advancement potential	
Ability to earn a higher rate of pay	

Bridget also considers the pros and cons of part-time employment.

Advantages	*Disadvantages*
Flexible work schedule	Less chance at advancement
A few benefits	Lower rate of pay
Some vacation time	

From this internal brainstorming, it is clear that she doesn't see herself taking part-time employment.

Interpretation: Bridget looks back at the sign telling her to choose between making a career change and staying in the same field. Since the sky is cloudy on the imaginary path she is taking, venturing into something new is questionable. She will definitely use the same career to work full time in a banking environment.

Activating the Solution: Bridget is temporarily satisfied with her decision. She feels if she cannot obtain employment in banking, she will find a job in the manufacturing environment.

EXERCISE

Making a Choice at the Crossroads

Imagine that you are driving down a road. The road splits in three directions. These directions correspond to three occupational choices. Each road has a sign that designates the type of occupation lying at the end of the road. Imagine yourself selecting one of the paths or directions. How would you label this path?

_____

_____

_____

As you travel down this road, what do you experience? Is it smooth? Easy to travel on? Winding? Obstacles? Note your experience and how this corresponds to your career change activities.

_____

_____

Do you come to a place where a bridge is washed out so you have to turn around or make another choice? If so, what would that choice be?

_____

_____

If you are having difficulty traveling this road, create a scene where you experience a smoother ride. Ask your intuitive mind to show you a symbol describing what you need to do to have a smoother ride. Use one of the interpretation techniques to unravel the symbolism. What have you uncovered?

_____

_____

_____

COMPANY TRANSITIONS: STAYING OR RELOCATING

Many people want an easy, magical way of deciding whether to stay with the same company or go elsewhere to seek their fortune. Can any formula determine how long one should remain at the same job site? The answer to this question could easily take the rest of this chapter, but it gives me the opportunity to remind you that making such a decision can be relatively simple and direct by using the IPS formula. In addition, options that haven't even been considered can come forth to help the decision maker arrive at a clear, decisive resolution. The individuals in the following cases use IPS to find out how to make an expedient job change within their company.

CASE 1: COMPANY MOVING: SHOULD I STAY OR LEAVE? **Background**: The group that I work for has been merged with another division. As a result, my work group will be relocated to another site. That location will be determined within the next few months. The problem is do I stay with this company or seek another job?

Problem: Do I stay with this company?

Centering: I start becoming relaxed as I listen to an environmental tape. I repeatedly state the affirmation, "I am receptive to my intuitive thoughts."

Receptivity: Relaxing on the couch, I take several "hang-sah" breaths to relax and expel the tension from my body. The sound of the ocean on the tape and the breathing help cleanse my body from within and without, leaving me relaxed enough to ask this very important question. Should I stay with my current company?

Imagery: The image that I picture is that of an isolated pond on a cool autumn morning. It reminds me of duck hunting where the mornings are spent watching the still water and the rising mist. In this quiet pond surrounded by cattails and woods, there is not a ripple or sound.

Interpretation: After I draw an amplification diagram around the term "quiet pond," the following associations emerge: stable, peaceful, serene, complacent, cool, picturesque, relaxing, and reflective. The word that strikes me the most is "stable." The word stable literally translates to job stability, which means not changing jobs at this time. If I don't change jobs, I need an answer to the following question:

♦ How long should I work for my current company? The image of a meadow with a mountain stream meandering across it comes readily. I can look across the meadow and see the mountains rising in the background with the stream winding toward the mountain.

Further Interpretation: I do not need any technique to unravel this image, which is clearly showing me I will be keeping my job in the foreseeable future. This makes me feel more comfortable and at ease to see my future in this way.

Resting Period: It has now been several days since I did the IPS and I still feel good about the decision to stay with my current employer and job.

Activating the Solution: A customer who is seeking to fill a position has recently sought my interest through a recruiter. I feel comfortable declining this offer even though I am curious as to what may have come of it.

CASE 2: CREATING CHANGE WITHOUT CHANGING JOBS. **Background**: Bruce is wondering about joining another social service organization. He likes change, and in some ways the thought of changing jobs is exciting. He enjoys the job and his coworkers but is becoming more concerned about things like securing benefits and a consistent salary now that he is 40 years old. He craves some kind of change. That change may be from his current to a new set of responsibilities, or perhaps a move to another organization.

Problem: Should Bruce stay at his current social service agency?

Centering: Bruce listens to a meditation tape guiding him to the woods. Because he often goes to a cottage on Lake Michigan, it is easy for him to project himself to the trail in the woods that leads to the beach. He especially likes the sound of the waves washing on the beach and the sea gulls flying overhead.

Receptivity: He takes several "reenergizing" breaths to relax and then, to become even more relaxed, he goes into the "autogenic" technique.

Imagery: He feels relaxed but has difficulty retrieving any symbol or image. He decides to do clustering using the nucleus term "leave agency" and forms clusters around the words "challenge" and "change."

Interpretation: As Bruce is going through this exercise, he realizes that he could be running away from the problems and frustrations he has been experiencing with his boss.

He also realizes that he can have challenge and change right at this agency. If he leaves, he could end up with similar frustrations or worse, so he decides to stay for the present time. Here is the clustering that led him to his decision.

Resting Period: For three days, he ponders the problem and increasingly feels better about staying at the agency.

Activating the Solution: The more he thinks about the problem, the more he is aware of a little voice saying, "Stay at the agency; forget about the problems with the boss; do what you do best; see what needs to be done and do it."

The exercise helps Bruce see that his anger and frustration with his boss should not be the deciding factor in his decision to leave. He is self-motivated and doesn't need his boss to galvanize him into action. For now, Bruce clearly hears his inner voice telling him, "Stay, reenergize, focus on personal growth and growth of the agency." However, he will continue to network and keep an eye out for other opportunities.

EXERCISE

Making the Decision to Stay or Leave

You are working for a company and they are closing your division. You are given two choices, to relocate to another division or leave. You have to give your answer quickly. How would you make this instant decision?

_____

_____

_____

Now, try looking at the wallpaper or something in your environment that can serve as a focusing object. Stare for 10 seconds and then create the following imagery to help you respond. Ask yourself the question, "Should I relocate or leave?"

Do doors open or close?

_____

Can you see your name on a door or desk?

_____

Is someone shaking your hand and welcoming you on the team?

_____

Are you doing work that is familiar (the same job) or unfamiliar (a new job)?

_____

From this information, would you relocate to another division in this company or leave?

_____

CASE 3: MOVING UP OR MOVING OUT. **Background**: The bank I work for is a financially strong and viable financial organization. Yet there is limited advancement for women into the upper ranks of management. The top of the organization is dominated by males, with only a few women managers even close to the upper ranks. As a female officer of the bank, I am committed to either moving up in the organization or leaving the company for greater opportunities. I have the skills and education to move into upper management and need to make a decision so I can formulate my future plans.

Problem: Can I feasibly advance to the upper management ranks within the bank and be recognized for my work?

Centering: To become centered, I sit in a cushy chair on my porch at the beach house and focus my eyes on the rolling waves approaching the shore. I slowly close my eyes and listen to the waves softly pounding on the edge of the beach.

Receptivity: I take several "total" breaths and hear the wind as I imagine myself walking alone on a desolate tropical beach. I settle down onto the soft sand next to a palm tree to think and receive valuable information about my future.

Imagery: I ask myself some questions and wait for the reply in the form of an image or a word.

♦ Do opportunities for advancement into upper management exist for a woman of my knowledge and education? I ask for a symbol showing me what my future might hold at this bank. I see myself looking into the sky and immediately see a dark rain cloud hanging over the blue water. This signified that stormy times are coming and advancement in the time I desire will be difficult. I pursue with further questions.

♦ Will I be able to move into a more challenging position within the organization in the next two years? I picture two doors in my mind. One is open with a light inside while the other is dark and closed. After posing this question, the closed door immediately comes into my view. I am disappointed and know that I will not be able to move to another area. This is exactly what my manager said at my last promotion by indicating that I would be at my current branch for at least three years.

♦ When should I consider a job change? In my mind, I look across the water and immediately see a bright and shining snowflake. This affirms that a job change will be made in the winter, which is just a few months away.

Interpretation: I go over the images in my mind and try to put them together. My entire imagery has to do with the weather, which makes sense since I am doing the IPS process in a very receptive outdoor area. The cloud symbol gives me an indication that I should move on in my career; the snowflake imagery indicates that winter will be the best time. I try to amplify the images to receive more information or clearer symbols, but my mind is blank and too busy analyzing what I have already seen.

Activating the Solution: The images affirm that although I am educated and experienced, I am still a female in a male-dominated company. Consequently, my opportunities at this time are limited. According to my intuitive problem-solving, I will look forward to a move coming within the next six or seven months of this year. This makes sense to me as I have been considering change. More companies may be hiring in the coming months as we pull out of the recession. I now realize that deep inside I have been restless for some time in this organization. My IPS experience brings that particular fact to the surface. I truly feel confident that it will be best for me to move on to a more "woman friendly" company for advancement.

EXERCISE

Chart Your Way to Clarity

Are you choosing between several job possibilities? Put all these options into a pie-shaped graph divided into three or more sections. Each section represents one of the job opportunities waiting for you. First, identify these opportunities by listing each option.

1. _____

2. _____

3. _____

4. _____

5. _____

Your intuitive mind will help you "cut up" the pie. First, drift into the alpha level as you use a centering and a receptivity technique. Then, imagine that a pie-shaped graph is right in front of you. Indicate which section is largest. This is the job opportunity you want to pursue.

Which is the smallest slice? This indicates the least likely possibility for you to pursue.

What do you notice about the other slices? Are they thick, thin, somewhere in between? Does this suggest they are contenders for your attention?

Making the Change

Leo Buscaglia recalls how his intuitive decision to leave an excellent job as an academic administrator, in spite of the unanimous advice to remain where he was, led to the greatest single experience of his life. Friends and associates all warned him that he should not give up the high-salaried prestigious position he had achieved at an early age, telling him that he would be unlikely to find another job as good.

But Leo's inner voice told him that life had more to offer. He wanted to see the world, to interact with many different people. So, instead of staying securely in his academic niche, he sold everything and traveled around the world for three years. He headed for the small villages of Nepal, and elsewhere, where he lived among the people. His inner voice had not led him into darkness. As he says now, "It is always light where it leads me."

Interestingly, after three years away, he returned to find two jobs open, one at the University of Southern California (USC) and the other at the University of California, Los Angeles (UCLA). He applied for and was given the post at USC, which he remembers as the happiest job of his life. Buscaglia says, "I really think that without risks, life is worthless. Risk opens doors and windows, and I like the airing out."

In the previous section, the transition challenge basically focused on movement within the company. Now, the individuals want to step out and make the transition to a completely different setting. In the first two cases, they debate the benefits of staying with the tried and true or stepping out and experiencing a new environment. In the third, the question is how to get the "right" offer.

CASE 1: SHOULD I TAKE THE JOB OFFER? **Background**: Joe is offered a position in sales management. The position will offer new challenges and responsibilities, greater visibility, the potential of future advancement, and more money. The one catch is the extensive travel required by anyone holding this new position. Joe has always been a "family man," and his responsibilities have recently increased with the birth of their baby and the purchase of a new house. Joe is very perplexed. While he is satisfied with his current job and greatly values the time he spends with his family, he is also attracted to the challenge of seeing if his recommendations for the sales area reorganization could really work.

Problem: Should Joe accept the new job offer?

Centering and Receptivity: Joe decides to take a day off in the middle of the week. He loads up his fishing gear and takes off for the lake. After he arrives, he launches the boat and navigates out to the center of the lake. He fishes for awhile and begins to relax by ridding his mind of all the "clutter." After awhile, he pulls in his line and lies down in the bottom of the boat while it drifts aimlessly. He gazes at the clouds as they sail by and he becomes very still.

Receptivity: As the boat slowly rocks with the waves, Joe feels all tension released from his body.

Imagery: The image of a car becomes apparent. As Joe examines the car further, he notices that the wheels are actually clocks and that the hands on the clocks resemble keys.

Interpretation: In his relaxed alpha level, Joe feels that the car represents the traveling required by the sales job and the advancement possibilities that come with the position. Joe feels the clock wheels indicate time away from family. The key hands contain the clue that he needs. They are finely articulated, rich antique gold with exquisite detailing and patina. This promotion is his vehicle toward additional prosperity in the future and can unlock all sorts of challenging possibilities for future advancement.

Further Interpretation: Joe feels more comfortable about the opportunity but is still concerned about the travel and time away from the family. As he returns to the car symbol, he gains a clearer sense of satisfaction. The resolution of that issue is based on his ability to be proactive in managing his time, including his travel schedule. As the car seems to represent his vehicle traveling into the future, he intuitively knows his future is unfolding.

Activating the Solution: Joe feels confident about accepting the sales management offer. His sense of conviction about this decision is so strong that his wife also knows this is the right decision.

CASE 2: LEAVING TO PURSUE A NEW INDUSTRY.

Problem: Do I pursue a new industry?

Centering: I affirm that my intuitive mind will lead me to the right answer.

Receptivity: Sitting in a relaxed position, I start to breathe deeply and imagine receptivity coming in on the inhale and distractions leaving on the exhale.

Imagery: I keep asking if I should stay put and accept the broker's position or switch industries. At first, I can get no imagery, but then I find myself thinking of the birds chirping outside, and an image of a sparrow comes to me.

Interpretation: Using amplification, I come up with the following associations to the sparrow: free, fly, quick, speedy, dark color, and aggressive. The "free" word ties in with freeing myself from my current employer. I also think "fly" means to fly away from the nest that I have become comfortable with. Also, the aggressiveness of the bird tells me to not be afraid to experiment and try a new industry to work in.

Resting Period: During the next few days, I continue to process my interpretation of this imagery.

Activating the Solution: I realize that I have a clear-cut opportunity to explore a new challenge in my work career. Since doing this exercise, I have contacted some corporate recruiters who have put me in touch with some new and interesting job possibilities. I am confident that the decision to "fly" away from my present work situation is correct.

CASE 3: HOW DO I GET A NEW COMPANY TO NOTICE ME?

Problem: What approach can I use to be hired by the company of my choice?

Centering: I go into the quiet back yard and lie down, concentrating on the sky and staring at the big white clouds.

Receptivity: I take several "hang-sah" breaths and relax my body with the "tense and release" exercise. It goes slowly at first, but then I lose myself in the clouds and find myself playfully watching them drift along. I have fun attaching labels to some of them based on what they represent to me. My relaxed body and clear mind help me feel completely receptive.

Imagery: I create an image of three ducks swimming peacefully on a pond. The pond is still and the ducks seem to be swimming in unison with no particular duck being the leader or the follower. The pond is set in the countryside among the farm fields and woods.

Interpretation: At first it is hard for me to see any association between my image and the problem I am addressing. However, after applying the amplification technique it becomes clearer. First, I take the image of the ducks. Ducks fly and swim. They are flock birds and have leaders and followers. They look out for one another by warning each other of impending danger. When in the pond, they adjust the size of their world to the size of their swimming space; hence, it becomes smaller in the winter due to freezing and larger in the summer. They quack and waddle. Also, they can be clever and determined. Next, I look at the pond and its relationship to the surrounding landscape. The pond could represent various things, like tranquility or boundaries, safety for some, water and plant growth, smooth and defined, fish and bugs, turtles and snakes, frogs and salamanders.

The image of the ducks on the pond not only represents where I am in my job search but that I need to resolve my question. The pond represents a limited environment and the feeling of being apart from the rest of the world. The ducks on the pond are all in the same situation, however, just swimming around. That is what I have been doing to a degree, swimming around. At times I feel as if I am in this unique place, set off from the rest of the world. The fact that there is no leader or follower indicates no plan and a sort of random motion. These feelings lead to my next question.

What do I need to do to break this cycle of random motion and perceptual limitations? In an instant I receive the image of a group of people at a small social gathering. I am standing in the middle of them. This image brings to mind the associations of party, social talk, laughter, people, interaction, networking, cooperation, and cliques. This image is directing me to network. Picking up from where I left off with the image of the ducks and the pond, the images are telling me not to be isolated and random but to use my contacts to be more social and network. The answer to the question of how to get an interview with my chosen organization is to not try to do it myself but to ask other people to assist me with that contact. My next step will be identifying those individuals and the best time to contact them about their assistance.

MOVING TO A NEW CAREER

The following cases address the dilemmas of changing careers.

CASE 1: SHOULD I CHANGE CAREERS. Background: I have been involved with computers and their use in a manufacturing environment for the last eight years. Previous to that, I was involved in many different kinds of pursuits. Lately, I feel that I am in a rut and should try a new field.

Problem: Should I change careers?

Centering: I sit in a chair and look at a painting on the wall that always makes me feel good. I repeat the word "relax" several times.

Receptivity: I do a "progressive relaxation" by starting with my feet and hands working through the midsection of my body up to my head. I then imagine myself walking along a secluded beach at sundown on a peaceful summer evening.

Imagery: I see small waves lapping against a sandy beach.

Interpretation: I know that *first impressions* are always right, and I acknowledge my immediate strong feeling that this imagery is of the ever-changing or sifting sands. While a beach looks the same from day to day, the sands that make it up are different or reorganized. This applies to my current job as well. What I do changes all the time, requiring versatility and flexibility.

Activating the Solution: Since I enjoy this type of environment, I should stay in my present field. By doing the exercise, I realize that I am getting the variety that I enjoy.

CASE 2: DECIDING WHAT TYPE OF WORK TO DO. Background: Keith is determining what type of work he should pursue for career satisfaction. This could be management in general or a job requiring technical skill.

Problem: What type of work should Keith do?

Centering: Keith focuses on a white lily sitting on the table.

Receptivity: By using several "hang-sah" breaths, he begins to relax and become receptive to his intuitive processes. He then counts down from 10.

Imagery: The term "career path" comes to his mind.

Interpretation: To interpret the imagery, he uses the word association technique to make the following chain of associations:

Career Path→ long road→hard drive→trucking→carry→weight→responsibility→ determination→purpose→service→need→useful→facilitator *management*

Activating the Solution: He feels that management is the right career path to pursue since it would use his inherent managerial characteristics in combination with his desire to accomplish more than simply earn a paycheck.

CASE 3: CHOOSING THE RIGHT OPTION. Background: Bob has the challenge of selecting the most desirable career opportunity. IPS helps him pick the right option in a very creative way.

Problem: Is the most desirable career opportunity in sales, operations, or ownership?

Centering: Bob focuses on the clouds outside of a plane window.

Receptivity: The "hang-sah" breath is used to become receptive. Bob also envisions himself in his deer hunting stand in the woods. From there he begins to elicit imagery.

Imagery: The images that come up are hockey puck, horse, and Northern Lights.

Interpretation: He uses amplification and word association to clarify these three images.

1. Hockey puck

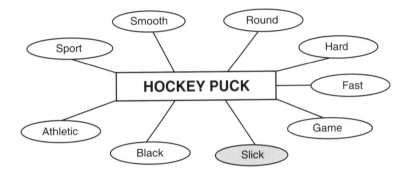

hockey puck→game→fair→toll→pay the price

All these associations remind him of sales.

2. Horse

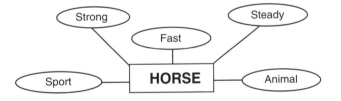

horse→race→run→fear→scared stiff

Now he is thinking of operations.

3. Northern Lights

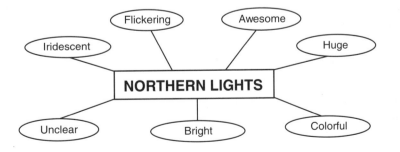

Northern Lights→beautiful→wife→kid→family→love

These associations relate to ownership.

Resting Period: He waits about one week and reviews his interpretations.

Further Interpretation: At first he is concerned that his intuition only better defines his three career opportunities in a more creative way. By using amplification alone, he determines the following:

Hockey puck   =   Sales
Horse   =   Operations
Northern Lights   =   Ownership

Then, by adding the "Ah'ha!" from his word association, he adds a new "column" or dimension and ends up with the following:

Hockey puck   =   Sales   =   Pay the price
Horse   =   Operations   =   Scared stiff
Northern Lights   =   Ownership   =   Love

Activating the Solution: Clearly his intuitive mind is showing him the order he should pursue:

First choice   =   Ownership
Second choice   =   Sales
Third choice   =   Operations

EXERCISE

Create a Job: Follow Your Fantasy

Are you undecided about what occupation you want to pursue? Are you thinking of changing careers? What type of job position would you like to hold? What is your dream work setting? Write down your thoughts about your "dream job."

_____

Directions: Become centered as you focus on a flower or leaf from a plant. Then take several "total" breaths and "tense and release" each set of muscles. In this fantasy, you have the license and opportunity to create any job of your choice. Stretch your imagination to see yourself in your "dream" job. What is your title and what are some of the details of your job description?

_____

_____

_____

_____

Where are you working? What type of environment or setting are you in?

_____

Put the scene into action by seeing others around you actively engaged. What do you "see" in this setting?

_____

Can you "hear" the conversations taking place around you? What is being discussed?

_____

How do you "feel" in this setting?

_____

Take note of this complete scenario you are creating. Then, every day for two weeks, take 15 minutes to become centered and receptive and play this script in the theater of your inner mind. Then, record your results of this fantasy journey.

_____

_____

_____

CASE 4: DECIDING WHEN TO RETURN TO WORK. Coming back to work after a long absence, whether due to time taken to raise children, recovery after an illness, or a much needed rest and repair, is a dilemma faced by many.

Background: Dale retired from the "work world" to raise her two young children. During this time, she enrolled in graduate school to prepare for an advanced position when she returns to the workplace. She is not clear about the right time to return to work. Using IPS, she receives some instant feedback concerning this decision.

Problem: Is spring 1995 the right time for me to return to work?

Centering: To become centered, I listen to soft background music while sitting on my porch.

Receptivity: I do the "hang-sah" breath and "progressive relaxation." When I feel relaxed, I pose my question about returning to work.

Imagery: Suddenly, a yellow light is blinking on and off as the words flash in my mind—Caution! Prepare to stop! Yield!

I then ask, "Why?" and using internal brainstorming, I create a blackboard to write my options down. I see

children	free time
home	school
husband	stress
$	future

Interpretation: Since the word "children" is highlighted, I probe to find out: What about the children? The original words are erased and replaced with the following:

young age	child care/baby-sitter
level of maturity and understanding	*my attachment to them, our relationship*
sense of security	*our ability to adapt to change*
fear	uncertainty

Activating the Solution: I realize from doing this exercise that my fears about returning to work are about me, not about how my children will handle the change. I could return to part-time work and arrange for excellent sitters when I am away. My children love being with other children in a preschool setting, so day care would be enjoyable. For now, that leaves me with my own adjustment to the upcoming change. This exercise has shown me that I need to concentrate and work on preparing myself for returning to the workplace. Looks like spring 1995 is the right time!

VENTURING INTO A NEW BUSINESS

In Case 3, Bob decided that ownership or going into his own business was the most suitable career direction. Now let's see how Bob considers what type of business to pursue. The individuals in the following three cases are also considering how to go solo and start a business.

CASE 1: DECIDING ON THE TYPE OF BUSINESS.

Problem: What type of business start-up should Bob pursue?

Centering: Bob closes his eyes and imagines a shell from the beach.

Receptivity: The "hang-sah" breath is used to help him become more receptive. Once again, he imagines himself in his deer hunting stand in the woods. He begins to elicit imagery.

Imagery: The images he sees are spur, train, book, gun, and star.

Interpretation: Again he uses word association and amplification to clarify these images.

1. **Star**

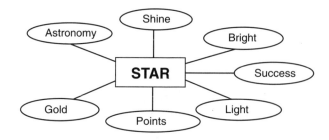

star→bright→smart→Bob

2. **Spur**

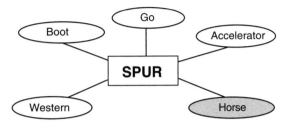

spur→star→shine→shoes→feet→wet→water

3. **Train**

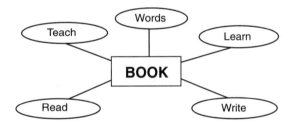

train→teach→student→student of life→life→live→love

4. **Book**

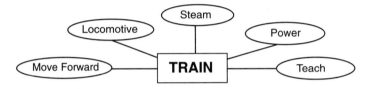

book→read→red→color→vibrant→alive→risk

5. **Gun**

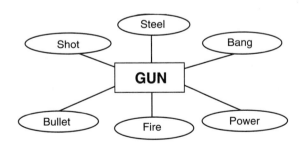

gun→bullets →shot→gun→steel→rob→thief→criminal→jail

Resting Period: Once again, Bob waits a week before reviewing the associations.

Further Interpretation: Initially, his logical mind makes the interpretations of the images more complex. The "train" throws him off, making him think of "training" as a business start-up. This is only partially correct. It is true that he has ambitions to teach, but he is not really enthusiastic about a training business. Training, teaching, or coaching is only part of his future, with his preference for teaching or coaching at the college level. The images of the spur, star, and gun do not seem to "fit" with the teaching profession. There is, however, a connection with a potential business start-up in his past that comes from the horse association to the word spur. About a year ago, Bob and his wife discussed starting a horse ranch and boarding service in Traverse City, Michigan. They had several conversations with local friends and decided not to pursue it at that time.

Activating the Solution: It is now time to revisit this potential business start-up. Bob will conduct a more comprehensive study of this opportunity of starting a horse ranch and boarding service.

CASE 2: EVALUATING THE RISK.

Problem: How can I start a business of my own?

Centering: I sit quietly in my living room listening to a tape of harp music.

Receptivity: I do the "reenergizing" breath and then start my countdown to become more receptive.

Imagery: The imagery that comes to mind is that of a cliff. I am picturing that I am at the end of a trail and I come to a cliff over a very deep gorge. At this location, I have to make a decision on how to approach the situation. I need to decide how to get to the bottom of the gorge. The following graphic represents the predicament I face and the resolution.

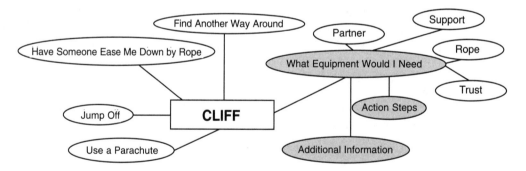

Interpretation: I interpret this imagery as a sign that I really do need to investigate the possibility of being a business owner. Once I can gather additional information, I will intuitively readdress this issue.

Activating the Solution: Here are the action steps I need to make this a reality:

1. Research areas to determine what businesses are available (Identify need and profit perspectives.)

2. Determine current personal financial position.

3. Determine available funding (personal investors, federal assistance and partnership).

4. Determine support from girlfriend and family.

5. Evaluate personal commitment.

6. Determine long-term career potential.

7. Evaluate current career potential.

8. Based on logic and intuition, make decision on whether or not to continue the process.

CASE 3: ARE YOU READY TO START A BUSINESS? **Background**: Paul and his family enjoy the comfort of the steady checks associated with full-time employment with a *Fortune* 500 company. However, Paul wishes to own his own business some day. Several ideas for new businesses and/or new products have come to mind while he is sleeping or running. He realizes that many of these ideas have ended up being pursued and developed by someone else, several months or years after he has made his initial discoveries. Paul calls this the stagnation of his entrepreneurial spirit. Although these ideas come quite freely, the nerve to quit his job and pursue an idea does not come as freely.

Recently, an idea developed quite suddenly that he has discussed with his wife, and both of them feel quite comfortable pursuing this concept. Paul is feeling scared and pressured as he wonders if he should quit his job and begin this small business. He resorted to IPS to help him decide if he should chase the dream of being the head of his own business.

Problem: Am I ready to run my own business?

Centering: He focuses on the picture of a geometric shape for about 5 minutes and then repeats the words "family" and "peace."

Receptivity: Feeling quite tense about making this decision, he takes several "ha!" breaths followed by the "tense and release" technique.

Imagery: He concentrates on thinking about a stoplight.

Interpretation: The red light reinforces the feeling to stop. He then asks

♦ Is this really a good idea? The feeling he has makes him want to get up and GO! This is a dilemma, when his imagery says no to him but his gut says yes to the idea. The next thought is to see if his wife should be the businessperson. The same stop feeling prevails.

He then asks,

♦ Is the idea a good business decision for me? This time no real feeling comes to mind, so he takes it as a caution.

♦ Is my family ready to undertake this business idea? The feeling of stop again prevails.

The final question he presents is

♦ Is this a worthy business decision for a good friend? The feeling is that he needs to go over to the friend's house and talk to him about the idea.

Activating the Solution: Paul wants to implement this business idea but feels that the caution is appropriate. A partner might be the answer. Since the response from his friend is so positive, he will include this person's involvement in his new business adventure.

What personal problems do you want to resolve? Let's go to Part Five to examine the gamut of personal problems that can be readily resolved with the IPS process. I'm sure you will find problems similar to your own somewhere in this Part.

Part Five

ACTIVATING INTUITIVE PROBLEM-SOLVING FOR PERSONAL SUCCESS

In my role as teacher, therapist, spouse, parent, and friend, I always hear about "personal" problems. I'm sure you are familiar with many of these challenges. Let me share some "problems" that you might be able to identify with.

Problem 1: Judy wants to handle money more creatively so she can save for tomorrow and still enjoy today.

Problem 2: Elliott wants to sell his house but doesn't know if he should sell it on his own or enlist the services of a realtor. If he sells it on his own, he can price the house competitively and it will probably sell. If he uses a realtor, it may sell faster but he will have to raise the price to cover the realtor's commission. Since the higher price would probably discourage some buyers, he is still debating this matter.

Problem 3: Arnold wants to gain more insight into the most effective way to raise his 3-year-old daughter so he can build her self-esteem and offer her balance as she grows up.

Problem 4: Carol is the single parent of two children, works 40-plus hours a week, and also goes to graduate school. She wants to be a mother who will be there for her kids. Carol agonizes about how to find the important balance so she can have "prime time" with them and not lose her children in the whirlwind.

What personal problems have you experienced recently? Are you professionally fulfilled but still searching for your ideal love or perfect partner? Is yours the "weighty" problem of "packing on the pounds" and then wondering how to lose the excess weight? Have any health challenges assailed you recently as you look for the quickest way to mend the aching back or sore legs? I know many people face incredible trials and tribulations building a dream house or adding on to their current residence. Are you performing the ultimate balancing act trying to give equal time to your multiple responsibilities from work, family, social, religious, and perhaps academic demands?

Did I get your attention and perhaps "hit a nerve"? In this unit, you will see how people have applied the IPS process to some of these vexing situations.

Let me remind you of the theme that, like a river, goes winding throughout this book. You can change your focus and engage the intuitive mind through the IPS process to find a solution to any problem or situation. In the next two chapters, you will see how seemingly insoluble problems are resolved so personal needs with family and friends are met, major decisions are accomplished, and solutions are found so time and financial needs can be managed successfully. I am certain you will be able to relate to several of these challenges and, most important, find solutions yourself and by applying IPS to your nagging dilemmas.

Chapter Fifteen

USING INTUITION TO CREATE VIBRANT HEALTH

Now, the history of science makes clear that the greatest advancements in man's understanding of the universe are made by intuitive leaps at the frontiers of knowledge, not by intellectual walks along well-traveled paths. Similarly, the greatest scientific thinkers are those who rely on sudden intuitive flashes to solve problems.

ANDREW WEIL, M.D.
The Natural Mind

People today are becoming more responsible for taking care of themselves. As they have become increasingly informed about the perils of certain life-style "killer diseases," they have empowered themselves to take responsibility for keeping healthy and physically fit.

In this chapter, you will discover how intuitive problem-solving can be applied to health concerns, including eradicating stress, improving physical health and finding the right exercise program.

HOW TO USE INTUITION TO MAINTAIN HEALTH

Good health is indeed wealth and characterizes the successful individual. The following cases illustrate how IPS has been used to address challenging health and physical fitness concerns.

To maintain optimal health, you can repeatedly imagine that you are perfectly healthy until the image portrayed becomes reality. At other times, the intuitive mind tosses us an image or key that unlocks the door to improved health. For example, when Jean wanted to help motivate her husband to stop smoking, she simply asked her intuitive mind to show her how to help him release this negative habit. The image of a mattress came to her, and after associating to that symbol, she realized how important her support was. She was shown that she could motivate him by being supportive, if and when he finally decided to change his behavior.

While this solution seems very simple, it illustrates how the intuitive mind can help the problem solver understand and resolve the problem. Notice what imagery is created to alleviate stress in the next case.

How to Alleviate Stress

The word "stress" is constantly emphasized in the media. Many people choose to postpone dealing with stress until tomorrow rather than confront it today. After a major health crisis, Judy realized she could no longer ignore stress but had to attend to the disabling effects immediately. You will see what appropriate solution she implements in Case 1.

CASE: RELIEVING STRESS. **Background**: Judy read an article about the type of woman who was likely to have hormonal difficulties caused by stress. Immediately she saw herself in this type of person, in her early thirties, never married, very athletic, very organized, always wanting to do things the right way, very active outside of work, and working in a corporate setting. According to the medical report, this type of woman is actually under a great deal of stress, which often goes unnoticed. This kind of stress can lead to health problems that could eventually cause serious damage.

> *Problem*: What can be done about the stress in my life?
>
> *Centering*: On my desk at work I have a hand-drawn Christmas card of an angel with doves on her wings. I focus on the doves in this picture.
>
> *Receptivity*: I take several "total" breaths and then relax by letting go of everything that comes to mind. As I focus on one of the doves on the card, I let go of my worries and responsibilities.
>
> *Imagery*: I keep looking at the dove and trying to think of what this might signify. To me a dove always meant peace, joy, happiness, and freedom.
>
> *Interpretation*: The following amplification shows all of my associations to the dove symbol.

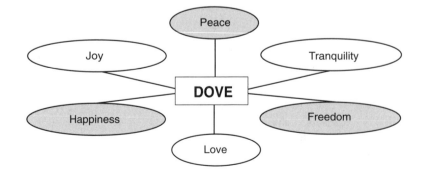

A feeling of peace comes when I think about the dove. In addition to peace, I feel happiness and notice my cares vanishing in the wings of the dove for a while. I think of freedom as not bound or fixed by any rules. I know that in my own life I am a very rigid person and feel fixed by my own set of rules. I have placed a great deal of pressure on myself to do things in a certain manner at exact times. I begin to see that the dove represents more of a freeing sensation than any of the other associations, including peace. I realize that the dove is showing me that I have to be free of restrictions or less bound to my own rules and pressures.

Resting Period: At this point, I let go by putting things out of mind, feeling more relaxed, and trying not to worry about the things around me. Just focusing on being free from all the restraints placed upon myself is making me feel more peaceful.

Further Interpretation: I realize how I have been pushing myself needlessly. Now I can release that pressure and truly bring the needed peace and freedom into my life.

Activating the Solution: I am becoming more aware of the times I push myself a little too hard. I am beginning to decline when my schedule is full and someone wants me to do something. Also, I have to be more aware of my rigidity and am learning not to take myself and my work too seriously. I can release the rigid restraint and feel freer every day.

EXERCISE

Alleviating and Reducing Stress

I can reach into my big bag of "stress busters" and pull out many ways to help you manage stress successfully. Remember, stress isn't something outside of you—it is between your ears, which means you have the power to do something about it. Let me give you ten stress busters, then you can come up with some of your own.

- Learn to breathe deeply.

- Plan your free time.

- Do not evaluate yourself on the basis of what you think you should have.

- Don't set unattainable goals—be happy with what you are now.

- Learn to enjoy dull sermons and lectures—a good time to relax.

- Keep the faith—life without faith and hope is terribly empty.

- Listening to music of your choice is a great relaxer.

- Laughing is a great stress reliever. Find something comical in any situation.

- Apologize when you wrong someone—don't let guilt build up.

- Luxuriate in a warm bath or hot tub to soothe tension away.

How to Improve Your Physical Health

CASE: TAKING THE FIRST STEPS TO GOOD HEALTH.

Problem: How can I improve my physical health?

Centering: To be receptive to physical sensations, I see myself taking a long peaceful walk in the morning. It is quiet and the sun is warm and bright. There is enough time to focus on the leaf patterns in several trees. I notice how relaxed and energized I feel during the walk.

Receptivity: I take several "hang-sah" breaths followed by the "tense and release" technique.

Imagery: I pose the question of how I can improve my physical health, and then I imagine a building. I go inside and see a pool, indoor track, weight machines, and lots of people doing different exercises. All the people look very trim and physically fit. Next, I see a straight short path that directly connects the building to my house. When an image of my appointment book comes up, I notice that the notation "club" is written in for every other morning. All these images led to several health-related questions.

- How can I quit smoking? While I am thinking about this, my chest becomes heavy and congested. It is hard breathing and I start to cough. I envision myself being enveloped by a black cloud of smoke. It smells awful and stale. Next I see myself smoking outside my home. The image changes and I am smoking outside my office rather than at my desk as I usually do. I see a chart listing the number of cigarettes I smoke daily. It shows a decrease down to zero over a month period. I next sense a very clean fresh smell and see myself in the store buying new clothes. The clothes are attractive and smell clean. Finally, I see my rosy face in the mirror and notice my teeth are much whiter than usual.

- How can I change my diet? As I begin to think about food, I feel very bloated and full. The number 6 appears. I can smell fresh fruit and see my favorite fruits in a dish. There is a huge pile of vegetables on top of some fish and bread. There appear four cups of coffee, ten glasses of water, and a bottle of vitamins. I see myself writing down what I am eating. On the table is a book on nutrition and diet. Finally, I see myself driving past all the fast-food restaurants where I usually stop. I lose my appetite because the sight of these restaurants makes me nauseous. My stomach feels tight and trim and my clothes do not seem as tight as usual.

Interpretation: The walking in the woods imagery is showing how this activity will give me more energy. The building is actually the athletic club in my neighborhood. The path between the club and my house emphasizes walking there to work out. The appointment book reminds me to schedule regular times for exercise. Seeing the word "club" prompts me to rejoin the club and resume my workouts.

The imagery about smoking is showing me the way to quit and emphasizes the practice of smoking outside rather than at my desk. If I do this, the majority of my smoking will be cut out. The troubled breathing and heavy chest signal the bad effect smoking is having on my health. Experiencing the smell shows how I am stinking up my office, home, car, and clothes. I know I will be cutting down gradually over a one-month period after seeing the chart of my smoking consumption. My reward for quitting smoking will be buying new clothes with the money I presently spend on cigarettes.

The diet imagery becomes clear, showing me that I should eat fruits and vegetables six times each day. The image also alerts me to drink less coffee and more water. Driving past the fast-food restaurants reminds me to stop going there. Then, I will not only feel healthier, but my waist will get slim and clothes will fit better.

Activating the Solution: The imagery provides me with several solutions to current health problems. The first commitment is to make physical exercise a regular part of my life by rejoining the club. Then, I will stop smoking by tapering off my consumption. I have already started to eat regular meals consisting mainly of fruits and vegetables.

EXERCISE

Create a Positive Reality to Improve Your Health

This exercise is inspired by Shakti Gawain's "Creative Visualization" technique.[1]

What aspect of your health would you like to improve? Is there a debilitating habit you would like to eliminate? Do you want to exercise regularly? Stop smoking? Change your food intake? Focus on any facet that you want to improve and do the following steps at least twice a day, on a daily basis, until you have eliminated this habit or enacted the desired change.

1. Pick a goal—something that you want to do or achieve (I would like to stop smoking).

   My goal is _____

   _____

2. Make an affirmation out of it by stating it in a simple sentence, in the present tense, as if it were already true (e.g., My clothes smell so clean now that I no longer smoke).

   My affirmation is _____

   _____

3. Use whatever imagery is strong to help you feel as if the affirmation were already true. You can close your eyes and imagine what it would be like if it were true. Don't worry if you can't picture it clearly; just imagine it as best as you can.

   My "picture" is _____

   _____

4. Let go of it! Go about your life, but be sure to follow your intuitive hunches and flashes as the new changes are coming about.

   My experience in "letting go" is _____

   _____

CHOOSING THE EXERCISE PROGRAM THAT'S RIGHT FOR YOU

EXERCISE

The Red Suit: An Imaging Exercise for General Well-being

Imaginary jogging has been found to improve the effects of an exercise program. An amazing study involving two groups of cardiac patients was done at a Canadian hospital.[2] One group performed the actual exercises, a second group was asked to do them through imaging. The group who used imaging was found to recover more quickly than the group actually exercising.

Directions: Do the following exercise once a day, for 2 minutes every day.

Find a quiet place where you will not be disturbed. Close your eyes. Breathe out three times and see yourself putting on a red jogging suit and red sneakers. See yourself going out of your home and walking to the park. Enter the park and begin to run around it clockwise, becoming aware of everything you see. Become aware of what you sense and feel, of the wind passing you by. Become aware of your stride and your breathing. Notice the trees, grass, and sky. Complete the run by coming back to the point at which you started. Walk out of the park and back to your home. Take off your jogging clothes, shower, dry off, and see yourself putting on the clothes you are going to wear for the day.

Then open your eyes, look around the room and stretch your arms. At the end of one week, note how you feel. Is there an improvement in your vitality?

_____

_____

_____

How to Find the Right Exercise Program

CASE: FINDING A PROGRAM YOU CAN STICK WITH.

> *Problem*: What kind of exercise program can I stick with?
>
> *Centering*: I repeat that my intuitive mind knows the correct answer to my question.
>
> *Receptivity*: After taking several "hang-sah" breaths, I do the "stretching and breathing" technique.
>
> *Imagery*: I see myself in a gymnasium. The only exercise machine in the entire gymnasium is the Nordic Track exercise machine.
>
> *Interpretation*: I realize that the Nordic Track exercise machine will be part of an exercise program I can stick with.
>
> *Activating the Solution*: I will call the Nordic Track people to get more information.

In the next chapter you will see how to use IPS for clarifying communication problems with family members or friends.

Chapter Sixteen

USING INTUITION TO MEET CHALLENGES WITH FAMILY AND FRIENDS

Like the wolf, intuition has claws that pry things open and pin things down, it has eyes that can see through the shields of the persona, it has ears that hear beyond the range of mundane human understanding.

CLARISSA PINKOLA ESTÉS
Women Who Run with the Wolves

I acknowledge Jim Stark, the circulation sales manager for the *Muskegon Chronicle* in Michigan, for leading me to my "senses" by showing me how the five sensory receptors filter the intuitive input. He was impressed with the speed and accuracy of IPS resolutions and wanted to use this process to mend the communication gap that existed between himself and his two teen-age daughters. Here is Jim's account of how he improved communication with his younger daughter. Jim relates:

> There had been a communication problem between myself and my younger daughter since who remembers. She is a good daughter and one to be proud of, but we just couldn't communicate beyond surface matters. The fact was, we felt so clumsy that we rarely talked at all. I decided to "get into her shoes" and try to sense her environment—mental, spiritual, and social. She had about 50 different pairs of shoes at the time. It was one of the few things we joked about. As soon as I opened her closet and started going through her shoes (literally), it became clearer to me. She didn't know her role, that is, whose shoes she was supposed to fit into.

267

I could feel her anxiety and realized my own insensitivity. I have started letting her know that she doesn't need to be anybody but who she is. I told her that she is unique in and of herself. I have started listening, really listening to what she is saying.

It hasn't been an easy assignment, and this story doesn't end with everyone living happily ever. Talking to each other has become much easier, though. I now understand her position, and that makes things much easier. She is now working on understanding me. If I hadn't taken the time "to put myself in her shoes," we'd still be two total strangers connected only by our bloodline.

Jim Stark was pleased with his discovery, and he eventually shared it with other parents in the continuing education course he developed, called "Intuitive Parenting."

The sensitive area of communication is one of the challenges highlighted in this chapter. Reaching out to relate to other people multiplies the problems and feelings of the parties involved. Clear communication is vital to determine what needs are festering. Unfortunately, most of us become so preoccupied with our own concerns that we don't "hear" what the other person is asking or even "see" how they are feeling.

In this chapter, you will discover how IPS can be used for a variety of day-to-day challenges, including

- ◆ Communicating with family and friends.
- ◆ Love and marriage.
- ◆ Using intuitive problem-solving to make winning winning major decisions.
- ◆ Finding the best way to communicate with friends.
- ◆ Effectively communicating with children.

COMMUNICATING WITH FAMILY AND FRIENDS

The variety of issues that have been resolved in the next two cases by using the IPS process include finding out how to heal a long-standing family feud and reestablishing communication with a parent.

Building Bridges to Your Family

You might wonder if the substance of this first unusual and complex case came from a soap opera. Yet, it happened to one of my students, who still can't believe how the IPS process showed her one picture that was literally worth a thousand words. She was amazed that her intuitive mind could show her a picture of a long-standing family feud being resolved.

CASE 1: A FAMILY REUNION. **Background**: This personal problem involves my older brother and mother. My older brother discovered two years ago that he had a different father than the rest of the siblings in our family and that this father is still alive. He has never had a good relationship with my mother, so when he established a relationship with his father and the rest of his "new" family, mother became enraged and literally campaigned against him. He desperately wanted to heal the relationship with our mother, who continued to distance herself from him.

My sister-in-law was planning a huge celebration of about 250 people for my brother's fiftieth birthday. Though he wanted my mother to be there, I felt he was unrealistic in expecting her to come. I also knew that her presence would only cause all of us more pain. Mother made it clear that she didn't want to come and maybe put herself in a position of being humiliated. Then, six days before the party, Mother called and said she would come after all. She gave me a list of conditions that had to be met if she was to put in an appearance at the party.

In the past whenever my mother had attended social events at my brother's, she literally isolated herself in a corner, smoked all evening, and was offended if any strangers were invited to the gathering. Needless to say, after the events of the last two years, I really wasn't prepared for her to be at that party and wondered why she was coming. In fact, I could not imagine that she had the courage to come, much less the ability to behave properly if she did.

Problem: How can I help Mom to be comfortable at my brother's party?

Centering: I retreated to my bedroom study, gazed into a faceted crystal ball suspended from a lamp, and listened to the *Pachelbel Canon in D Minor* cassette tape playing softly in the background.

I kept saying the word "peace."

Receptivity: I took several "hang-sah" breaths and "progressively" relaxed my body until I felt totally receptive.

Imagery: I heard the word "wait" and then imagined seeing "the sun rising" and heard the sounds of a "waterfall." I asked, "What is my role in the weekend interactions?"

The response was "wait."

I then saw my mother, my brother, and his father standing together and being surrounded lovingly by both families! I couldn't believe it!

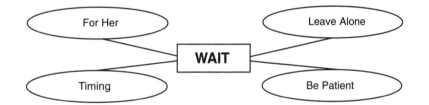

Interpretation: My amplification to the word "wait" was the following:

This left me puzzled, so I did a word association to the waterfall and rising sun.

waterfall→cleansing→healing

This suggested that my mother would have a cleansing and be healed of her negativity toward my brother.

rising sun→son (my brother) rising and being happy

Resting Period: I turned off the light and sat quietly listening to the music for several minutes.

Further Interpretation: My logical mind said it could never happen. This was wishful thinking for a hopeless situation. I thought my mother could never forgive herself and others for real or imagined slights. I then realized that I had to let go of this logical thinking and trust the intuitive mind to show me the greater good for my brother, mother, and family.

Activating the Solution: When I went to the airport to pick up my mother, they wheeled her off the plane in a wheelchair. As we drove away from the airport, Mother continually spewed negative comments. She was very nervous about the party and continued to list her conditions until my energy was drained.

However, much to my astonishment, my mother did exactly what I never imagined she would do. She was gracious all weekend. She faced my brother's father and his family with amazing strength and openness. A miraculous healing process began for my mother and the rest of the family. True to the IPS imagery that I had received, my brother, his father, and our mother stood together, surrounded by both families. The tears of joy that came throughout the weekend were indeed the water for cleansing and healing.

CASE 2: REOPENING COMMUNICATION WITH A PARENT. **Background**: At the age of 25, I went into counseling to explore my poor relationship with my parents. During the past four years, I have concentrated on my relationship with my mother. We have struggled throughout that time, since I realize I can no longer let her manipulate or control my life. As a result, our relationship has become so strained and tense that we have not talked for the past two years.

Problem: When can I reopen communication with mother?

Centering: I close my eyes and lie back in a lawn chair on the deck. I focus on the sound of the breeze through the leaves on the trees and the sound of the water rippling to shore.

Receptivity: I begin my deep breathing exercises by taking several deep "total" breaths. Then, closing my eyes, I concentrate on relaxing every muscle in my body by going through the "autogenic" technique.

Imagery: I pose several questions to establish a time, place, and vision of how this conversation with my mother will take place.

♦ Who will be there? I see my brother, mother, and myself at my brother's house. We are all talking. My brother is uncharacteristically serious and not like his usual worry-free, kidding-around self.

♦ When should we meet? I visualize a calendar and ask for a day and month to light up. First, I look at the total year. October becomes bright. Then, I visualize the days in October and see the 20th light up. Since my mother and brother live 120 miles away, I will need to drive there to meet them. When I look at the calendar I notice that the 20th is a Saturday, I know I have the perfect date.

♦ What will the outcome be? I have been putting this off forever and finally feel confident that I can meet my mother. I am wondering how my mother will receive me, and ask for a symbol to describe our conversation. In response, the symbol of a book emerges.

Interpretation: Many associations to this image of a closed hardcover book emerge during the amplification. These associations show the following:

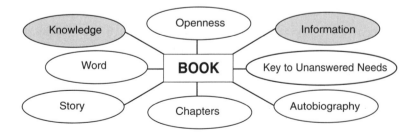

The "Ah'ha!" comes as I realize that this book holds the information and knowledge I need to share with my mother.

◆ How to open this book? The associations that come to mind are open page by page or pry open. What keeps coming to my mind is to open the book page by page, starting at the beginning and proceeding to the end.

◆ How will my mother respond to what is in the book? I see my mother crying. This appears to be a cry of relief because we are finally talking. I sense that she now understands what I have been through in the past few years.

Activating the Solution: I am now comfortable about reopening contact with my mother when we meet on October 20th.

EXERCISE

Wearing Your Parents' Shoes

When I taught child psychology at college, I stressed how the "child is father to man." No matter how old you are, you are the child that needs to become the father or mother who birthed you. To literally understand how they feel, you will follow the directions to get under their skin and become either parent, or both if you prefer.

Directions: First, get into the alpha level. Look at a focusing object. Then, affirm, "I will understand my parents' point of view" and follow that by taking seven "hang-sah" breaths.

As your parent, you are sitting down and contemplating a recent disagreement you the parent have had with your child. You want to present the parental point of view about the dispute.

What is it?

_____

_____

_____

_____

What would you like your son or daughter to say to you about this situation?

_____

_____

_____

_____

What action would you like your son or daughter to take to make amends?

_____

_____

How has this intuitively helped you understand the difficulty so you can mend this feud?

_____

_____

LOVE AND MARRIAGE

Love relationships often appear to present insurmountable challenges. When I was younger, for example, dating was a high priority among my friends during our high school and college years.

The Dating Game

The following two cases address crucial aspects of this process, namely, where to meet, and whether a breakup is the right thing to do.

CASE 1: WHERE TO MEET A POTENTIAL SPOUSE. **Background**: Renee tends to go to a lot of nightclubs with girlfriends but has yet to meet a man in that setting who is interested in a serious relationship. She knows it is possible because several friends have met their husbands under these circumstances, but that has not happened to her.

Problem: Where can I meet an appropriate person to date?

Centering: She watches the fan oscillating on the ceiling and becomes mesmerized.

Receptivity: Once again, Renee takes several "total" breaths and does some body stretches. She does a "progressive relaxation" by sending a message to each part of her body that it is relaxed. She imagines herself taking a walk in the woods and being very much aware of all the various sights and smells until she comes to her favorite place by the river.

Imagery: This time she imagines herself walking to the edge of a lake and reaches her hand down in the water until she feels an object. This article that she picks up in her hand is a silver antique cross.

Interpretation: The cross is beautiful, with exquisite detail. In the center of the cross is a round black jewel. But she is very puzzled by what this means.

Resting Period: Since this is the only image she retrieves during the IPS session, Renee decides to go for a walk. On the way back home, the answer comes as a strong "Ah'ha!"

Further Interpretation: The cross signifies that she might meet a nice gentleman by going to some of her church's social events. Although this seems obvious, Renee admits she never thought of meeting someone through church. Now, she decides to get more involved with the church activities so she can potentially meet somebody. When she does, she will be clearly prepared for her knight in shining armor, as signified by the black jewel in the center, to come along.

CASE 2: BREAKING UP IS HARD TO DO. **Background**: After dating Cindy for two years, we broke up two months ago. I am not sure if this was the right thing to do since we really get along well.

Problem: Is breaking up the right thing to do?

Centering: The affirmation I choose to repeat is, "My intuitive mind will lead me to the right answer."

Receptivity: I assume a relaxed position and take several "hang-sah" breaths to get into the alpha level.

Imagery: As I concentrate on our relationship, the image of a small ticking clock appears.

Interpretation: Using amplification, I come up with the following associations:

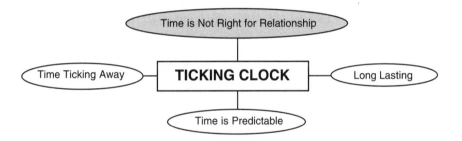

The flash finally comes as these associations showing the dynamics of our relationship are enlightening. We don't have a personality problem with our relationship, but the timing is all wrong. Cindy is three years older and wants a very "serious" relationship, while I am too involved with my career right now to make such a commitment. The intuitive input is showing me that we are not in the same time frame for the relationship to survive.

Activating the Solution: Cindy and I are still good friends and we openly communicate with each other. As I explain these insights, she agrees that we are in different stages of our lives and our relationship needs. The IPS exercise helps clear up the frustration that I have built up wondering whether the break up is the right thing to do.

USING INTUITIVE PROBLEM-SOLVING TO MAKE WINNING DECISIONS

Getting Married

During my interviews with leading male and female entrepreneurs, I asked them about the greatest risk they ever took. Quite a few gave the brief reply, "getting married." One pointed out, if you are not satisfied, you can't take it back as easily as you can return a purchase. The following case is concerned with the big "M," or marriage, question.

CASE: TO MARRY OR NOT. **Background**: Kelly has been dating her boyfriend for nine months, and recently he moved in with her. They are thinking of getting married, but both are indecisive about making this final commitment. Both have been married previously and neither wants to experience another divorce. Kelly notes that her boyfriend is more secure about getting married than she is because he has been divorced longer than she has. Kelly had a bitter divorce and is afraid of making another mistake.

Problem: Should I marry my boyfriend?

Centering: Kelly comes home from work and decides to take a hot bath to relax. To become centered, she concentrates on the tile pattern around the bathroom.

Receptivity: Sitting in the tub, she let the hot water ease her tense shoulders and muscles. She takes some deep breaths to clear her mind from the day's activities at the office.

Imagery: She closes her eyes and waits for an image to appear to help her resolve the marriage question. She sees a traffic light with the green light on, but then the yellow light starts to shine simultaneously. The yellow light is not as bright as the green light. The yellow light puzzles her, so she elicits reasons for why the yellow light might be shining. The words that appear are "caution," "be careful," "concern," "my fears," and "unsure." The phrase that she is drawn to is "my fears."

Interpretation: The green light is telling Kelly that marrying her boyfriend is the right thing to do. He is the person she will be happy spending the rest of her life with. The yellow light tells her that she still has some fears left over from her divorce which mainly center on being rejected and deserted.

Activating the Solution: Kelly thinks that living with her boyfriend prior to getting married will help her get rid of any fears and build more confidence about their being wed. They are planning to get married in six months, and Kelly feels the majority of her concerns will be answered by then.

Communicating with Your Mate

CASE: GROWING WITH A SPOUSE.

Problem: What can I do to improve my relationship with my wife?

Centering: Sitting by a lake and looking at the water, I affirm that my intuitive mind will show me what to do.

Receptivity: This is a wonderful setting in which to take several "reenergizing" breaths followed by the "stretching and breathing" technique.

Imagery: I see a clock.

Interpretation: Amplifying to the clock I discover the following:

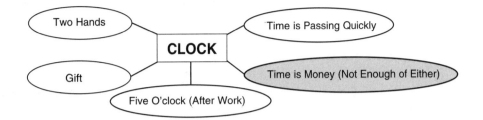

The two biggest reasons for our stress are time and money. I need to know which one to focus on to help us get along better this week. I see the word time.

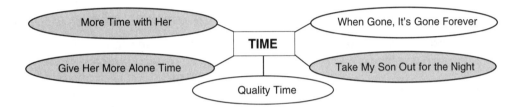

Activating the Solution: I need to take my infant son out for a night this week. My wife stays home with him all day and most nights while I am busy with school or doing homework. I am missing time with my wife and also need to spend quality time with my son. I will watch him Tuesday night and then get a baby-sitter so I can take my wife out to dinner on Saturday.

FINDING THE BEST WAY TO COMMUNICATE WITH FRIENDS

CASE 1: MAKING NEW FRIENDS. **Background**: Sue laments that she has been so busy with her work, family responsibilities, and going to school that she has not pursued social activities in her spare time. She did, however, become very close to her next-door neighbor for about two years. Then, she suddenly realized she was being taken advantage of as shared confidences were exposed to other neighbors. Sue abruptly ended the relationship because the trust that she cherishes in any relationship was violated.

Problem: Will I be able to find and maintain a close female relationship?

Centering: She focuses on a triangle with a small delicate flower bloom in its center.

Receptivity: Sue goes through the "autogenic relaxation" technique and does the "countdown" to relax thoroughly.

Imagery: She poses the following questions:

♦ Will the person be someone I already know or someone new? Sue visualizes two hands: one with the word "old," and the other with the word "new." She closes her eyes and waits until one becomes more dominant. Since both images reflect the same intensity, she decides to stop and relax by taking ten more deep breaths. She visualizes the hands again and finds they still appear the same. She begins to get a bit discouraged until an intuitive flash shows two close friends: one, a new friend, and the other a person she already knows.

◆ Will I meet the new person at work, school, church, or a social outing? Sue visualizes a set of steps and puts "work" on the first step, "school" on the second step, "church" on the third step, and "social outing" on the fourth step. As she visualizes herself walking up the steps, she finds herself feeling very comfortable with the step that represents church.

◆ Will I meet the new friend during a service or spiritual class? Sue becomes still and visualizes the word "service" on the right side of the altar and the word "class" on the left side of the altar. She continues to shift her emphasis back and forth. She feels drawn to the right, to "service."

◆ What is the first initial of the name of the person I already know?

To visualize the answer to this question, Sue decides to mentally write each letter of the alphabet on cards and string these cards on a line that can easily be moved with a pulley and string. She pulls the string as the cards parade past her in succession. She needs to go through the alphabet only one time, because the letter "L" flashes vividly. She tries to think of anyone she knows whose first name begins with the letter L. The only person that she can think of is Lisa, the wife of one of her husband's clients.

Interpretation: The IPS shows the potential of having two good friends. One is a new friend that Sue will meet at church during a service. The other friend may be Lisa.

Activating the Solution: Sue decides to give Lisa a call for a lunch date and to remain open and receptive to any new friends coming into her life through the church setting.

CASE 2: PATCHING UP A FRIENDSHIP.

Problem: When would be the right time to patch up some differences with an old friend?

Centering: Mike opens his day planner and stares at a page with a colorful geometrical picture to become still.

Receptivity: Since he feels terribly stressed, Mike takes three "ha!" breaths to relax and then does the "tense and release" relaxation technique. Then, looking at the sky, he focuses on the abstract reflections in the clouds. He becomes more aware of the sun shining through the windows, brightening the room and providing a sense of warmth and security.

Imagery: He wants to actively retrieve imagery and decides to use the images of the calendar and clock to determine when this amend should be made. He visualizes a calendar that has all 12 months of the year. Slowly, he turns one page at a time and stops at the month of October. Next he sees a calendar for the month of October with 31 days on it and waits for a day of the month to be highlighted. The 8th becomes more pronounced on the calendar.

He wants to find out what time of day would be best for the contact and visualizes an analog clock with the hour hand sweeping slowly around the face. He remains receptive as the hands slowly circle the face of the watch. After a few seconds, the hour hand stops at 11:30 A.M.

Next, he begins to visualize how the meeting will go and looks for any symbols that might show any information about the event. He imagines meeting his friend in a restaurant. The only image shows his friend smiling, which suggests a positive experience.

To find out if the meeting should take place over breakfast, lunch or dinner, Mike visualizes a wheel with three categories on it in a pie graph format. He visualizes the wheel spinning slowly past a marker which, when it stops, points to lunch.

Interpretation: Mike and his friend will have lunch on October 8th at 11:30 A.M. to patch up their past differences.

Activating the Solution: Mike eagerly notes the date in his day planner and looks forward to contacting his friend for a lunch appointment.

EXERCISE

Reestablishing Communication with a Friend

Sit quietly and think of a friend that you feel estranged from at this time. You are both standing face to face. Let your intuitive mind show you who takes the first step toward the other. Who is it?

_____

_____

Let your intuitive mind tell you what you need to say. What are your words?

_____

_____

Your intuitive mind will give you an "image" showing you what must be done to restore peace and harmony. Use any interpretation technique to analyze this symbol.

My interpretation is:

What is your intuitive insight about how to heal the breach?

_____

_____

_____

_____

CASE 3: HANDLING A CONFRONTATION. **Background**: A couple of months ago, I had to confront a friend about something she did. I shared a secret with her and not leaking this information to others in the same business as my husband was vital. Although I had a "gut feeling" that I shouldn't tell her, I also knew I would have trouble keeping the secret. Somehow I felt that if I didn't tell her, I would end up lying to her. Later, I found out that she actually did tell a couple of people. Unfortunately, they were friends of my husband's biggest competitor. When I found out that she divulged the confidence, I went to confront her. I lost my temper and blew up, which is most uncharacteristic of me.

Problem: Was I wrong to confront Carol so strongly.

Centering: Looking out the window, I focus on the budding daffodils. Unfortunately, my anger escalates, and I lose my concentration. When this happens, I close my eyes and affirm that "I am relaxed."

Receptivity: I take three "total" breaths and then go into the "abbreviated autogenic" relaxation technique.

Imagery: I ask the question to see if my outburst was justified. All I saw was a mule standing in a field. That was all, but what came to me right away was an old joke about a stubborn mule. This mule wouldn't work for the farmer, so the farmer cajoled, pleaded, and offered it treats. When that didn't work, he threatened and yelled at the mule, which also didn't work. Finally, he picked up a 2 x 4 and whacked it on the head. A guy passing on the road stopped and asked why he was beating the poor animal, and the farmer replied, "I'm not beating him, I'm just getting his attention!"

Interpretation: When I recalled this "tale," I realized that I wasn't being hard on my friend but just trying to get her attention. I really appreciated how my intuition was using a sense of humor to get me to lighten up and relieve my tension.

Activating the Solution: My intuition is clearly telling me to ignore the issue. I take responsibility for not being more up front to begin with by telling her that I couldn't discuss a confidential situation. Now that I "got her attention," I don't think she will ever betray a confidence again. I'm glad I realized that it was a mistake made by both of us. I'm sure in the future I will use better judgment in such a situation.

EFFECTIVELY COMMUNICATING WITH CHILDREN

When challenges with children abound, taking the appropriate action and/or saying the right words is critical. IPS was used in the first case to validate the right time for toilet training, to create improved communication between a mother and her four year old in the second case and to help a parent discover how to motivate his 17 year old to do well in school, in case number 3.

Heeding the Needs of the Young Ones

CASE 1: TOILET TRAINING.

Problem: Is Jeremy ready to be toilet trained?

Centering: I close my eyes and repeat the phrase "I am relaxed" several times.

Receptivity: After taking a couple of deep breaths, I do some shoulder shrugs and ankle roll exercises to relax these tense parts of my body.

Imagery: I ask the question and hope that a stoplight or cards with a yes/no will appear. Unfortunately, this doesn't occur but I do see a green circle/ball.

Interpretation: I amplify to this and retrieve many associations, but nothing seems to make sense.

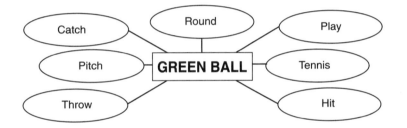

Suddenly, it dawns on me. The green ball is my stoplight image showing the color green, which means go. This shows me that Jeremy is ready to start toilet training.

Activating the Solution: The following weekend, I start the toilet training. After one and a half weeks, I think maybe I have misinterpreted the green ball since I have been having a lot of difficulty with the toilet training. Finally, after two more weeks, Jeremy is doing great. He tells me when he has to go to the bathroom and is having very few accidents.

CASE 2: APPLYING DISCIPLINE. **Background**: Donna talks about her second-born child Krista, who at four years old is most difficult to discipline. Trying to reach out and understand her, Donna poses the following IPS problem:

Problem: How can I better communicate with my daughter and put myself in her shoes to understand her thoughts and position?

Centering: I focus for a few minutes on the flowers sitting on the table.

Receptivity: Then, I take several "total" breaths and do a "progressive" relaxation.

Imagery: Immediately I picture a very bright sunshine.

Interpretation: Doing an amplification shows me the following:

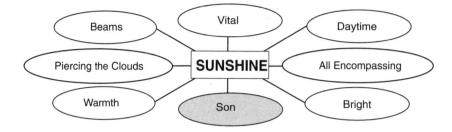

Quentin, my first-born child, is a year and a half older than Krista. He was the best baby a woman could have and continues to be an easygoing, good natured little guy. Anything is OK with him as long as we're together. Now Krista has come along and has demanded more attention right from the start. She continues to be a determined, highly spirited little girl. She "knows" what she likes and dislikes, and what she wants or doesn't want. And she isn't shy about telling you. Many of her personality traits are very positive. She will *never* be one to say "I can't" or "I don't know how." She will find a way, no matter what! And that is terrific! She's got high energy and great determination. If channeled in the right direction, she'll succeed in anything she tries. As I look at the "sunshine" symbol and the word "son" jumps out at me I clearly know why I have problems with Krista. I am assuming that I can handle Krista as I did Quentin. Now, I know that I need to deal with each of them differently.

Activating the Solution: Although I'm not sure *how* I will change my approach with Krista, I am now very much aware of the mistakes I have been making and will correct myself in the future. They are two unique children, and I need to tailor my communication with each of them individually. I look forward to the results of this new awareness and consequent plan.

CASE 3: SCHOOL MOTIVATION. **Background**: Here is Ron's story about his 17-year-old daughter who is starting her senior year in high school.

My wife and I know that she is capable of more than the below-average work she is doing. Over the past few years, it has become apparent that she does not know how to study and is not motivated to do so. We have tried many things, including tutors, a learning center, setting strict study hours each night, and even limiting some outside activities in an attempt to motivate her.

Problem: How can I help my daughter, Becky, become motivated to do well in school?

Centering: Using a "koosh ball" as a focusing object, Ron concentrates on relaxing and repeats the phrase "I will help Becky."

Receptivity: He concentrates on breathing slow and easy as he repeats the phrase.

Imagery: Ron sees a silver plane flying through the sky.

Interpretation: He tries word association to get some insight into this situation.

plane→freedom→encourage her to leave the nest→stop trying to influence her

This chain of associations doesn't work so he decides to try again.

plane→a trip→her desire to go to Europe next summer

The "Ah'ha!" comes as Ron remembers Becky's keen desire to go to Europe next summer.

Activating the Solution: Ron decides to try an incentive program in which he will underwrite the trip costs based on a scale related to her grade point average.

Understanding Your Child

Use the metaphor technique to help you get a better understanding of your child. See your child as (1) a song, (2) a game, or (3) a movie. Clarify any images with any of the interpretation techniques.

Song: My image is

_____

_____

Interpretation is

Game: My image is

_____

_____

Interpretation is

Movie: My image is

_____

_____

Interpretation is

What have you learned intuitively from this exercise about your child?

_____

_____

_____

_____

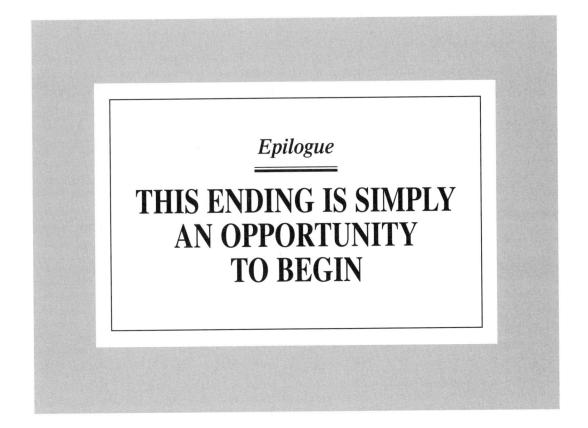

Epilogue

THIS ENDING IS SIMPLY AN OPPORTUNITY TO BEGIN

People with high levels of personal mastery do not set out to integrate reason and intuition. Rather, they achieve it naturally—as a by-product of their commitment to use all resources at their disposal. They cannot afford to choose between reason and intuition, or head and heart, any more than they would choose to walk on one leg or see with one eye.

PETER SENGE
The Fifth Discipline

THE LAST WORD OR TWO

I teach a course in a Masters in Management program called, "Whole Brain Thinking for Managers: Integrating Intuition and Logic." At the end of a semester, I notice how amazed and excited the students are with the intuitive discoveries they are continually making. Many are not finding something new but are simply "reinventing the wheel." They are now attaching a label to something they have always done. They have always been able to make a quick decision without having sufficient facts, for example, or wander into a new area to make a judgment call. Often it seemed to be a "lucky guess" or "coincidence" when they knew so much about an unexplored area. Now, more confidence is placed on the hunches that guide them through the quick decision or quick call. After learning the IPS process, the flashes that come instantly are imbued with respect as they lead to the right choices and connections.

Most important, I have seen how using intuition has empowered so many people to cope with continual change and chaotic upheaval at work and in their personal lives. You too will be continually amazed and delighted by the wonders of your intuitive mind as it quickly accesses its own computer base to retrieve a word or idea you haven't used for some time.

You never know how or why your intuitive mind will present a particular symbol until you unscramble the picture. When you delve into the underlying meanings of the images and symbols, don't forget to suspend all judgments so the right meaning can emerge.

That is your ultimate aim in anything you do—to be "whole brain" in your thoughts, feelings, and actions. That is the power of intuition—to mobilize this unused ability and become whole. Now that your intuitive skills have been developed, you are ready for "whole brain" integrated thinking. To echo the sentiments expressed at the beginning of this book, your challenge for effective functioning entails utilizing input from both sides of the brain. Anyone functioning with just one part of the total mind or brain is sadly incomplete. You are truly an intelligent person when you utilize both your intellect and intuition for better decision making, problem solving, and innovating new perspectives.

I am often asked, "Where does the intuitive mind come from? Is it "out there" or "in here"? My belief is that all intuition is in fact spiritual as we tap the energy from the God source within us. I recently read a sociological survey that divides the issue of religious authority into two groups—those who see God within themselves and those who see an external source of spiritual authority.

My perspective belongs to the first "group," as I feel we receive intuition from our indwelling "spiritual source" that emanates from a God mind. We receive all the intuitive knowledge and wisdom we need to resolve our problems from this "spiritual source."

I was pleased and affirmed to hear Leo Buscaglia underscore that our inner voice can also be called the voice of God. He likes the concept that God speaks only in whispers that we may not hear because, one, we don't believe it; two, we don't listen; or three, we plow ahead and make all kinds of mistakes that go counter to our own needs and personalities. Buscaglia believes that the inner voice is clear but that so much static is created, personal static that we create ourselves, that we can't hear it. When we *do* hear, we don't trust our own voices. And we are much more ready to listen to the voices of others than to what our intuition tells us. He emphasizes that our intuitive voices are generated inside ourselves, but we are reluctant to accept them and therefore can miss whatever messages are coming from the God in us.

One of my students, Bill, devised this daily affirmation.

I have intuitive knowledge to unlock....I am growing more quiet in my mind.... The new quiet I am feeling eases the journey down my path.... My fears are abating: I am growing confidence and trust in myself.

EXERCISE

Reflection:
A No-Exercise Exercise

What type of intuitive experience are you more aware of at this point?

_____

_____

What facets of your intuition would you still like to develop?

_____

_____

My final gratitude is to all the people who have taught me how to use and exercise my intuitive muscle. I can only end by sharing the sentiments of Dr. Jonas Salk,[1] which express how I feel every waking and sleeping moment of my day.

It is always with excitement that I wake up in the morning wondering what my intuition will toss up to me, like gifts from the sea. I work with it and rely upon it. It's my partner.

Blank page 286

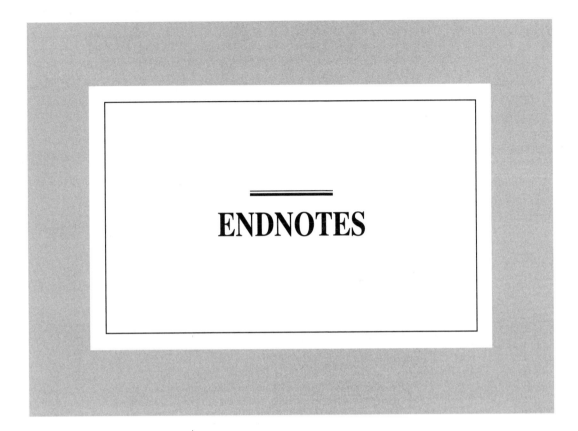

ENDNOTES

Introduction

1. As part of a research grant from the Charlson Research Foundation, in Excelsior, Minnesota, I interviewed 64 top-level business leaders across the country from October 1991 through February 1992. From March to June 1993, an additional 35 managers and leaders had been interviewed. I have drawn on their responses throughout the book. Their responses have also been incorporated in a paper delivered at the Centennial Annual Convention of the American Psychological Association, in Washington, DC, on August 14, 1992.

2. Although I never met Dr. Salk, my debt to him is immeasurable—reading his views on intuition is a most enlightening experience. I recommend his book, Salk, Jonas (1983). *Anatomy of Reality*. New York: Columbia University Press. An interesting article entitled "A Conversation with Jonas Salk" was written by Peter Stoler (March 1983), *Psychology Today*.

3. Naisbitt, John and Aburdene, Patricia (1985). *Re-Inventing the Corporation*. New York: Warner Books.

Chapter One

1. Barker, Joel (1992). *Future Edge*. New York: William Morrow.

2. These excellent videos about the paradigm process are "The Business of Paradigms," "Power of Vision," and "Paradigm Pioneers." For more information, call Charthouse Learning Corporation 800-328-3789 or write to 221 River Ridge Circle, Burnsville, MN, 55337.

3. Barker, Joel (May 1992). "New Thoughts on Paradigms," *Industry Week*.

4. Vaughan, Frances (1979). *Awakening Intuition*. Garden City, NY: Anchor.

5. Jung, Carl. (1923). *Psychological Types*. New York: Harcourt Brace.

6. Using a satellite dish to represent intuition was inspired by Laurie Nadel from the following source: Nadel, L., Haimes, J. and Stempson, R. (1990). *Sixth Sense*. Englewood Cliffs, NJ: Prentice Hall.

7. To explore the view of intuition as a logical skill, see the articles of Weston Agor and Herbert Simon in Agor, Weston, ed. (1989). *Intuition in Organizations*. Newbury Park, CA: Sage.

8. Already cited in note 4, I encourage you to read this priceless book of Frances Vaughan (1979).

9. Peterson, Wilferd (1991). *The Art of Creative Thinking*. Santa Monica, CA: Hay House.

Chapter Two

1. Dean, Douglas and Mihalsky, John (1974). *Executive ESP*. Englewood Cliffs, NJ: Prentice Hall.

2. Agor, Weston (1984). *Intuitive Management*. Englewood Cliffs, NJ: Prentice Hall.

3. Agor, Weston (1986). *The Logic of Intuitive Decision Making*. Westport, CT: Greenwood Press.

4. Drucker, Peter F. (1980). *Managing in Turbulent Times*. New York: Harper & Row.

Chapter Three

1. You can read a fascinating account of the ultradian rest response in Chapter 9 of Laurie Nadel's book (1990), *Sixth Sense*. Englewood Cliffs, NJ: Prentice Hall. Your ultradian rhythms occur every hour and a half. At this time, the body is in the alpha level so you can naturally tune into your intuition. Validate, for yourself, the times when you slow down and can use an intuition break.

Chapter Four

1. The story of J. P. Morgan is in Dean, Douglas and Mihalsky, John (1974). *Executive ESP*. Englewood Cliffs, NJ: Prentice Hall. There are fascinating accounts describing how well-known "business pioneers" let their intuitive hunches lead them to success.

Chapter Six

1. Rico, Gabriele (1983). *Writing the Natural Way*. Los Angeles: Tarcher.

2. Buzan, Tony (1983). *Use Both Sides of Your Brain*. New York: E. P. Dutton.

3. Wycoff, Joyce (1991). *Mindmapping*. New York: Berkley Books.

4. I would recommend the following two books on color interpretation: Gimbel, Theo. (1980). *Healing Through Colour*. Essex, England: C. W. Daniel Company, Ltd., and Hills, Norah, ed. (1979). *You Are a Rainbow*. Boulder Creek, CA: University of the Trees Press.

5. The most extensive research has been done by Max Luscher and can be found in Luscher, Max (1979). *The Luscher Color Test*. New York: Random House.

6. Agor, Weston (1986). *The Logic of Intuitive Decision Making*. Westport, CT: Greenwood Press.

7. As part of my continuing research on the use of intuition in decision making, I inquired about how people use their quiet time and take the needed time to relax. The preliminary results are described in Emery, Marcia (August 1992). "Intuition: The Inner Counselor Speaks." Paper presented at the annual meeting of the American Psychological Association, New Orleans, Louisiana.

Chapter Seven

1. Vaughan, Frances. (1979). *Awakening Intuition.* Garden City, NY: Anchor.

Chapter Eight

1. Agor, Weston (1986). *The Logic of Intuitive Decision Making.* Westport, CT: Greenwood Press.
2. Capacchione, Lucia (1988). *The Power of Your Other Hand.* North Hollywood, CA: Newcastle.

Chapter Nine

1. There are many excellent books to read about dreams. I highly recommend Stanley Krippner's book (1988), *Dreamworking.* Buffalo, NY: Bearly Limited. Dr. Krippner (1990) has also edited a wonderful compendium titled *Dreamtime and Dreamwork.* Los Angeles, CA: Tarcher. Another classic is Ullman, M. and N. Zimmerman (1979). *Working with Dreams.* Los Angeles, CA. Tarcher.
2. Delaney, Gayle (1988). *Living Your Dreams,* rev. ed. New York: Harper & Row. Also, see Delaney, Gayle (1991), *Breakthrough Dreaming.* New York: Bantam.
3. See (May 1985), "Meditation, Lucid Dreaming May Be Related Dream States," *Brain Mind Bulletin.*
4. Ullman, M. and Krippner, S. with Vaughan, A. (1973). *Dream Telepathy.* New York: Macmillan.
5. Reported in Vaughan, Alan (1991). *The Power of Positive Prophecy.* London: Aquarian Press.
6. My precognitive dream research has been reported at many of the annual meetings of the Association for the Study of Dreams as the references suggest. If you are interested in any of these papers, please write to me and request the title(s) of your choice.

   Emery, Marcia (1984). "Precognitive Dreams." *Dream Network Bulletin,* Vol. 9, pp. 4–5.

   Emery, Marcia (June 1987). "Identifying and Interpreting the Intuitive-Precognitive Dream." Paper presented at the meeting of the Association for the Study of Dreams (ASD), Arlington, VA.

   Emery, Marcia (June 1988). "Successfully Programming the Intuitive-Precognitive Dream." Paper presented at the meeting of the ASD, Santa Cruz, CA.

   Emery, Marcia (June 1990). "Exploratory Dream Studies: Part Three, The Timing Influences of Astrological Correlates." Paper presented at the meeting of the ASD, Chicago.

   Emery, Marcia (June 1991). "Exploratory Precognitive Dream Studies: Part Four. Programming the Precognitive Dream." Paper presented at the annual meeting of the ASD, Charlottesville, VA.

Emery, Marcia (June 1992). "Exploratory Precognitive Dream Studies: Part Five. Astrological Indicators of Precognitive Dreams." Paper presented at the annual meeting of the ASD, Santa Cruz, CA.

7. Vaughan, Alan (1991). *The Power of Positive Prophecy*. London: Aquarian Press. Vaughan, Alan (1982). *The Edge of Tomorrow*. New York: Coward, McCann, Geoghegan.

8. For an excellent account of Edgar Cayce's dream interpretation methods, read Thurston, M. (1987). *Dreams: Tonight's Answers for Tomorrow's Questions*. New York: Harper & Row.

Chapter Ten

1. Vaughan, Frances. (1979). *Awakening Intuition*. Garden City, NY: Anchor.

Chapter Fifteen

1. Gawain, Shakti (1978). *Creative Visualization*. Mill Valley, CA: Whatever Publishing. Also, see Gawain, Shakti (1986). *Living in the Light*. San Rafael, CA: Whatever Publishing.

2. Epstein, Gerald (1990). *Healing Visualization: Creating Health Through Imagery*. New York: Bantam.

Epilogue

1. Providing the Salk references again will be a reminder to treat yourself by reading any accounts of this great man. See Salk, Jonas (1983). *Anatomy of Reality*. New York: Columbia University Press. Also, see Stoler, Peter (March 1983). "A Conversation with Jonas Salk," *Psychology Today*.

ADDITIONAL RESOURCES

Supplementary Reading

Use the books on this reading list to supplement your intuitive practice activities.

To avoid repetition, I won't repeat the references already cited in the endnotes but suggest you go back and review those sources as well.

Adair, Margo (1984). *Working Inside Out*. Berkeley, CA: Wingbow Press.

Bastick, Tony (1982). *Intuition: How We Think and Act*. New York: John Wiley.

Estés, Clarissa, (1992) *Women Who Run with the Wolves*. New York. Ballantine Books.

Goldberg, Philip (1983). *The Intuitive Edge*. Los Angeles: Tarcher.

Goldstein, Joseph (1976). *The Experience of Insight*. Boulder, CO: Shambhala,

Jackson, Gerald (1989). *The Inner Executive*. New York: Simon & Schuster.

Johnson, Robert (1986). *Inner Work*. New York: Harper & Row.

Kautz, William and Branon, M. (1989). *Intuiting the Future*. New York: Harper & Row.

Reed, Henry (1991). *Dream Solutions*. San Rafael, CA: New World.

Rosanoff, Nancy (1988). *Intuition Workout*. Boulder Creek, CA: Aslan.

Rowan, Roy (1986). *The Intuitive Manager*. Boston: Little, Brown.

Segaller, Stephen and Berger, Merril (1989). *Wisdom of the Dream*. Boston: Shambhala.

Savary, L., Berne, P., and Williams, S. (1984). *Dreams and Spiritual Growth*. New York: Paulist.

von Oech, Roger (1986). *A Kick in the Seat of the Pants*. New York: Harper & Row.

Windsor, Joan (1987). *Dreams and Healing*. New York: Dodd, Mead.

Windsor, Joan (1985). *The Inner Eye*. Englewood Cliffs, NJ: Prentice Hall.

Wonder, J. and Donovan, P. (1984). *Whole Brain Thinking*. New York: William Morrow.

Zdenek, Marilee (1983). *Right Brain Experience*. New York: McGraw-Hill.

Audiocassette Tapes

"A Breathtaking Experience," by James D. Emery, M.M.

"Meditation Through the Seasons," by James D. Emery, M.M.

"Receptivity Exercises," by James D. Emery, M.M.

"Intuitive Problem Solving," by Marcia Rose Emery, Ph.D.

"Exploring Your Dreams," by Marcia Rose Emery, Ph.D.

"Precognitive Dreams," by Marcia Rose Emery, Ph.D.

These audio programs are available from

Intuitive Management Consulting Company
P.O. Box 68044
Grand Rapids, Michigan 49516
(616) 949-3574 FAX (616) 956-3135

Join the Intuition Network

The purpose of IN is to promote the applied use of intuition in decision making, to share new knowledge on how to use this skill as it becomes known, and to promote ongoing research on intuitive processes for practical use in organizations.

To receive further information about IN write to

Jeffrey Mishlove, Ph.D., Director
Intuition Network
Institute of Noetic Sciences
475 Gate Five Road, Suite 300
Sausalito, CA 94965

Join the Association for the Study of Dreams (ASD)

To receive further information about ASD write to

P.O. Box 1600
Vienna, VA 22183

Source Notes

The author gratefully acknowledges the following people for their permission to quote material from interviews with the author:

Larry L. Adams, page 154.

James B. Adamson, pages xvi, 74, 224.

Richard Antonini, pages 74, 184.

Joel A. Barker, pages xv, 3, 5, 23.

Barrie Bechtel, page 150.

Steven Bernard, page 118.

Geoffrey Bloom, pages xvii, 227.

Leo Buscaglia, Ph.D., pages 12, 74, 247, 284.

Thomas Carnegie, page 50.

Darwin Clark, pages xvi, 27.

Peter C. Cook, page xv.

Kenneth DeHaan, pages xiv, xvii.

Richard M. DeVos, page xiii.

William Gonzalez, page 149.

Dan Henslee, page xv.

Judith Javorek, page xv.

Carol Lopucki, page 238.

Charles McCallum, page 184.

Frank H. Merlotti, page 237.

Dorothy M. Morris, page xv.

Bruce Nyenhuis, pages 49-50.

Mary Kay Russell, page 106.

Sally Rypkema, page 118.

Dr. Jonas Salk, pages xiv, 21, 285.

James Schiltz, page 150.

Carol Valade Smith, page xvii.

James W. Stark, pages 73, 154, 267.

The author gratefully acknowledges permission to use portions of the following copyrighted material:

Agor, Weston. "Manage Brain Skills to Increase Productivity." *Personnel*, Volume 63, page 42 (August 1986). NY: American Management Association, all rights reserved. Reprinted by permission, page 187.

_____. *The Logic of Intuitive Decision Making*. Westport, CT: Quorum, an imprint of Greenwood Publishing Group, Inc. Reprinted by permission, pages 23, 118, 145.

Bergson, Henri. *Creative Evolution*. Lanham, MD: University Press of America. Reprinted by permission, page 101.

Caddy, Eileen. *Footprints on the Path*. Findhorn Forres, Scotland: Findhorn Press. Reprinted by permission, pages 153, 209.

Estés, Clarissa Pinkola, Ph.D. *Women Who Run with the Wolves*. NY: Ballantine Books. Reprinted by permission, pages iv, 267.

Gawain, Shakti. *Reflections in the Light*. San Rafael, CA: New World Library. Reprinted by permission, page 173.

Goldberg, P. *The Intuitive Edge*. NY: The Putnam Publishing Group, Jeremy P. Tarcher. Reprinted by permission, page 145.

Hilton, Conrad. *Be My Guest*. NY: Prentice Hall Press/a Division of Simon & Schuster, 1987. Reprinted by permission, page 204.

Naisbitt, J. and P. Aburdene. *Re-Inventing the Corporation*. NY: Warner Books, Inc. Reprinted by permission, pages xiv, 67.

Peters, Thomas J. and Robert H. Waterman, Jr. Selected excerpts from *In Search of Excellence: Lessons from America's Best-Run Companies*. Copyright ©1982 by Thomas J. Peters and Robert H. Waterman, Jr. Reprinted by permission of HarperCollins Publishers, Inc., page 101.

Peterson, Wilferd. *The Art of Creative Thinking*. Santa Monica, CA: Hay House. Reprinted by permission, page 17, 35.

Segaller, S. and M. Berge. *Wisdom of the Dream*. Boston, MA: Shambala Publications. Reprinted by permission, page 159.

Senge, Peter M. *The Fifth Discipline*. Copyright © 1990 by Peter M. Senge. Used by permission of Doubleday, a division of Bantam, Doubleday, Dell Publishing Group, Inc., page 283.

Thurston, Mark. *Dreams: Tonight's Answers for Tomorrow's Questions*. NY: HarperCollins Publishers. Reprinted by permission, page 172.

Weil, Andrew. Excerpt from *The Natural Mind*. Copyright ©1972 by Andrew Weil. Reprinted by permission of Houghton Mifflin Company. All rights reserved, page 261.

Vaughan, Frances. *Awakening Intuition*. NY: Doubleday, a division of Bantam, Doubleday, Dell Publishing Group, Inc. Reprinted by permission, pages 8, 13.

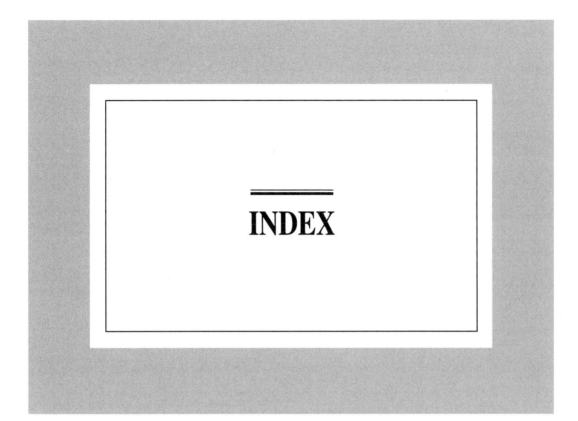

INDEX

Emotions
  and distortion of intuition, 115-116,117-118
  intuitive cues to, 13
  negative emotional influences, 116
  positive emotional influences, 116
Employees
  dissatisfaction with support staff, 212-215
  evaluation of, 225
  hiring decisions, 224-225
  motivating for teamwork, 201-203
  new employees, adjustment of, 219
Environment, intuitive cues to, 13
Executive ESP, 23
Exercise
  choosing exercise program, 266
  imaginary jogging exercise, 266
  and intuition development, 149-150

F

Family
  communication problems, 123
  discipline of children, 279-280
  healing family relationships, 268-272
  motivation for school, 280-281
  toilet training of children, 279
Fantasizing
  alpha to omega technique, 88-89
  and imagery, 87-88
Fear, and intuition, 116
Fireman, Paul, 227-228
First impressions, 19
Free association, 19
Freud, Sigmund, 107, 160, 169
Friendships, 275-278
  making new friends, 275-276
  resolving differences with old friend, 276-278
Fry, Art, 4
Future Edge (Barker), 5

G

Gawain, Shakti, 265
Global Intuition Network, 291
Gonzalez, Bill, 149
Gut feelings, 9, 11, 13, 22, 36

H

Handedness, use of subdominant hand, 156

Health
  choosing exercise program, 266
  creative visualization exercise, 265
  imaginary jogging exercise, 266
  steps in improvement of, 264-265
  stress reduction, 262-263
Hess, Leon, 204
Hilton, Conrad, 204
Hiring decisions, 224-225
Howe, Elias, 160

I

Imagery, 27, 149
  accessing images, 84-86
  activation of, 86, 87-88, 93-96
  alpha to omega technique, 89-89
  color images, 112-115
  and daydreams, 87-88
  evaluation of, 90-93, 94-95, 133-134
  exercise for, 70
  guided imagery exercises, 71-73, 80-81, 132-133
  interpretation of, 27, 32
  and intuition, 18, 19
  and senses, 74, 79-84, 87
  and symbols, 101-103
  use in business, 68-69
Imagination, and relaxation, 65-66
Internal brainstorming, 134-139
  example, coping with stress, 135-137
  exercise for, 137-139
  process of, 135
Interpretation methods
  amplification, 103-107
  clustering, 109-110
  mind mapping, 110-112
  word association, 107-109
Intuition
  and dynamic people, 23
  examples of, 7
  keys for development of, 18-19
  levels of intuitive experience, 13
  nature of, 8-9
  and subconscious, 17-18
  terms related to, 11-12
Intuition development
  and affirmations, 40-42
  alpha waves, 38-39
  associations for, 291
  audiocassettes on, 291